For
Shirin & Jal,
with our kindest regards
& every best wish

Muriel Box &
Gerald Gardiner

April 17. 1983

Ex Libris

Shirin Dastur Patel

REBEL ADVOCATE
A Biography of Gerald Gardiner

REBEL ADVOCATE

A Biography of Gerald Gardiner

by

MURIEL BOX

LONDON
VICTOR GOLLANCZ LTD
1983

For Carol and Leonora

© Muriel Box 1983

British Library Cataloguing in Publication Data

Box, Muriel
  Rebel advocate
  1. Gardiner of Kittisford, Gerald Austin, Baron
  I. Title
  344.2'0092'4   KD632.G/
  ISBN 0-575-03269-3

Printed in Great Britain at the Camelot Press Ltd, Southampton

Ah, my Lords, it is indeed painful to have to sit upon a Woolsack which is stuffed with such thorns as these!

The Lord Chancellor in Iolanthe
W. S. Gilbert

He did not throw himself about or rant or impersonate a Harrow-and-Magdalen "hearty". Some people thought him cold. But that was not my impression. "Austere", perhaps, but not cold. The austerity was the outward manifestation of a rigorous self-discipline and self-control. On matters of law reform there was a warm-hearted zeal and a deep commitment, made the more effective by precise and temperate expression.

Wolfenden

CONTENTS

LIST OF ILLUSTRATIONS

Cadell, George Howe, Pamela Brown and Jane Baxter (*photo Westmore-land Studios, Oxford*).

Following page 178

Off to court at a swinging pace (*photo Sport and General Press Agency*).

Gerald in his robes as Lord Chancellor, 1964.

Gerald taking the chair at a board meeting of the *New Statesman* (*photo John Hillelson*).

The Queen sharing a joke with Gerald in the Law Courts at the opening of the new Queen's Building in the Strand (*photo Sport and General Press Agency*).

The Chancellor conferring degrees on the Open University graduates, 1973 (*by courtesy of the Open University*).

Gerald and fellow graduates, after receiving their degrees from the Open University, 1977 (*photo Hulton Press*).

Gerald and Muriel Box at Mote End on their engagement, 1970 (*photo William McQuitty*).

Gerald and the author, at Sydney Harbour, before leaving for Hong Kong, 1973.

ACKNOWLEDGEMENTS

On laying down my pen with a sigh of relief after several years' toil and research on this biography, I nevertheless realized that the work was still incomplete without an acknowledgement of the debt I owed to my husband's many friends and colleagues who contributed personal impressions and versions of events in his life which were not to be found in public records and were therefore unavailable to me.

All these people gave generously of their time and effort, and in expressing my gratitude I would like to add that they provided me with material which revealed sides of Gerald's character and details of his career during the period when he was a complete stranger to me (roughly sixty years). My thanks go to Lady Browning (Dame Daphne du Maurier), Lord Wolfenden, Mr and Mrs Wilson Wiley, Mr C. H. Rolph, Mr Tom Sargant, Sir Neville Faulks, Mr Wilfred Button and his colleagues in the Lord Chancellor's office, Lord Elwyn Jones, Sir George Coldstream, Mr Hume Boggis-Rolfe and Miss Pat Malley; and to Sir Harold Wilson, who kindly permitted me to quote from his book *The Labour Government 1964–1970*, which came as a gift inscribed, "For Gerald in friendship, with recollections of great days and the contributions thereto of the greatest Lord Chancellor of this century, and with the writer's compliments and best wishes".

I appreciate the help given me by the staff of the British Library at Colindale for providing references I needed from *The Times* and other newspapers, and of the London Library for their promptness in finding *Auschwitz in England*, an excellent account of a Nazi concentration camp and the Dering case in 1964, also the invaluable sources of information from *Hansard*, and the book which illuminated the E.T.U. trial, *The Road from Wigan Pier* by Lady Olga Cannon and Mr J. R. L. Anderson. I am also grateful to all the other publishers and authors of books from which I have quoted, the titles of which appear in the Bibliography.

But without the patience, conscientious attention to detail and persevering research of my Editor, Mrs Sheila Bush, I doubt whether the book would ever have emerged as it is today. I offer my sincere thanks to her, and also to Miss Livia Gollancz for her own careful perusal of the manuscript in its last stages.

I cannot let it go at that. The Gardiners also provided me with family data and anecdotes from Gerald's life; principally Carol, his daughter, and his nephew, Robert Gardiner; but naturally I owe most to the subject of this biography, who never spared any effort to guide me to the official documents or the correct accounts of his career, and assist me with details which only he could give of his early life before becoming a member of the Bar.

M.B.

ALTHOUGH ENVIRONMENT PLAYS a distinct rôle in the formation of character, heredity also shares in the creation of a personality. Gerald Gardiner's forebears for this reason are interesting, since they have clearly had an influence, however remote, on the kind of man he eventually became.

A certain degree of sex discrimination becomes apparent when family trees are being traced; the male line seems to be of paramount importance, the female members of the family receiving scant attention unless they prove to be of exceptional historical or social renown. Even allowing for such imbalance, several features emerge from Gerald Gardiner's family tree. Over the years – centuries, almost – the names of clergymen, lawyers and soldiers constantly recur, members of the church predominating. None of the clerics was in the least outstanding, the most nearly so being the rector of Uplowman in Devon, Lewis Sweete (1553–1613), who became the archdeacon of Totnes; while three hundred years later F. E. Gardiner (Gerald's uncle) eventually reached Truro Cathedral as sub-deacon and canon. The rest were very minor clergy who held quiet country livings in the parishes of Kittisford, Langton Budville and Badialton in the county of Somerset.

Among those who preferred the law were two in the late sixteenth century, whose careers bore a certain analogy to Gerald's own. They were Alexander Webber, M.A., of Magdalen College, Oxford, and his nephew, William Webber, both barristers-at-law of the Inner Temple. There the resemblance ends, for neither went on to become Lord Chancellor.

Perhaps at this point the business of the family name should be clarified. It was originally Webber, not Gardiner. The change occurred in 1748, when a later William Webber, on reaching the age of twenty-one, assumed the name of Gardiner in accordance with the terms of a will made by his grandfather, John Gardiner, whose only son had died in infancy and who wished the name of Gardiner to continue. The Webber name was safe anyway, and, since William stood to inherit all his grandfather's estates and money if he called himself Gardiner, the change was not only sensible but highly advantageous.

William Gardiner (as he now was) and his descendants continued to lead peaceful and uneventful lives in their tight-knit communities, never venturing far afield, until suddenly one of them plucked up courage and took himself off to become proprietor and minister of the Octagon Chapel in Bath, which still stands in its charm and beauty to this day. He was Gerald's great-grandfather, John Gardiner (1757–1838), who combined two professions, spiritual and legal, being a barrister of civil law of Glasgow and of the Middle Temple, London, as well as a Doctor of Divinity of Oxford University. His wife hailed from Glanmere, County Cork, thus injecting some Irish blood into the family's veins for the first but not for the last time.

The Irish are always to be depended upon for the unexpected, and the Rev. Dr Dionysius Lardner, Gerald's great-grandfather on the maternal side, was no exception. Possibly he contributed to the rebellious streak in Gerald, who, brought up in a strict Conservative tradition, diverged sharply on becoming an adult and opted for socialism instead of the Toryism of his father.

Dionysius Lardner, born in 1793, the son of a Dublin solicitor, followed his father's profession for a short time, but soon abandoned law to take holy orders. Entering Trinity College, Dublin, he obtained his M.A. in 1819 and LL.D. in 1827, then, instead of devoting himself to the ministry, changed his mind again in favour of a literary and scientific career. While at the university he took prizes in metaphysics, logic, mathematics, physics and ethics. A series of lectures on the steam engine gained him a gold medal from the Dublin Royal Society and later led him to urge Lord Melbourne and the government to open a steam route to India via the Red Sea. Incidentally, he put forward the idea of building steamships to cross the Atlantic.

He married at twenty-two a young woman, Cecilia Flood, of independent fortune and violent temperament who five years later, after bearing him three children, ran off and lived clandestinely with a Mr Murphy of the Irish Customs, by whom she had an illegitimate daughter. Her whereabouts remained hidden from her husband for the following nine years, but during that time Dionysius himself was carrying on an affair with Anne, the wife of one Samuel Boursiquot, a vivacious young woman whom he had known from childhood. Barely two months after Cecilia's departure Anne, who already had four offspring, gave birth to another, a son who was christened Dionysius Lardner Boursiquot.

Samuel, apparently a complaisant, elderly husband, made no

objection when Lardner became a lodger in his house during the confinement and stayed on for the next seven years, possibly because he paid the rent and all the other expenses of the house and made himself financially responsible for the upbringing and education of the boy who in later life called himself Dion Boucicault, and who, we must assume, was Gerald's great-uncle. His name, and that of Dionysius, were often mentioned in the Gardiner family as illustrious relatives, but Dion's origins were not revealed. One of the most prolific playwrights of the Victorian era, he was not only to write and produce over two hundred plays but to act brilliantly in many of them. *London Assurance*, which was put on at Covent Garden in 1841, was his first great success, and it was also the first time that he was billed as Dion Lardner Boucicault; for five years he had acted under the name Lee Moreton. It was as if he were afraid to use his real name until he had proved himself a success in the eyes of his celebrated father.

When Dr Lardner was appointed to the first Chair of Natural Philosophy and Astronomy at University College, London, in 1827 and went to live there, Anne Boursiquot left her husband, followed him with her children, including Dion, and set up house near his lodgings in Golden Square. Although Lardner obtained a divorce from his wife in the Ecclesiastical Courts of Dublin in 1832, he was unable to get his complete freedom to marry again until he brought his case to the House of Lords, where an Act had to be passed before it was granted seven years later. But by this time his relationship with Anne had ceased, and a year later he stopped his monthly allowance of £60 to Dion. He had become financially embarrassed through his involvement in a scandal that not only shook the academic world and London society but forced him to abandon his career and flee the country.

He had met a Mrs Mary Heaviside, and his passionate association with her turned into a *cause célèbre* whose repercussions continued to be felt for the next five years.

Tradition has it in the Gardiner family that he met the lady on a visit to Bath in the season, but it may have been in Brighton, where she lived with her husband, Captain Richard Heaviside, a cavalry officer in the Dragoon Guards. Although happily married for fifteen years, with three children, Mary Heaviside fell madly in love with the celebrated professor (then in his mid-forties), and he fell equally overboard for her. For several months the couple tried unsuccessfully to cope with their tricky situation, Mary even resorting to opium in a suicide attempt to deliver herself from it. In the end they could bear it no longer and eloped in order to live together. This was in 1840.

Her husband immediately set off in hot pursuit, and finally the couple were run to earth in a Paris hotel. Without waiting for explanations, the Captain started laying about Lardner brutally with his stick, forcing him to take shelter under a piano to avoid the savage caning, from which situation he was eventually rescued by the hotel proprietor. Mary refused to be intimidated or to return to England, and shortly afterwards the couple sailed to the U.S.A., where for the next five years they lived in the patient hope of Heaviside bringing a divorce.

Instead he brought a case against Lardner for seduction, and was awarded £8,000 in damages. Mary, it seemed, was a very valuable asset! Eventually Heaviside obtained a divorce from his wife in the Ecclesiastical Court, but since he showed no intention of proceeding further to the House of Lords the Lardners continued to live for some years in sin, quite prosperously, as it turned out.

In New York Dionysius had made the most of his talents by arranging a series of lecture tours all over the States. This, together with the publication of his works in America, netted him £40,000, an astronomical sum by the standards of the day. In 1845 he and Mary decided to return to Europe, and took up residence in Paris. On learning of their arrival, Heaviside at last relented and took his case to the House of Lords, where he was granted a divorce.

The Lardners, thus able to marry, did so but remained in Paris, where Mary gave birth to two daughters, Susan (Gerald's grandmother) and Helen. Dionysius went on to produce a vast amount of work of infinite variety, having completed in 1849 his twenty-year stint on the *Cabinet Cyclopaedia* in 133 volumes, for which he was best known. Ten years later he died, leaving a considerable number of books popularizing science, physics and astronomy to be printed and reprinted more than fifteen years after his death. Some of his theories were considered dubious and inspired Thackeray to satirize him as Dr Dionysius Diddler in the last *Memoirs of Mr Charles J. Yellowplush*, and also in the *Miscellanies*.

Meanwhile the Rev. George Gregory Gardiner (a son of John Gardiner) had settled in Paris and become minister of the English church in the Avenue Marboeuf. Having left his father's Octagon Chapel in Bath several years previously, he had married, gone to Bonn and produced a family of nine children. The only one who concerns us here is his seventh son, Robert Septimus Gardiner, Gerald's father.

Mary Lardner, now widowed, and her two daughters were members of the Rev. Gardiner's congregation, and they became close family friends during the years that followed. When the Franco-Prussian war of 1870 broke out, and fears for their safety arose, Mary was offered fatherly advice on behalf of her daughters. The Rev. Gardiner expressed in ominous tones his view of the invading army:

"We all know about the licentiousness of the German soldiery. Your two girls must be got out of Paris at all costs!" His warning was taken seriously, and resulted in the Reverend's son Robert, then a fourteen-year-old schoolboy, being deputed to accompany the young ladies away from the capital to Dieppe, where, as everyone thought, they would be out of harm's way. The reverse happened.

Inside a year the war was over, yet this had given Susan Lardner time enough to meet and fall in love with Count von Ziegesar, a dashing Prussian officer in the army of occupation. Neither knew the other's native tongue, and they conducted their courtship in French. Marriage quickly followed and they went to Berlin, where their daughter Alice was born in 1875. The marriage proved a failure, and Susan and her daughter eventually returned to Paris. Although there was no divorce, neither the Count nor his wife ever set eyes on one another again, and the only time his name was mentioned thereafter in the family was on his death, when the question of his grandsons inheriting the title was broached. This happened to be just before the First World War, when anti-German feeling was very strong, and the Gardiner boys, who were at school at the time, refused the offer.

How the Count's descendants came to be British was brought about by Robert Septimus Gardiner.

By the year 1880 he had developed into an enterprising young man, a graduate from Grenoble University, speaking French, German and English fluently. These assets enabled him to obtain a position with a Quebec firm as a glove salesman. Occasionally he travelled to Europe, and during these visits paid his respects to the Lardner sisters in Paris. He became infatuated with Susan's little daughter Alice, and secretly determined to marry her the moment he had made his fortune. This promise was eventually fulfilled, though the wedding did not take place for many years: Robert Septimus remained a bachelor until he was nearly forty, by which time he had become a prosperous man of affairs in London.

From an early age he sported a dark beard, apparently to create an impression of himself as a businessman of experience and substance.

This gave him a striking resemblance to the Prince of Wales (later King Edward VII), as shown by the portrait of him painted by Philip de Lazlo. Since he never shaved off the beard, it must have been advantageous to him. He was soon to leave the glove company far behind as he steadily rose in the world to become managing director of a gas company in Newcastle, and eventually a highly successful entrepreneur. Other talents developed as his social life expanded, enabling him to take a flat in London and indulge his love of music and the theatre. He started the Lyric Club which engaged famous artists to sing on Sunday evenings, an innovation strongly disapproved of by his father, since it violated the Sabbath. He composed music and sang a little himself, one of his numbers, the *Lyric Polka*, proving popular with the club. As he grew more affluent he acquired a private box at Covent Garden, as well as at Drury Lane and Epsom. While dabbling in the entertainment business he somehow managed to be present at the quarrel between Gilbert and Sullivan over the new carpet for the Savoy Theatre which irrevocably dissolved their partnership.

He became a director of the Alhambra and was subsequently elected chairman of its board. This was at a period when the famous music-hall was in a very bad way, and Robert Septimus determined to rescue it from bankruptcy. Taking out all the front stalls, he put in comfortable armchairs as an added attraction which improved matters; and he also engaged original and first-class acts from abroad, which successfully put the Alhambra on its feet again.

In 1896, after his long intended marriage to Alice von Ziegesar, he gave up his Buckingham Palace Road flat and installed his twenty-one-year-old bride in a house in Cadogan Square, and from that time his business interests began to supersede his theatrical ones. He branched out into the shipping business by forming the Pelton Steamship Company and Pelton Colliery Company, and when the First World War broke out he had secured contracts to export coal to France and Belgium in his own ships. It was an extremely profitable operation, and out of the proceeds he provided, during the war, a hospital for French officers at Le Touquet, for which he received the Legion of Honour. For his ability to supply coal to Belgium at a critical time he was awarded the Belgian Order of Leopold, and after the war secured for himself a knighthood from the Lloyd George National Government of 1922. This he obtained by donating £15,000 towards a newspaper called the *Near East*, whose finances were in a far from healthy state, and which represented British interests abroad. To rescue it from failure was considered a worthy objective and deserving of recognition.

Meanwhile, Alice had been busy on her side. She had borne him three sons, Cyril, Gerald and Nevile, in 1897, 1900 and 1902 respectively. She was a rather quiet, reserved mother with a gentle demeanour, who devoted the time she could spare from rearing a family to painting and writing. She produced a book of poems, *A Garland of Roses*, which her husband paid to have printed, but a novel she wrote never saw the light of day.

The family lived at 67 Cadogan Square for nearly a decade, and probably would have remained there had Gerald not fallen seriously ill and nearly died. Both parents were abroad at the time, but were hurriedly summoned home to cope with what had at first been diagnosed as appendicitis, but which subsequently developed into peritonitis. Gerald's recovery was slow, and for many months he had to be carried about the house on cushions. He remained delicate as a child and, despite his father's almost over-zealous care, suffered every childish complaint that was going. Yet in later life he was rather proud of his record at the Bar, for in 40 years he did not miss a single day's work through illness.

Whether or not it was his son's frail health or some other factor which influenced Robert Septimus to leave Cadogan Square is not known, but in 1907 he bought a large mansion in Kent, near Canterbury, called Hardres Court. There his staff gradually accumulated, and finally consisted of a butler, housekeeper, cook, two footmen, three house-maids, lady's maid, kitchen and scullery maid, two chauffeurs, about ten gardeners, a carpenter, electrician, odd man, bailiff and two gamekeepers. Besides the bailiff he had a personal secretary to help run his shipping interests and supervise the large kitchen-garden and the many-acred farm on which Jersey cows, beef-stock and poultry were raised.

It was a leisured country life which the family led and continued to lead until the early nineteen hundreds, when the fortunes of Sir Robert Septimus Gardiner, which had suffered from the partial collapse of the colliery business after the war, sharply declined owing to the general depression. When this happened he prudently sold Hardres Court and moved, with Alice, to 84 Brook Street in Mayfair, whence he kept a fatherly eye on the careers of his three sons.

*

As soon as Gerald's health improved, he was sent to Dr Bull's preparatory school at Westgate-on-Sea. He was then eight years of age, and despite the fact that he hated every minute and described it later as "a dreadful place where I was constantly beaten along with the other boys" he remained there until he was ten. His parents visited him regularly, each time finding him profoundly unhappy and subject to weeping on their departure. Finally his father removed him to another establishment, Heatherdown at Ascot, which his elder brother Cyril had attended and where the régime was more humane and attractive. However, Gerald's three years at Heatherdown came to a sudden end when his father discovered that the headmaster was interfering sexually with the pupils, his son among them. He removed him at once, forcing the head to resign, and thus causing the school to decline thereafter and ultimately to close.

During the holidays the three brothers played tennis, cycled around the leafy lanes and paid visits to the Vicar's children who lived next to Hardres Court. They did not have to go far to hear the Rev. Newman preach, for their place of worship was conveniently in their own grounds and was called Upper Hardres church. On high days and holidays the boys were encouraged to produce their own entertainment, consisting of short plays, sketches, recitations and songs, in which all three sang and acted before an audience of friends and relatives invited by the Gardiner parents. Thus from an early age they developed a confidence in their talents and overcame any shyness when appearing in public, which was to stand them in good stead later in their chosen careers.

Vacations were not wholly given over to pleasure, for more often than not, depending on their progress at school, the Gardiner boys received private coaching from a tutor engaged by their father, who appeared determined that they should not lag behind in anything.

He rented a house near Pitlochry for several years running, and here the boys were encouraged to participate in shooting, fishing and grouse drives on the moors. Their Scottish Sundays were rather confusing affairs for the children, since a decision had to be taken as to what they could or could not do on the Sabbath. Sometimes they were allowed to play bridge but not tennis, at other times tennis but not bridge. Church-going was customary, but after their mother became a Roman Catholic, when Gerald was about twelve, their attendance tended to be infrequent. Religion meant a great deal to Alice Gardiner, but she never forced her particular faith on her sons.

Other holidays were spent abroad at Monte Carlo or Mentone, sometimes with their parents, sometimes not. When they were small Ostend was selected as a good seaside resort to which they were despatched with a nanny and a tutor, who allowed them greater freedom than they experienced at home. The three boys enjoyed roaming along the sands, indulging in their own brand of fun and games while the tutor and nanny, having taken a fancy to each other, indulged in theirs, of a somewhat different but equally enjoyable nature. No harm seems to have resulted from this laxity, for on the whole they were well-behaved children. Gerald, however, displayed one act of disobedience which forever after brought him fame within the family.

While holidaying in Belgium one summer, when he was only a few years old, the parents decided they should all visit the Brussels Exhibition. For some inexplicable reason Gerald refused point-blank to go. No amount of persuasion, coaxing or pressure had the slightest effect on the stubborn child, who was led protesting from their hotel. His protest being ignored, he announced his intention of keeping his eyes shut during the entire tour. Despite the threat, which he firmly carried out, the family remained unmoved. As they passed one exhibit, a woman waxed sympathetic at the sight of a little boy with closed eyes being pulled along, and was unable to refrain from exclaiming censoriously: "Fancy! Dragging a poor blind kid to an exhibition like this! Disgraceful!"

Sometimes the Gardiners visited their great-aunt Helen Lardner in Paris, as well as their grandmother Susan, the Baroness von Ziegesar. They stayed with her in the Rue Kléber where she had an apartment, and amused themselves playing dominoes with the old lady, being rewarded with a chocolate every time they beat her, or listening to her as she sat performing gracefully at the piano, very erect and elegantly dressed in gowns always trimmed with high lace collars.

No mention was ever made of Count von Ziegesar, possibly because the boys found their own father extremely intimidating, with his thick black beard, slightly bulbous eyes and vibrant voice which had the effect of inhibiting, rather than inviting, confidences. Adults, on the other hand, found him attractive, warm and friendly, especially at dinner-parties where he shone as the perfect host with a fine taste in wine and a fund of amusing stories and anecdotes. An unusually strict sense of time, and of its practical importance, sometimes had unexpected results. When his brother, Evelyn Gardiner, arrived at Hardres Court with an invitation for the weekend, the rather vague old Canon of Truro was greeted with: "Delighted to see you, my dear fellow! Now, what train are you leaving by?" Not the least discourtesy was intended, rather the reverse: Robert Septimus was simply anxious that Evelyn should not miss his train home on the Monday.

Talking to Gerald when he was still a schoolboy at Harrow, his father shot a query at him with arrow-like swiftness. "Tell me, my boy, who d'you think is the greatest living Englishman?"

Gerald, utterly taken aback and struck dumb with shyness under the intent gaze levelled at him, gulped and, after some hesitation, blurted out: "Winston Churchill, I suppose."

Robert Septimus exploded. "Churchill? That —. My God!" Angrily striding away, he left Gerald sorely baffled. Winston at the time was out of favour with the Conservative party, having joined the Liberals, but the boy was unaware of this. His mother, finding him alone and miserable, inquired the reason, and on learning it laughed.

"Why, darling," she said, "when he asked who you thought was the greatest living Englishman, you should have answered '*You*, father!' and everything would've been all right." This was the first and last time Gerald remembered his mother showing a touch of humour.

Just before the outbreak of World War I, Gerald entered Harrow. His recollections of the five years spent there were far from happy. The intense coldness of the building in winter, due to shortages of coal and other fuel, caused him to suffer severely from chilblains. To make things worse, each boy was forced to take an ice-cold bath every morning to keep up his morale, and this hated ritual was something Gerald never forgot. There were also certain shortages of food which increased as the war went on, a situation the hungry boys resented but could do nothing about.

On arrival Gerald was placed in the bottom form, one lower than he should have been, thus enabling him to win first prize at the end of term for being "best in the form". He considered this somewhat spurious, yet it must have encouraged him a little, for while remaining in the middle group of boys for the rest of his time there he was awarded the junior reading prize and later the senior one. His good speaking voice was apparently his only asset, for his work generally was undistinguished and his popularity was not enhanced by his dislike of games and sport. Except for his rôles in school plays (he took the part of a girl in *David Garrick*) he became convinced on leaving school that he was a failure in everything.

For the Harrow masters he had little respect, the only exception being the gifted Townsend Warner (father of the writer, Sylvia Townsend Warner) and the Rev. Kittermaster. The former was an excellent teacher who instilled in him a great love of English literature, while the latter, a Borstal chaplain before coming to Harrow, widened his social and spiritual horizons at his most impressionable age.

Kittermaster was a dedicated Socialist, a pacifist parson, whose sermons, unconventional in theme and phrasing, impressed themselves on Gerald's memory to such a degree that he remembered them vividly forty years later. He was a humane, kindly man who thoroughly understood the psychology of boys and knew instinctively how to manage them. One day Gerald happened to mention that his father was coming down to see him, and Kittermaster immediately invited them both to have tea with him in his house. Gerald accepted, but warned him that his Socialist views might not go down well with his Conservative father and it would probably be wise to avoid mentioning them. This was agreed, and when the afternoon arrived Kittermaster behaved impeccably. Unfortunately a copy of the *Nation* (later the *New Statesman & Nation*), lying among some periodicals on a table, caught the sharp eye of Robert Septimus. He was inwardly enraged. On being seen off by Gerald afterwards, he remarked with intense indignation: "To think a son of mine should be at a school where the *Nation* is openly read and displayed by the masters! Nevile's down to follow you here, but now, of course, he'll go to Eton!" And he did.

Not knowing anything about the paper Gerald's curiosity was naturally aroused and he started to read it. Finding the contents interesting and informative he continued doing so assiduously. Many years later Kingsley Martin, its editor, was to invite him on to the board of the amalgamated *New Statesman & Nation* as a director, and later still, on the death of G. D. H. Cole, he was elected chairman and was able subsequently to advise the paper on several libel actions brought against it. His business acumen also proved a valuable asset, discovered when he drafted the ingenious constitution of a "self-perpetuating trust" known as the *New Statesman Publishing Company*, whose directors own all the voting shares in the paper (they are a holding company) and who cannot dispose of them except to Board nominees, thus protecting the paper from an attempted "take-over" (there have been several attempts). He continued as chairman until he resigned in 1964 to become Lord Chancellor.

When the announcement of his appointment came out in the press Kittermaster, by then a frail old man of eighty-seven and very near his end, wrote him a letter:

My dear Gerald, my very dear Gerald,

There is a great compulsion upon me to write to you, though so old and feeble a creature I am that the effort to write a letter is almost too much for me.

The compulsion arises from two causes. Firstly, the *Sunday Times* reporter has lately been persecuting me to give him news of you as a schoolboy, as I daresay you saw in the long article about you published in the paper. I was not well reported. The only item of interest, which might have amused readers but which I did not like to record, was that your father forbad you to enter my house, Dame Armstrong House, ever after you had brought him to tea with us, and he had seen a copy of the *Nation* on my study table. Do you remember that? The other reason is that I have just had occasion to answer a very long letter from an undergraduate of 20 years old at Sussex University.

The writer is a clever, interesting ex-Lancing boy who lived near us at Angmering-on-Sea and whom I more or less shepherded through a difficult adolescent stage. He is a tremendous individualist and in many ways an idealist and a rebel. Well, I found myself writing to him, the "disciple" of my old age (I am 87), my last disciple, and telling him of you, my earliest "disciple".

I told him that one of the saddest things to me in my old age was to see so many promising young rebels and idealists become smug, complacent, conventional, prosperous middle-aged men who laughed at their youthful enthusiasms. I told my boy that you were the one *notable exception* and that, for all your name and fame at the Bar, you had never lost your glorious reforming rebel streak.

I begged him to be like you and to remain a rebel and an idealist all his life. I said that I was not asking him to hold your views necessarily, but to imitate your character. So perhaps, dear Gerald, you will have an indirect hand in passing on the torch of sincerity and truth.

How I wish I could see you again before I die. And Margery wishes the same . . .

Dear Gerald, I love you as much as ever I did. I don't expect an answer.

Ever,
Kitter.

Commenting many years later in an interview on television about the quality of his schooling at Harrow, Gerald remarked: "It wasn't a very good education. . . . In history I twice got up to George I, then found myself in a form that was starting again at William the Conqueror. And Lord Bath, who was in the same house as I was, told me about five years later that he never got beyond George I either. Of course schools change, you know. I expect they're up to George II by now."

While he was at Harrow a strong friendship sprang up between Gerald and a fine young classical scholar, Stephen Tomlin, who wrote poetry and professed very left-wing views. These may have been a reaction against the views held by his father, a Judge in the Chancery Division of the High Court, who later became Lord Justice and then a Law Lord. Stephen often went to stay with an aunt who lived in Kent not far from Hardres Court, so that during the holidays Gerald spent a great deal of time in his company. On leaving Harrow Stephen became a sculptor, studied under Frank Dobson and later produced a bust of Lytton Strachey which is now in the Tate Gallery. His marriage to Strachey's niece, Julia, was not of long duration, and he died, apparently of blood poisoning, while he was still quite young, which lost England a promising and gifted artist.

The views of Stephen Tomlin, combined with those of Kittermaster, might be seen as the beginning of Gerald's change of attitude towards contemporary society. Contrary to his parents' acceptance of the *status quo*, he gradually became suspicious of the Establishment, but his views did not crystallize into action until well after World War I had ended and the years of the great depression had set in. During the General Strike of 1926 he still reacted as any young man with a strictly conventional upper-class background was expected to do. He joined the Special Constabulary Reserve in the belief that law and order had to be maintained in that period of strife, but by the time he resigned in 1932 his convictions had undergone a radical change, and many years later he looked back and spoke with considerable regret of his temporary service as a Special Constable, as though he regarded it as a blot on his record.

BEFORE HIS STUDIES ended at Harrow in 1918 Gerald passed Responsions, thus enabling him to go to university. His father had put him down for Magdalen College, Oxford, but meanwhile he was eligible for military service at the end of July. Expecting to be called up at any moment, he determined to make the most of his vacation, which was one of the happiest he ever remembers, spent pleasantly hay-making at Hardres Court.

During his five public-school years, in company with other Harrovians he had joined the Cadet Corps and done a stint of square-bashing. The war, in its fourth year of mud, blood and misery, was now in its death throes, but thousands of young men were yet to be slaughtered before the final collapse of Germany and victory for the Allies. The training of cadets had included at one point a competition between units of the corps in which Gerald took part. In readiness for this exercise he changed one day into his uniform and, in turning to leave, tripped and fell against the sharp edge of a chest-of-drawers, hitting his temple. He remembered nothing of what followed, but was informed subsequently that he had gone through the entire exercise correctly, finally returning to his room, where he immediately collapsed, unconscious. The school doctor diagnosed concussion and kept him in a darkened room for three days until he recovered, seemingly none the worse for the incident.

At the beginning of August he reported to Bushey in Hertfordshire for his military training in the Coldstream Guards Cadet Battalion, where he remained for several months. A few older men from public life also joined up at this time to help voluntarily in the war effort, among them the celebrated actor Gerald du Maurier. Soon after his arrival the idea was mooted of providing the trainees with some sort of entertainment, whether by du Maurier or not is uncertain, but a play was put on which he not only produced but acted in as well. This was *Vice Versa*, a comedy adapted from the famous novel by F. Anstey.

Du Maurier played Bultitude Senior while Gerald was cast as Bultitude Minor. During rehearsals everyone was on tenterhooks, for the nonchalant and experienced du Maurier never seemed able to remember his lines. On the night, however, he astonished the company by taking the prompt so adroitly that the audience were quite unaware of anything untoward happening.

Daphne du Maurier, writing to me in 1977 about the episode, described Gerald (Gardiner) as "Surely a star turn! The best-looking young man I have ever seen in my life, and I was only eleven! Although, heaven knows, he has risen to a different stardom in the law and politics, who knows, he might also have been another Larry Olivier!"

World War I dragged on, September came and went, but the final scenes of the tragedy were painfully protracted., The long-desired Armistice, eventually declared in November 1918, at last brought relief to some of the combatants. Within a month of the end Gerald had become a Second Lieutenant in the Coldstream Guards and was transferred to Wellington Barracks in Chelsea, where in the matter of a few weeks he was demobilized.

Many hundreds of thousands of war veterans had to wait until February or March 1919 to get their "ticket", which resulted in frustration and deep resentment and caused a Guards division to be brought back from Flanders to deal with "a certain amount of trouble" (as General Sir Henry Wilson, Chief of Imperial Staff, modestly understated in his diary on February 7th). That Gerald was unaware of what subsequently happened may seem surprising, but, since the nature of the "trouble" was kept under close wraps by those in power, none of it was allowed to leak into the papers. The Guards had to cope with angry, rebellious troops with fixed bayonets holding up the traffic in the centre of London and threatening to go to the Palace to get redress for their grievances from the King, while thousands of soldiers on Salisbury Plain refused point-blank to volunteer for the expeditionary force then being recruited to help combat the Bolshevik uprising in Russia. Later, on being put on compulsory draft to go there, they vociferously rebelled. Mutinous colonial troops were eventually placated and help to the White Russians had to be abandoned, for the Government came to its senses at last, albeit reluctantly, and realized that the war-weary troops had made their case and had had enough. The true temper of those times only emerged 60 years later when official records could be examined in detail.

Gerald left the Guards almost simultaneously with du Maurier, who returned to the theatre to pick up the threads and his managerial plans, but the two kept in friendly touch for some years. As a result of playing with him in *Vice Versa*, Gerald acquired a passion for acting and intended to make the stage his career. Robert Septimus, however, on hearing of his son's ambition, had very different ideas.

"My grey hairs will descend in sorrow to the grave if you ever become an actor," Robert Septimus pontificated. Then, seeing Gerald's keen disappointment and perhaps remembering his own real attachment to the theatre in his youth, not to mention a sneaking regard for it still (which he deviously concealed), he attempted persuasion and suggested a compromise. "Now, if you'll take my advice, dear boy, and go up to Oxford, you can qualify for the Bar, then if you find you don't care for it you can do whatever you choose afterwards. Think about it."

Thinking about it only served to convince Gerald that a future without participation in the theatre would be a bleak and unattractive one. To cross his father in anything was, he had always felt, extremely difficult and usually a rather hopeless venture, yet he desperately wanted to act. His dilemma was acute. After examining the problem in as reasonable and logical a manner as he could muster, he reduced it to a simple formula.

"Assuming I'm a failure at whatever I attempt," he told himself pessimistically, "it will be easier for me to go on the stage after failing at the Bar, than to go to the Bar after failing on the stage!" Having extracted this small grain of comfort from his decision, he communicated it to Robert Septimus, who accepted it and proceeded with alacrity to make plans for his legal future. If he had been told then that Gerald would one day reach the highest position in that profession, he would have been astonished, yet, thanks to his intuitive understanding of his son at that time, his choice of a career was instinctively the right one. As for Gerald, as he was later to discover, on the surface the two professions have much in common. "Once I got started in the law," he said, "I found it fascinating, and better than long runs. You write your own part and there's a good deal of acting in it, of course."

Several months now stretched ahead which had to be filled before he could enter Oxford. His father decided these must not on any account be squandered on frivolous pursuits, and arranged for him to spend six of them in Tours, learning to speak fluent French with a family who spoke no English.

Unfortunately, Tours at that time was full of other young men sent by their fathers from England with exactly the same purpose in mind. Inevitably they sought one another's company and went around the town together conversing in their mother tongue instead of the one they were bidden to learn. Gerald was no exception. When he returned to

Hardres Court at the end of the summer, having acquired only a passably good accent and slightly improved fluency, his father, who spoke the language like a native, was not exactly impressed. He continued to hope.

Shortly after arriving home Gerald learned to his chagrin that he had a further examination to sit before he could go up to Magdalen, which involved achieving a certain standard in Latin. This he found daunting, for since being in the army he had neglected the subject – he hated it anyway – and after a year had forgotten nearly all he had ever learned. Robert Septimus, realizing that he would never get through unless something was done about it, immediately sent him to a well-known crammer's establishment in Maidenhead. The man in charge was a master named Oldenshaw, who had been for several months President of the Union at Oxford. He proved an excellent coach, for Gerald passed his examination – but only, as he asserted later, because he pronounced an entirely new theory about Macbeth which impressed his examiners as highly original. He kept no record of this, and no amount of memory-jogging has ever produced it.

Meanwhile his brother Cyril had also been of some concern to his father, for being the eldest son he had not escaped active service and the rigours of war. He had joined a Kent regiment, the Buffs, and fought in Flanders, where he was wounded in the chest towards the end of hostilities. He had always been somewhat of a problem to Robert Septimus but a favourite with his mother. When the war was over and he had recovered from his wound, he was sent out to South America accompanied by a doctor, partly to recuperate and partly to make a career for himself. While he succeeded in the first he presumably failed in the second, for some time later he was back again in England and his father, not knowing what on earth to do with him, shipped him off to Australia, where he worked for a while on a sheep farm. Not exactly caring for this type of work, he abandoned it and found himself in Melbourne one evening having a drink with Seymour Hicks, the world-famous actor-manager, who apparently took a fancy to his fine speaking voice and personality and invited him to join his company. The offer was accepted.

When Robert Septimus heard the news he did not turn a hair, which always seemed to Gerald rather odd. Perhaps he had become resigned to the limited extent to which he could control his sons' affairs. In any case Cyril prospered and married Barbara Brandon, a well-known actress in Australia, who was also a member of Hicks' company, and eventually, when Colin Clive had to leave the cast of the war play, *Journey's End*, in London, took over his part and played it successfully for several years.

During the months of preparation and study before going up to Oxford, Gerald's emotional life had received a disturbing jolt from which he had emerged not entirely unscathed. He experienced his first love affair with a pretty young war widow whose husband had been killed in the fighting.

Gladys Howard and her father, a military man, were old friends of the Gardiner family and sometimes guests at Hardres Court. On one of their visits a romance developed. Judging from his photographs, Gerald at this time was a slim young man of six foot two, fair haired, with arresting blue eyes, and possessed of a beautiful speaking voice, like his brother. He found the Howard girl most attractive and they were well matched physically, though mentally (according to Gerald) they were worlds apart. Other young men reacted in the same way to Gladys Howard, especially a Major Mills who was several years her senior. She was then about twenty-one, a year older than Gerald, and sophisticated enough to realize the advantage of having two men rivalling each other for her affection. After a while things reached the point where she felt the need of advice concerning the choice of her future husband, and set about acquiring it in a rather bizarre fashion.

She had a very real admiration and respect for her father-in-law, Lord Howard of Glossop, who lived in the north of England and was fond of his late son's wife. An invitation to spend a holiday with him gave her the opportunity to include both Gerald and Major Mills as guests, thus paving the way for her to hear Lord Howard's views on their suitability as possible partners.

The two men eventually found themselves travelling north with her, and seemed to accept the situation without any particular embarrassment. At the end of the holiday, and after she had consulted her father-in-law on her matrimonial prospects, Gladys Howard broke the news to Gerald that she had decided to marry Major Mills. One of her reasons for rejecting Gerald was his inexperience with women, which apparently found no favour in her eyes. She advised him to remedy this as soon as possible if he wished to succeed with them. Gerald, although cast down, accepted the rebuff without rancour, but his hurt feelings affected his natural shyness and lack of self-confidence with women for the rest of his life.

*

The prospect of studying law for the next four years scarcely filled the young Gerald Gardiner with enthusiasm. No rooms were available for him in his college during the first year owing to chaotic conditions existing after the war, so he settled into lodgings in the Iffley Road to begin life as an Oxford undergraduate.

More to his liking was the opportunity to take an active interest in the theatre, which he found one of the dominant features of the university at that period. Very shortly after arriving at Magdalen he joined the Oxford University Dramatic Society, and within months he had established himself with this quasi-professional group, which was steadily increasing its reputation for putting on fine performances of classical plays with a growing number of talented actors drawn from the university. Its semi-professional nature arose from the fact that twice a year it hired a director, usually from the London stage, as well as the services of a West End actress to augment an otherwise male cast, in order to put on a play at the New Theatre in winter and another in the open air in summer. The director was paid £50 to produce, but the leading lady regarded it as a signal honour to be selected to play in an OUDS production and received nothing for her engagement. Since, however, the performances were always reviewed by the London critics, a considerable amount of valuable prestige attached to the star roles, which received reviews in the press, not to be sneezed at by any ambitious young actress.

The OUDS came into being in 1885 in a rather unusual way. Attendance at the Oxford theatre was strictly out of bounds to undergraduates during term-time, which meant that the evening before a new term commenced a large contingent of them made a beeline to the local Playhouse to make sure of their last chance to see the current show without being gated.

The quality of productions left a great deal to be desired, the plays themselves, mostly third-rate farces and vulgar comedies, being badly acted and even more atrociously directed. Arthur Bourchier (later to become one of London's renowned theatrical producers) was in one of these "pre-term" audiences at the Playhouse, full of excited young avatars of the drama, when he noticed as the show went on that the leading actor continued to wear the same pair of trousers over a period of thirty years! Others noticed this, too. It so outraged the young men that they rose in a body and stormed the stage, where several undergraduates violently debagged the unfortunate actor.

The following day Arthur Bourchier, triumphantly flourishing the trousers, was met in the High Street by the Vice-Chancellor, the great Jowett of Balliol, who asked him what he thought he was doing. Momentarily at a loss for a satisfactory explanation, the intimidated Bourchier fell silent. Next morning he was summoned to a meeting with the Vice-Chancellor to explain his behaviour. He arrived fully prepared to defend himself and the others who participated in the debagging incident.

There would be no repetition of the trouble at the Playhouse, he explained, if the management presented shows that had some merit, instead of the puerile stuff the undergraduates had to put up with. They deserved something better. Also, he continued, waxing more eloquent as he was not interrupted, why should the theatre be out of bounds to them during term-time? It would be far more beneficial if they were free to see good plays, well acted and produced, at any time during term; and come to that, was there any reason why the undergraduates shouldn't provide their own entertainment? It couldn't be worse than the shows the Playhouse had been giving during the last few years, and might be a great deal better.

Jowett apparently thought there was something in the idea. He eventually agreed to lift the ban on theatre-going during term-time and consented to the undergraduates putting on their own plays, provided they included a Greek one every four years and presented none written within the previous thirty years. This compromise was accepted with enthusiasm, although in effect it meant their choice was practically limited to classical plays. In no time at all the OUDS was formed by Bourchier, rehearsals began on its first play and from then on it never looked back.

At the time Gerald arrived on the scene the enterprising director, J. B. Fagan, had been asked to produce *Antony and Cleopatra* the following winter, and had accepted the offer. Gerald hoped to be included in the cast, and would have been but for the fact that he failed his examination at the end of his first year and was sent, for the second time, to the crammer, Oldenshaw. It was a great disappointment, for the production turned out to be a very fine one, with Cathleen Nesbitt playing Cleopatra opposite an astonishingly handsome young Antony called Cecil Ramage. During rehearsals their emotional relationship in the play obviously had a deep effect on them, for they fell in love, and by the time the play opened in December 1920 they had already decided to marry as early as possible. How the marriage progressed is revealed in

Cathleen Nesbitt's autobiography, *A Little Love and Good Company*. Her long and successful career continued into her nineties, her last appearance being in the New York production of *My Fair Lady* in 1980. In the media she is often referred to as the lover of the poet Rupert Brooke, almost never as the wife of Cecil Ramage.

Oldenshaw's coaching, meanwhile, eventually bore results, for on his second examination attempt Gerald passed, which must have been a source of relief to Robert Septimus. Since there were no further exams until the finals, which were not until three years hence, his son considered he was free to abandon serious study for the time being and devote himself to the theatre, which seemed infinitely more important.

Besides acting in several plays for the OUDS he accepted the offer to manage a production of *The Pretenders*, but this apparently failed to absorb all his energy, for he joined another amateur group, the Oxford Harrovian Dramatic Society, whose producer, Thorold Coade, put on plays which were performed in the speech room at Harrow; *The Speckled Band* gave Gerald the chance to play Sherlock Holmes to the Watson of Malcolm McCorquodale, who later entered politics and became an M.P.

Thorold Coade, a very energetic drama enthusiast, also ran another company of amateurs which toured the local Oxford villages, giving performances when and wherever possible. He delighted in good plays, and managed to persuade professional artists to take a role in them occasionally. When he put on Wilde's *Importance of Being Earnest*, in which Gerald took the leading part, Beatrix Lehmann joined them as Lady Bracknell. On another occasion G. K. Chesterton's *Magic* not only charmed the Oxford undergraduates but went over to Harrow with Anthony Eden and Gerald alternating in the role of the Duke. An Oxford contemporary described him as a very good actor with a beautiful voice.

Then there were the "Smokers", which came round regularly each year and were considered highly improper by some. They were variety performances which included songs, sketches and satirical skits on the particular play that had been presented by OUDS that season, and took place in the club dining-room for three consecutive nights. Following the West End theatre fashion of having "magazine-programmes", Gerald produced a similar one styled "Devised, Designed and Directed (in fact written) by G.A.G. with profuse apologies to the proprietors of magazine programmes". Contributing to the smokers was a young man from Wales, delighted to be learning the rudiments of his craft. His name was Emlyn Williams.

No opportunity for a celebration was ever missed by the undergraduates, and there were plenty of opportunities. A popular choice was boat-racing. Gerald, who normally disliked participating in any kind of sport, was somehow persuaded in his first year to row in a Magdalen College four. Perhaps, as he explained, it was because he always liked to try anything once. His crew happened to be successful in beating the other four, and later went on to the customary drinking party held in the college that evening.

Port wine was the main drink being served, and the session turned into a lengthy one with Gerald determined to discover what it was like to get drunk. This was again a desire to try everything once, and he found it dispiritingly slow. After downing glass after glass he was still stone cold sober. Disappointed, he held out his fourteenth for a refill, then the fifteenth, followed by the sixteenth. No result. Down went the seventeenth impatiently. *Wham!* He was out like a light! It must have required considerable strength and stamina to carry Gerald's unconscious body home to his lodgings in the town that night, but his convivial chums accomplished it without mishap. As far as he can remember he never repeated the "experiment".

The Oxford and Cambridge boat-race gave Gerald his first chance on radio. The OUDS, who always celebrated the event with a lighthearted show, offered it to the BBC in 1922. Gerald played a newsreader satirizing events of the day. Whether Gerald du Maurier heard this and was reminded of his talented colleague of Bushey days is doubtful, but he asked Gerald if he would care to act professionally opposite Tallulah Bankhead in *H.R.H.*, a play he was presenting. His rôle was to be that of the Prince of Wales, whom he slightly resembled at the time. Gerald, highly delighted to receive such an offer from someone so prestigious in the profession, had immediate thoughts of a dazzling success awaiting him on the stage. He was all agog to accept the wonderful opportunity offered by du Maurier, but once more he had reckoned without his father.

Robert Septimus, on learning of his intentions, vetoed them immediately, reminding him of his promise to qualify for the Bar, and that he was in duty bound to finish his stint at Oxford. Faced with such opposition Gerald either had to make a stand and face the unpleasant consequences or carry out his promise. Again he was beset by doubts. How really talented was he as an actor? Perhaps he was only a gifted amateur. If he turned down du Maurier's offer, would the opportunity ever occur in the future? What if he proved a failure? He was never to know the answers to his questions. Feeling unsure of himself and at the same time hating to break a promise, he finally gave in and agreed to stay on at Oxford.

Gerald lost nothing by declining du Maurier's offer, for when *H.R.H.* went into production the title was changed to *The Dancers*. His part raised serious objections from the Lord Chamberlain, who considered that the character whom it portrayed bore too close a resemblance to the Prince of Wales. This resulted in its total elimination from the play. A new character, that of a Russian Grand Duke, was introduced and subsequently played by Scott-Gatty for 344 performances.

Having agreed to stay on at Oxford, Gerald did not lose interest in the theatre; if anything, he clung to it with ever renewed vigour. He became a moving spirit in the OUDS' many productions, finally being elected its President in 1922. During that time he acted Orlando in *As You Like It* opposite Joan Buckmaster's Rosalind, Horatio in *Hamlet* and Cleonte in *Le Bourgeois Gentilhomme*, and spoke the Prologue to *Henry IV, Part I*. In an earlier performance of this play, many years previously, Cosmo Lang had undertaken the Prologue, and on its revival, when he was Archbishop of York, he was invited to see it. He signed the visitors' book Cosmo Ebor and many thought this must be the signature of some actor of that name! Gerald would have preferred a more exacting rôle, but since he had been neglecting his studies on becoming President, he felt some serious swotting was indicated. Playing a minor rôle was better than being excluded altogether, especially as the production was an outstanding one, designed and directed by J. B. Fagan with Gyles Isham playing Hotspur. As well as Gerald, those who played subsequently with Gyles and were later to become famous professionals were Patrick Waddington, Tyrone Guthrie and Richard Goolden. In *Hamlet* the following year Robert Spaight appeared as the First Player and – seated in the corner but admonished: "Don't prompt unless there's a dead emergency" – was Emlyn Williams, who described Gyles' Hamlet as "a romantic and vital presence embodying youth and breeding – quite electric".

During the following ten years, while struggling to establish himself in the legal profession, Gerald found time to be a member not only of the Windsor Strollers, but also of the Old Stagers of Canterbury, playing with them whenever possible. The opportunities to participate, however, grew fewer and fewer as the law involved steadily more of his time, and eventually his association with the two societies petered out a few years before World War II.

Interest in the OUDS was a different matter. It never waned, and in 1946 he was so troubled by the state of its finances that he organized a gala matinée which turned out to be most successful. A surprising number of luminaries in the London theatre, and many lesser lights, offered their services, and so put the OUDS firmly back on its feet again.

One of the events contributing to the near insolvency of the OUDS occurred when John Fernald engaged the celebrated Max Reinhardt to produce *A Midsummer Night's Dream*. Fernald was justifiably proud of persuading the great German producer to direct it for the extremely modest fee of £50 for the week. On the day of his arrival, Fernald and members of the committee went down to Oxford railway station to welcome him. When the train drew in Reinhardt emerged smiling from his carriage, followed by an entire posse of stage hands and electricians. The committee was stunned. Reinhardt they had made arrangements for, but not his huge entourage, all of whom had to be accommodated somehow, which was the last thing they had envisaged and knew they could not possibly afford. Nevertheless it was managed, but years passed before the finances of the OUDS recovered from the shock.

It was in the face of such difficult problems that Gerald's equanimity and air of imperturbability led to a society being formed in Magdalen calling itself the S.R.G.G.H., the Society for Ruffling Gerald Gardiner's Hair. There is no doubt that he had an unusually calm mien during crises, disasters never seeming to rattle him, and when he accepted responsibility for a job it was carried out with meticulous care. Most undergraduates referred to him and remembered him as quite unflappable, a quality which was to prove indispensable when he became an advocate. And – unlike many people whose gifts exceed the average – everyone liked him at Oxford.

During his four years there, Gerald's participation in theatrical activities, while dominating his life, did not by any means wholly fill it. He indulged in other pursuits which, although he found them less fascinating, were intriguing and mind-stretching.

Soon after his arrival at Magdalen he discovered the existence of the debating society, and in no time at all became involved with the Oxford University New Reform Club, which had a wide range of political objectives. It had been formed in 1920 by Gerald Howard of Balliol, and in 1922 the freshly formed committee headed by Gerald, its new President, felt that a change of programme was urgently needed.

The club did not support any particular political party, but set out with a definite and clear policy evolved along new lines to meet post-war problems and instigate reforms to deal with them. These suggested reforms were many and varied, including such controversial subjects as divorce, prostitution and homosexuality, in addition to the recurring problems of Ireland, taxation, agricultural and foreign policy. When Gerald's father, now Sir Robert, discovered that his son was president of a club advocating that homosexual acts between consenting adults should no longer be regarded as a criminal offence, he declared that if he had known about it in time he would have made it his business to come to Oxford and put a stop to it.

Gerald's introduction to politics at this early period can be attributed in great part to the influence of the New Reform Club, for by the time he came down from Oxford his political opinions had obviously taken root. Many of the club's objectives remained with him for the next forty years, and many were eventually achieved when he was in a position to deal with them in the House of Lords. The most important issues he concerned himself with then were reforms in the law relating to divorce, homosexual offences, legal punishment for suicide and capital punishment. All these were first put forward by the New Reform Club in 1922 and pigeon-holed in Gerald's retentive memory. By those who wished for no change in the *status quo* they were regarded as the reforms of a "left-winger", and Gerald, commenting in an interview over fifty years later, had this to say of them: "Those on the right are just as sincere as those on the left, but the great advantage of being on the left, though it's unfair, is that if you live long enough you live to see your dreams come true. Whereas if you're on the right, you only live to see your worst fears confounded."

Concurrent with his involvement in the New Reform Club were his interests in the Oxford Union, which were shared by a number of other young men who carved distinguished careers for themselves later in life. Robert Boothby shared a suite of rooms with Gerald in his third year, and other contemporaries, though not all at Magdalen, were Evelyn Waugh, Beverley Nichols, Hore Belisha, Charles Morgan and Michael Tandy (brother of Jessica Tandy). Among the well-known speakers whom the Union persuaded to attend debates were G. K. Chesterton, Hilaire Belloc and Lloyd George. When the great Welshman came one evening to defend the Treaty of Versailles, Gerald spoke against the Asquithian Liberals (represented by a Mr Pringle, M.P.), the dominant party in the Union. There was keen argument just then about the reparations a bankrupt Germany was being forced to pay. Gerald supported the idea that the reparations were so excessive that they couldn't possibly be paid, and that it would be better for the world to get the country back on its feet and trading again than to try to starve it into submission.

Another outstanding debate was on the subject of contraception, an almost forbidden topic at that time. Gerald's side, which was strongly in favour, won a resounding victory over the opposition. When Dr Marie Stopes came to Oxford some months later to address a Saturday night meeting in the town hall on family planning, the Vice-Chancellor of the university banned it for undergraduates on the grounds that it was not a fit subject for discussion. Whereupon Ruskin College, which believed in free speech but not in contraception, threw their hall open to her and the meeting took place. Gerald was then in his fourth year and in 1924 had been elected President of the Union (the first to be elected from Magdalen College for many years). He decided that this was an opportunity to show solidarity and joined Marie Stopes on the platform. There is no record of what his father said on this occasion!

During his last summer at Oxford, the Union was invited to take part in a debate with a college in the Eastern states of America. Although Bates College was small, it had won a reputation for winning most of the debating competitions in the U.S.A., and now, with the help of several other famous North American colleges, a series of debates was mooted with the Oxford team.

The offer was accepted with enthusiasm. Robert Septimus approved of the idea and gave Gerald a cheque for £70 to enable him to sail a week earlier than the scheduled date so that he could spend some time enjoying the country prior to the hectic fortnight planned for the Oxford Union, which turned out to consist of one-night stands. Among those who joined Gerald were Douglas Woodruff (later to become Editor of *The Tablet*), Christopher Scaife, the poet, and Arthur Bagnall, who had been President of the Union before Gerald.

The Oxford debaters chose two subjects, "The French occupation of the Ruhr" (the American colleges mostly opted for this), or "The League of Nations" (Canada's choice). The latter was a touchy subject, for although it was President Wilson's brain child the U.S.A. had originally refused to join the League, only later changing its mind. The serious nature of the debates was rejected at Columbia, where a more light-hearted note was struck. Their subject was announced as "The Statue of Liberty Faces the Wrong Way".

The visiting group soon found that no two methods of debating could have been more unlike than the English and American. The Oxford Union tended to spice their speeches with wisecracks and witty jokes to enliven the debate, whereas the Americans were deadly serious in their approach, talking in a fast monotone in order to get in as many arguments as possible and so receive more marks from the judges at the end. The Oxford group also found that the Americans went into strict training for three months before the event, renounced smoking, and engaged coaches and readers to research the subject for them. As a great favour to the visiting team, the Americans agreed to give up their judges who normally nominated the winner and adopt the English style of debate, which meant that the outcome was decided entirely on votes from the audience as to which was the better team.

The debates were conducted in a distinctly formal atmosphere. On each side of the platform was a table, behind which hung the Union Jack and the Stars and Stripes respectively, while in the chair the state senator was ensconced to provide any necessary guidance to the teams. The Americans, having done their homework, had meticulously card-indexed all possible arguments and questions with the relevant answers and filed them away in a box which they kept for reference on their table. The English team was puzzled during one of the debates by a curious ticking sound which fell on their ears from time to time. Eventually they discovered that it was their opponents flicking over their card index in order to check up on the appropriate answers. At another college they learned that the American side had sent spies in advance to learn what the Oxford Group's arguments were, in order to be better prepared for their own debate.

The audiences varied slightly. At Harvard the function was held in the Boston Symphony Hall, where theatre prices were charged for admission, but in Dartmouth the audience consisted mainly of students. On the whole the Oxford Union came out of the venture with some distinction, for the audiences, delighted by the humorous vein which ran through their speeches, voted nearly every time in their favour.

Before they returned to England they had the privilege of being received at the White House by the celebrated President Calvin Coolidge. He turned out to be a somewhat monosyllabic gentleman who did not appear to know where they hailed from.

"Oxford, sir," they explained.

He reflected for a moment or two, then: "Very old, Oxford," was his sole comment.

On his return there Gerald learned that he had obtained his degree – fourth class. While disappointing, this was not entirely unexpected, since the time he had spent studying during the past four years was distinctly out of proportion to that spent on the OUDS and the Oxford Union. A slight consolation was granted to him when his college invited him to stay on for another year, ostensibly to study for his Civil Law degree, but in reality in recognition of the fact that for the first time in fifty years a Magdalen man had been elected President of the Union.

Gerald was most happy to accept, but within a few weeks he had effectively blotted his copy-book by creating a new record. He was the only President of the Union to be sent down during his term of office!

The editor of the famous Oxford magazine, *Isis*, was partially instrumental in bringing this about. Michael Tandy, who had recently taken over the editorship and found it something of a burden, had asked Gerald to be its sub-editor. To this he rather reluctantly agreed, feeling that he already had too many irons in the fire. A short while later Tandy came to him with an article written by a woman undergraduate which he said Mr Gull (commonly known as Gully), the proprietor of *Isis*, would not allow him to publish. The article was a strong and cogent indictment of the restrictions and old-fashioned rules practised in the women's colleges, which the writer, who had just gone down, found insulting and inhibiting to her sex compared with the more liberal ones existing in the male colleges.

Tandy felt it was a good article and should be published, and Gerald concurred. The writer of the piece was Dilys Powell, who later blossomed into our foremost film critic. After some consideration they decided to issue it as a pamphlet at threepence a copy, the cost of printing to be shared equally between Gerald and Michael. The pamphlet duly appeared and was put on sale on the streets of Oxford. It would have gone on selling but for the heads of the women's colleges, who complained in harsh terms to the proctors. Gerald and Michael were summoned to justify their conduct, which was regarded with the utmost severity. Knowing that if Michael, who was still studying to get his degree, was sent down it would be a severe set-back to him, Gerald explained to the proctors that the whole thing was entirely his own idea and little, if any, blame attached to Tandy. Consequently Gerald was sent down while Tandy was gated for the rest of the term, which turned out to be beneficial for him in the end as it forced him to concentrate on his studies instead of on frivolous things like the editorship of *Isis*.

Since Gerald had to resign from the magazine in what he felt were rather ignominious circumstances, it was a pity he could not foresee the kind of glowing tribute *Isis* was to pay him in the distant future after his successful legal cases hit the headlines. "The more we contemplate our idol, the more does he paralyse us with awe. A prince among barristers!"

He went back to the bosom of his family in dubious mood. As they considered his future, neither he nor his father could have been exactly cheered by the opinion of his Magdalen tutor, Mr Segar, who gave it as his considered opinion that Gerald would never achieve any succcess in a legal career. However, contrary to what might have been expected, Robert Septimus reacted to his return with unusual equanimity. Perhaps the fact that his son had acquired a reputation as a speaker and had been elected President of the Union, as well as President of the OUDS, compensated for the fourth-class degree and for having been "sent down". In any case, Gerald cannot remember his father being in the least put out by his last escapade, or by Mr Segar's views. Instead he took the practical and sensible step of sending his son to study law with Messrs Gibson and Weldon, the well-known tutors for the Bar examinations. He spared no expense in furthering Gerald's career, and continued to do so for many years to come.

After several months' tuition, Gerald passed his examinations and was admitted to the Bar in 1925.

AMONG THE PEOPLE visiting Oxford during the early nineteen-
twenties was one who was to play a significant rôle in the future life of
Gerald Gardiner. At a party to which the lady had been invited,
probably by his close friend, the actress Auriol Lee (he is a little hazy as
to exactly where and how they met), he found himself introduced to a
vivacious, elegant young woman with a lively air of sophistication and
wit, who immediately attracted him. She, in her turn, charmed by his
personality and good looks, found they had much in common, since she
loved the theatre and everything connected with it as enthusiastically
as he did. They soon began to see quite a lot of each other.

Lesly was the daughter of Edwin Trounson, J.P., of Southport. At
the time of meeting Gerald, she was not living with her parents, but in a
small flat of her own in London. Gerald soon learned of her extremely
unhappy youth, followed by a marriage which had been equally
miserable, if not downright disastrous. As an imaginative, high-
spirited child Lesly had early run into trouble at school and was
severely punished by her puritan parents, who decided that she should
change to a convent education in the hope of improving her conduct.
Some of her trivial misdemeanours were dealt with by her mother
over-zealously to the point of harshness: for instance, by subjecting her
daughter to confinement in a dark cupboard for several hours, and on
other occasions forcing her to contemplate a series of medieval
paintings, horrifying in their ferocious cruelty, the memories of which
haunted her for many a year.

After she left school her parents, at a loss to know what to do with her,
sent her off to Paris for a year or two to study art, the only thing for
which she showed any aptitude. When she eventually returned home
they married her off to the son of a wealthy chemist in the Midlands.
The marriage was doomed from the start. Lesly discovered that her
husband was an acute alcoholic, and during his drunken bouts he
treated her abominably. Later the birth of a child, although a partial
consolation, could not wholly compensate her for the misery she
suffered at the hands of her husband. In the end, and in utter
desperation, she left him and gave her little son into the care of his

grandparents while she went to London to seek a way out of her wretched situation. It was then that she and Gerald met.

Meanwhile her husband, whose health had deteriorated alarmingly since she had left him, and who had been forced to have treatment at a home for alcoholics, had fallen in love and had an affair with his nurse, which gave Lesly the chance she had long wanted. She sued for divorce and successfully obtained it in 1925, the year Gerald became a member of the Bar. By this time they were deeply in love and eager to get married, but his financial prospects were scarcely promising. All he could offer Lesly to live on was the £700 a year his father allowed him during his Oxford years. How much longer this would continue, and whether the idea of marriage might adversely affect the situation, was highly problematical. Gerald was enough of a realist to know that his earnings at the Bar during the first few years would be negligible, but something had to be done. Eventually he approached his only source of monetary aid: his father.

Much depended on Sir Robert's reaction at meeting Lesly for the first time. He found her socially very attractive (she was a fine bridge player), a lively conversationalist and, being a great reader, well informed – all qualities he admired. In fact, he was so impressed by her personality that he generously agreed to continue Gerald's allowance, thus enabling the couple to marry. Before the year was out the ceremony took place in the Chapel Royal, Savoy, between a young man of twenty-five and a bride ten years his senior, a fact he was not to discover until after the knot was tied.

There were other surprises in store for him, one of which took several decades to emerge. The expensive honeymoon which the couple enjoyed in Monte Carlo was made infinitely more delightful by additional money that Lesly helpfully supplied. Unknown to Gerald, she had charmed a "loan" of £500 from one of his barrister friends just before the wedding. It was thirty years before he discovered this, and the fact that it had never been repaid. She explained that she had borrowed the money solely because she wanted him to enjoy a carefree honeymoon without the worry of its cost!

The couple returned to London and settled down, in a small flat, to learn the delicate art of living together, something they were to find increasingly difficult as the years went by. Lesly's casual attitude towards money, combined with a real generosity towards her friends, presented Gerald with a complex and sometimes baffling personality. He began to dread her forays into the West End, which generally resulted in some extravagant purchase for their home he knew they could ill afford.

Earning a living at the Bar was none too easy in 1925, for there were far more barristers than briefs to go round, and many young men were leaving the profession because they could not wait for work to come their way. Gerald's pupilage began in the chambers of St John Field, and cost at that time £100. He found himself sharing a small, cramped room with several other pupils at 2 The Cloisters; among them was Hartley Shawcross (who later became Attorney-General in the Labour Government of 1945). The office was run by a head clerk, Mr Adam, whom Gerald regarded as somewhat of a martinet. Later, in 1928, a young man named Wilfred Button entered the same chambers and began his pupilage.

Speaking to Wilfred Button in the eighties, I asked him if he had any recollection of Gerald at that time.

He smiled. "It's such a long while ago – so many years have passed since then that only one thing remains vivid in my memory. One evening in the early thirties, it must have been, I happened to be working late in the office when Mr Adam stopped to chat with me on his way out. He ended by remarking: 'You know you're working here with a very exceptional fellow, don't you?' Mystified, I asked whom he meant. 'Gerald Gardiner, of course. You mark my words, he'll go to the top of his profession.' He then leaned forward and stared straight into my eyes and repeated: 'And when I say to the top of his profession, I don't mean just the top. I mean to the *very* top!' With that he left me."

This prophetic statement was echoed later by Wilson Wiley, a solicitor who sent Gerald many briefs over the following years, for the two had been contemporaries at Oxford. He too remembered Adam remarking that Gerald would undoubtedly become Lord Chancellor. "His capacity for work was extraordinary, and he took endless trouble with his briefs, yet had the gift of appearing to do everything without effort. When Lesly held bridge parties, which usually lasted until about 11.30 or 12, he never excused himself on the score of work, even if he had a heavy case coming up next day and a lot of papers to get through. He studied them thoroughly until five or so, and then went to bed for a couple of hours. I remember reading an opinion of his which concluded with the words: 'I feel so strongly about this case that if I'm wrong I will pay all the costs' – and there can't be many barristers who have ever said that!'"

Gerald could scarcely have written in this vein when he was beginning his career, for his income was non-existent for some time. His work consisted mainly of writing drafts (or devilling, as it is called) for his chief, and attending St John Field's cases, and also attending interlocutory summonses in the High Court, for all of which he was not paid.

For the first year his income was nil, the second year it was the same, and for the third it jumped into the three guinea bracket in payment of a brief to take a note for St John Field on the only occasion when he appeared in a County Court case. The action was between two women dog-owners, and the question to be decided was whether a dog with one testicle which had descended into its scrotum could be regarded as a "fit" dog for all normal purposes. Apparently it could, and St. John Field won the day.

These three years had not been kind to the Gardiners, for during them Lesly had suffered a serious blow from which she never completely recovered. Her young son Neill, to whom she was devotedly attached, suddenly died of meningitis at the tender age of nine. The tragedy affected her health, and for years afterwards she could not bear to hear his name mentioned. Eventually she recovered sufficiently to make up her mind to repair her loss by having another child, or perhaps she may have felt that, as she was nearing forty, delay in doing so might be risky. Whichever it was that decided her, Lesly gave birth to a daughter on December 5th, 1929. She was christened Carol, and from that day forward became a focus of love and attention for her mother and Gerald until she left England 28 years later and went to work in the U.S.A. Even then the affectionate link was unbroken, for whenever she returned to England the time was generally spent in her parents' company.

Fortunately, in the thirties Gerald's income began a slow but steady rise from a lowly £140 a year to £750 and then £1,500, and by the end of the decade had mounted considerably beyond the latter figure. Gradually he broadened his experience by taking cases in the various County Courts around London, where he formed a very low opinion of the quality of the judges presiding. Their peculiarities and eccentricities struck him forcibly, leaving him with the impression that they were colourful characters rather than good judges.

At that time any barrister could apply for a County Court judgeship, his appointment depending solely on the Lord Chancellor's opinion of his qualifications, which were submitted on a long detailed form. Gerald felt that this method of selection called for reform and years later, on becoming Lord Chancellor himself, he tried out a new one.

The most promising applicants who submitted their names to him (about a dozen a year from each circuit) were asked to send in their qualifications. After carefully considering them Gerald later interviewed each one personally before making his final choice, for he considers the appointment of judges to be one of the most important functions of the Lord Chancellor, since, when things go wrong on the Bench, everything else tends to go wrong. He thinks too that circuit judges should hear both criminal and civil cases, because it is not good for them to be continuously involved in criminal cases. During the last half-century the standard of judgment in both High and County Courts has improved greatly, in his opinion, but progress has been a slow, gradual affair.

Like most Junior Counsel he was quick to learn the nuances and "tricks" of his trade. During an action in which an Irish K.C. found himself in a tight corner, he resorted to quoting an obscure passage in Coke (the lawyer's Bible) which had absolutely no relevance to the case in question. When asked afterwards by his Junior why he had gone to the trouble of quoting it, he said: "Sure, it'll take the other side a week to trace it, and by then the case will be over!"

Another action involving a theatrical entrepreneur who was suing an agent gave Gerald a refreshing angle on his profession. The entrepreneur, anxious to be helpful, asked Counsel if it would advance his chances if he sent some theatre tickets to the Judge trying the case. He was told firmly and categorically that this would be tantamount to bribery, and in no circumstances was he to do so. The case proceeded and was eventually won by the entrepreneur, who later thanked Counsel, saying: "I did what you told me. I sent those tickets to the Judge."

The barrister was astounded. "But I told you not to!"

His client beamed triumphantly back. "Oh, don't worry. I sent them in the name of the defendant!"

In the early thirties Gerald further widened his scope by joining the Midland Circuit, which, being the one favoured by St John Field's chambers and covering the towns of Bedford, Northampton, Warwick, Coventry and Birmingham, gave him first-hand knowledge of proceedings in the provincial courts. The most valuable experience gained as a Junior, however, was in being led by Sir Norman Birkett and Sir Patrick Hastings in the many libel cases in which they appeared. In Sir Oswald Mosley's libel action against the *Star* newspaper in 1933 he had the satisfaction, as Junior to Sir Patrick, of studying them both at close quarters, since they were opposing Counsel.

The spectacle of these two brilliant and outstanding advocates eloquently conducting their cases with cut and thrust served as a fascinating model, and taught him more than anything else the intricacies, not only of libel and slander law, but of the subtle art of advocacy. Whereas Birkett prepared his cases with great skill and thoroughness, his vast knowledge of the Bible and Shakespeare coming through to enrich his speeches, Pat Hastings' fine gifts as an orator exercised an almost magnetic power of persuasion over a jury. Their individual talents showed a marked difference, for when their reported speeches came under examination in the sober light of day Birkett's prose read impeccably, hardly a comma needing to be inserted, while Pat Hastings' speeches quite often verged on the incoherent in their most impassioned moments.

Another case in which they appeared opposite each other was that brought by Baron Victor de Stempel, a Russian aristocrat and naturalized Briton, against Mr Walter Dunkels, a rich diamond broker whose step-daughter had married the Baron, with whom later she had marital difficulties resulting in separation. The situation was complicated by the fact that Victor de Stempel was employed in the firm of diamond brokers run by his father-in-law's cousin, Otto Dunkels. When the troubles his step-daughter was having with her husband reached Walter Dunkels' ears, he remarked to Otto: "Victor is a Jew-hater and unfit to be employed in the business." He succeeded, after much pressure, in persuading Otto Dunkels to dismiss de Stempel, who promptly brought an action for alleged breach of contract.

Sir Norman Birkett, who appeared for the Baron, won the case and £6,000 damages for his client, but it was a long time before he received them. Walter Dunkels, extremely dissatisfied with the verdict against him, decided to take his case to the Court of Appeal, where he lost for a second time. Nothing daunted, and seemingly determined to ruin de Stempel at all costs (money being no object to him), he went on to the House of Lords for another try, but this time he changed his Leading Counsel. Sir Patrick Hastings, who had been acting for him so far, was not the best man to argue his case further in the Lords, since he was considered brilliant at cross-examination but less so in arguing fine legal points on appeal, and in this particular case he would not be required to examine witnesses but to show great legal expertise.

At this stage the Baron also chose to make a change, but for a very different reason. He could no longer afford his leading Counsel's fees. The £6,000 damages awarded to him two years earlier had still not been received, since they had been held by the court pending the outcome of both Appeals, and this put him in serious financial straits. He reluctantly came to the decision, therefore, to relinquish Sir Norman Birkett and take instead his Junior Counsel, Gerald Gardiner, who had been on the case through the previous hearings. Thus Gerald found himself appearing in the House of Lords opposite the new Leading Counsel engaged by Walter Dunkels, who turned out to be none other than the formidable Sir Stafford Cripps.

This gentleman, who was eleven years older than the Junior facing him, already had a considerable reputation, not only in the legal world but in political circles. He had risen rapidly in his profession, becoming a K.C. in 1927 and four years later Solicitor-General. It was during World War II, however, that he achieved great prominence in other directions. In quick succession he was appointed Minister of Aircraft Production, then President of the Board of Trade and, after hostilities ceased, Chancellor of the Exchequer. Widely known for his austerity and skilful handling of diplomatic relations, he was sent to Russia as a Special Envoy in 1940. All this, of course, was in the future; on that day in the Lords Gerald recognized him simply as the leading member of the Bar specializing in civil cases, of whom it was rumoured that, when offered a brief he did not care for, he would raise his fee to 1,000 guineas a day (with refreshers) in order to put the prospective client off. On this occasion it apparently did not, for the fee was paid!

It was the first time Gerald had conducted an appeal on his own in the House, and to have such an opponent must have been, to say the least, awe-inspiring. How he proceeded to handle it is not known (records are not kept of Counsel's speeches in the House of Lords), but the result must have been extremely gratifying. Walter Dunkels' appeal was dismissed, four judges concurring with one against, and Baron de Stempel was awarded his long-deferred costs.

As a result of his increasing experience in libel law, Gerald's name inevitably started to crop up whenever these cases were fought or defended. The Beaverbrook newspapers were not slow to take note over the years, and he eventually became standing Counsel to them and also appeared for *The Times* and the *Daily Worker*, whose policies could not have been more alien. It often surprises the layman that a barrister who is generally regarded as a tolerant non-racialist should accept a brief which results in the defence of a client with diametrically opposite views. There is a seeming anomaly here which appears to show an unethical aspect on the part of Counsel in legal cases, and which could be puzzling when Gerald's participation in the previous cases is considered. Most people were aware that he was a pacifist and a hater of racism, yet he agreed to act for Sir Oswald Mosley and Baron de Stempel, both of whom could not have been exactly *en rapport* with him, the former being associated with anti-Semitism and the latter, as a White Russian refugee from Soviet Russia, with anti-communism.

When questioned on this score, Gerald explained the position in which a barrister finds himself when accepting briefs. According to the principle at the Bar, laid down by Lord Erskine and continued by the Bar Council, a barrister, if free, is bound to appear for any client who wants him at a proper fee. It was in accordance with this principle that Gerald acted for Mosley and the British Union of Fascists, for the Communist Harry Pollitt and the *Daily Worker*, for Dr Alan Nunn May in the Soviet spy trial, and for a great many others with whose political views he was not in sympathy. An advocate is there, he says, to put his client's case, not to express his own opinion; and if he were to give his personal view in court by beginning a speech: "I think so-and-so . . ." he would, quite properly, be reprimanded by the judge.

During the thirties his reputation as a sound and reliable Junior barrister was increasingly recognized, and he found, rather to his surprise, that the legal profession was far more to his liking than he had imagined in his salad days. The fact that every case was different, and each about real things that mattered desperately to the person concerned, weighed heavily with him when he compared his present profession with the theatrical one which only a few years back had seemed so desirable.

As he remarked later in life: "If I had the chance to live it over again and was offered the choice between being a barrister on a miner's pay or being a miner on a barrister's pay, I'd be a barrister every time."

Shortly after Carol's birth her parents decided they needed a home away from London, and they began looking round for a house in Surrey. They eventually found The Briars at Oxshott, and thereafter Gerald began commuting to the Temple. They were not to remain there overlong, for Lesly, having a penchant for change, soon discovered a larger place, Hill House, possessing an attractive situation and extensive grounds, which she felt suited them better. There they settled down and lived until the beginning of World War II, the longest spell they ever spent in one house.

Every morning Lesly would drive Gerald to the station (she was an excellent driver) and meet him each night on his return, but although she ran their home with commendable efficiency and care and saw that Carol lacked for nothing, their married life was far from smooth. Though he never uttered a word of reproach or anger, Lesly's expensive tastes turned out to be a source of intense and continual worry to Gerald over the years, for he never knew from one day to the next how he was going to meet the bills which suddenly dropped into his lap, usually for a piece of fine furniture, an antique or some china that had caught Lesly's fancy and unexpectedly appeared in Hill House as a result.

The number of nightmarish hours spent tramping up and down, agonizing about writs and summonses ending in possible bankruptcy, never seemed to diminish. On one occasion, when he was desperate and found things seemingly hopeless, Robert Septimus came to the rescue, providing financial help for Lesly when she needed it.

Robert Septimus and Alice visited Hill House from time to time, but he was becoming increasingly infirm, and on November 16th, 1939, only a few months after war with Germany was declared, he died at the age of eighty-three. Alice felt his loss deeply, and after the funeral went to recover at the Convent of Our Lady in St Leonard's-on-Sea. Her appreciation of Gerald's help came in a letter to him a few days later, when she wrote:

It would be impossible for any Mother to have found greater support and comfort in her son than I did in you. Your prompt rallying to my side at the time when your dear father's illness became serious; your able handling of all those endless and difficult business problems arising at such a time; your personal loving sympathy in my grief; your readiness to consider any alterations I wished to make in what had already meant strenuous arrangements for you; your great devotion to my darling during his illness and the loving care you gave him – all these are memories which can never be effaced and which will remain with me so long as my own life still lasts . . .

Many years later, on looking back at his father's death, Gerald expressed regret at the lack of a closer relationship between them, since there were many things he felt they could perhaps have discussed to their mutual enjoyment, but the difference in age and temperament always seemed too wide a gulf to be bridged, and thus they remained enigmas to each other. There is no doubt that Gerald owed Robert Septimus a vast debt for his initial encouragement and financial support during the early years of his career at the Bar and later in his marriage, when he suffered strains that needed understanding and help which was always forthcoming. Although politically in opposite camps, they never quarrelled over their opinions, for Gerald retained a youthful awe of his father and avoided any provocative encounters by taking refuge in silence.

Although he would have been surprised had anyone suggested that he resembled Robert Septimus, Gerald's rebellious streak was possibly inherited from his father, who shocked his revered parent by introducing the Lyric Club to London, with performances on Sunday nights. This innovation was calculated to outrage the religious feelings of any Victorian family, and showed courage. The theatre and entertainment world held fascinations for both father and son: it was not until late middle age, when Robert Septimus ceased to be active in it, that he opposed Gerald's choice of a stage career, possibly because by then he realized its hazardous nature and wished his son to choose a more secure profession. Gerald's success as President of the Union convinced his father that he was fitted for the law, where he could best develop his talents; and so it proved.

Other eccentricities were shared by father and son: Robert Septimus never ate watercress or any fruit containing pips, on the ground that they might cause appendicitis. Gerald refrained likewise, but expressed a simple dislike of them. In most other respects they were poles apart, for he was as shy and retiring as his father was outgoing and sociable, while their politics were totally opposed.

Sir Robert, who had suffered severe shipping losses during the depression years of the twenties and thirties, nevertheless left sufficient money to keep Alice in reasonable comfort for the rest of her days, yet no more than that. She survived him by fourteen years and was fortunately spared a second loss in the family which occurred a year after her death. Her youngest son, Nevile, since leaving Oxford had entered the Civil Service in Washington and spent much of his life abroad, ending up in The Hague as Commercial Secretary in the Diplomatic Service. In 1954 he was posted from there to the Philippines, where he had the ill-luck to be bitten by a poisonous insect. He was rushed to the American Hospital, but despite all efforts to save him he died within 48 hours.

Following their move to Oxshott, Gerald contacted the local Labour party and joined it soon after. Unemployment at that time was near the million mark, and the fact that it was steadily becoming worse instead of better concerned him deeply, rousing him to take an active interest in the party which was trying to solve labour's problems. The Oxford University New Reform Club had already given him a desire to see a different and more equitable society than one producing hunger marches, particularly the army of unemployed led by the diminutive Ellen Wilkinson on the long trek from Jarrow to London to ask for help. Within a short while he became chairman of his local branch, and was able to give it any legal advice it needed.

Gerald's interest in law reform intensified during the period leading up to 1939. He became a member of the Haldane Society, originally a legal club formed in the late twenties and named after the first Labour Lord Chancellor, Viscount Haldane, who died in 1929.[*] There had been in existence for some years an Inns of Court Conservative Society, consisting mainly of Conservative barristers. The time came when many thought this needed to be balanced by one made up of lawyers of a different political persuasion. Thus a number of Labour lawyers formed the Haldane Society, which supported the Labour party and became affiliated to it in 1938. Membership of the party was also a prerequisite for joining the Haldane Society and enabled it to send a delegate to the annual Labour party Conference. The policy of the Society was to give legal advice to national and local organizations of the Labour party, Trades Unions and Co-operatives, and generally to promote the interests of the Labour party and further the cause of socialism.

Gerald soon found himself very active on its behalf, seeing in it an excellent chance of exercising his reforming zeal in various directions. Unfortunately war intervened and frustrated most of his efforts, and only years later, after hostilities had ceased, did they gradually begin to bear fruit. One example of this was his passionate conviction of the need to abolish the death penalty; he never lost an opportunity to address meetings up and down the country, sometimes to audiences numbering fewer than a dozen people. Not until the middle sixties, however, were his efforts successful.

During the "phoney war" period of 1939–40 he became involved in a legal contretemps concerning the imprisonment under Regulation 18B, on the direction of the Home Secretary, John Anderson, of a man called

[*] Not to be confused with his celebrated nephew, J. B. S. Haldane, the radical scientist.

Liversidge. There had been much criticism of this regulation* in the House of Commons, as a result of which several amendments were made to it. In 1941 Liversidge appealed against his detention in Brixton prison, and his case went to a second Appeal in the House of Lords. Lord Atkin, who believed that Liversidge should be released, dissented from four of his fellow judges in the interpretation of the Regulation, saying he had listened to "arguments which might have been addressed acceptable to the Court of King's Bench in the time of Charles I".

These were strong words, and roused the editor of *The Times* to indite a 1,000-word leader expressing his views of the case. Two days later this elicited a reply from Lord Maugham, the Lord Chancellor,† who took the somewhat unprecedented step of commenting on his distinguished colleague Lord Atkin. Explaining that, in accordance with the tradition at the bar, Counsel for the Home Office could not reply to Lord Atkin's dissentient speech, he added: "I think it only fair . . . to say that I presided at the hearing and listened to every word of their arguments, and that I did not hear from them, or anyone else, anything which could justify such a remark."

Gerald, who had followed the proceedings and discussed them with the Inner Temple fraternity, felt impelled to compose a letter in defence of Lord Atkin's judgment which he asked a sympathetic barrister to counter-sign with him. His colleague, however, excused himself from doing so on the grounds that he was hoping to be appointed a judge, and if he openly crossed swords with the opinions expressed in the House of Lords by four judges of the Appeal Court, this might damage his prospects with the Lord Chancellor. So on November 7th the letter went to *The Times* signed solely by Gerald.

Setting out the history of Regulation 18B in the House of Commons, he concluded:

What is one to think of an executive whose law officers now argue that the amended regulation now means, and must have been inten-

---

* *Regulation 18B*   The original Regulation 18B conferred on the Home Secretary an absolute discretion to detain persons if he was "satisfied" of certain things. On October 31st, 1939, upon a motion in the House of Commons to annul the regulations, grave dissatisfaction with this regulation was expressed in the House on the ground that it left the liberty of the subject to the sole discretion of the Home Secretary. The Government thereupon withdrew the regulations and agreed to amend them to meet this and other objections, the new Regulation 18B providing that the Home Secretary could only detain if "he has reasonable cause to believe" those things of which previously he had only to be "satisfied".

†Brother of the novelist, W. Somerset Maugham.

ded to mean, precisely the same as the regulation which was withdrawn?

It may be presumptuous for an ordinary lawyer to express a view upon the decision of the House of Lords, but as so distinguished a lawyer as Lord Maugham has thought your columns an appropriate place in which to comment upon part of a speech of another member of the tribunal, it may be permissible for a humble member of the Bar to follow his example and to say that, in places where lawyers meet, the view being yesterday expressed by lawyers of all shades of opinion was one of admiration for, and gratitude to, Lord Atkin for his dissenting speech, the contents of which appear to some ordinary lawyers to be unanswerable.

The letter landed him in hot water with the Benchers of the Inner Temple, many of whom were profoundly shocked by the presumption of a Junior Counsel in daring to criticize the judgments of the eminent Judges of Appeal. However, after it had been argued over at some length among them, the storm in a tea-cup blew over, the majority of the Benchers finally coming to the conclusion that if Lord Maugham wrote a silly letter to *The Times*, then he must expect a silly answer!

On reaching his fortieth year Gerald could not have foreseen the trick fate was about to play on him in the immediate future, resulting in an emotional upheaval which almost wrecked his marriage and permanently changed its fundamental nature.

A young colleague, many years his junior, who but for the outbreak of war would never have strayed into his orbit, won Gerald's heart and incidentally lost her own. It was no lighthearted, casual affair, though it may have begun as such when they found themselves working together, but as time went by it became desperately serious. Ultimately the problem of Lesly had to be faced, and Gerald, after much soul-searching, presented her with the truth and asked for a divorce. The situation was shattering for both of them. Lesly declared she would never in any circumstances give him his freedom, and he came away from a painful showdown with the uneasy impression that if they parted she might easily end her life. She was then over fifty and Carol was away at school; if she were left alone, Lesly intimated, there would be no point in going on, since her whole life revolved around her home and her husband and little else.

Despite these deeply emotive words, which Gerald knew had been uttered before as a kind of threat in similar situations with other couples, he was unable to put an end to the affair. In fact, it made him cling more devotedly to his love, to the point where he was prepared to leave Lesly and live with her without obtaining his legal freedom. Unfortunately this idea did not go down well with the object of his affection, who, while reciprocating his feelings, desired above all to have children of her own.

In the end she remained firm in her view that it would be totally wrong to bring them into the world to be disadvantaged later when they became adult. This was the main reason leading to the subsequent break-up of their relationship. Parting was an infinitely sad process, and accomplished only after distressing scenes with Lesly, who remained adamant throughout. As her rival was equally inflexible on the question of children, she and Gerald, realizing there was no other solution, eventually decided to go their separate ways but never lost touch. The lady married some time later and went abroad to settle down and raise a family. A friendly exchange of letters between her and Gerald has continued infrequently over the years, even to the present day.

It is a chapter in his life that he shrinks from mentioning, for, although he remained with Lesly until she died, his attitude towards her was never the same afterwards. At first a kind of armed neutrality existed between them, which very gradually was replaced by a resigned acceptance of the *status quo*, and finally of each other.

One morning in 1942 Gerald arrived in the Temple to find his chambers entirely demolished. Only a poker was rescued from the ashes of what the previous evening had been 2 The Cloisters. Soon afterwards he resumed work at 3 Hare Court, where fortunately accommodation was made available to the bombed-out, its erstwhile barristers being away on active service. The bombing of London, which had begun in earnest much earlier and continued unabated, decided him to enrol in the L.C.C. Ambulance Service. Five evenings a week, after court sessions were over, he would mount his bicycle and ride to Woolwich – which he had chosen because, with the nearby arsenal, it was the most dangerous place to be – manoeuvring his way over potholes and tramlines until he reached his post. Not too bad a journey by daylight, but in the blackout it was often perilous. One night, soon after the siren had whined its warning and searchlights spanned the sky, a local cinema crammed with troops and dock-workers enjoying a bit of relaxation with their girl-friends received a direct hit. In the chaotic aftermath Gerald, driving his ambulance to the hospital filled with wounded and dying, was shattered by a loud report. One of his tyres was punctured. The experience of climbing down and changing the wheel to the accompaniment of anti-aircraft guns blazing and all hell let loose was one he was never to forget.

As more and more men were drafted into the forces, young solicitors and barristers gradually faded from the legal scene, which was kept going by harassed, middle-aged and much older men who found themselves working twice as hard as they normally did in pre-war days. The barristers attached to various bodies like the Bentham Society and the Mary Ward Settlement worked for poor litigants for nothing, in their spare time, but as their number dwindled so the work became too heavy for those left behind to cope with. There was no legal aid as we know it today, and many people suffered in consequence. Gerald and many of his colleagues acted at that time as Poor Men's Lawyers for those unable to pay.

The situation deteriorated to such a degree by the third year of the war that he called a special meeting of Poor Men's Lawyers in order to discuss ways and means of improving matters. Various solutions were argued out by all concerned, but final agreement was never reached on how to remedy the problem and the whole thing fizzled out. Left with it unsolved, Gerald decided as a last resort to write to Lord Simon, the Lord Chancellor, setting out the difficulties they were experiencing and asking him what could possibly be done to improve matters, which had reached a stage where they could not possibly be worse. Lord Simon, realizing that legal aid was in danger of disappearing altogether unless something drastic was done, quickly appointed the Rushcliffe Committee to examine and report on the problem. Later this led to the Legal Aid and Advice Act of 1949, which established what is still the basis of our legal aid system today.

Ever since the start of hostilities Gerald had decided that when his call-up came he would go before a tribunal as a conscientious objector. This decision had been brought about largely through his association with the Rev. Dick Shepherd, the famous incumbent of St Martin-in-the-Fields, who had been an army chaplain in the First World War and had received the M.C. for rescuing men under fire. The experience influenced Shepherd to become a pacifist, and led him to take the view that the World War had been different in character from all other previous wars and that no person calling himself a Christian could possibly take part in another one.

The Shepherd family had been friendly with the Gardiners for many years, and Gerald had been much impressed by Dick's philosophy, but until World War II erupted he had not seriously considered his position in regard to it. When he did, however, he came to the conclusion that he was still in agreement with Dick's views, which coincided with those of Kittermaster, his old friend of Harrow days. The impact of these two men prompted Gerald to nurse the hope that, when he faced a conscientious objector's tribunal, he would be allowed to join a non-combatant service unit instead of rejoining the Coldstream Guards. Rather to his surprise, his call-up papers never came, and he found he was over military age for combat duties; this left him free to continue his career at the Bar, which by that time was extremely successful. However, instead of carrying on, as he was free to do, he decided to abandon it and join an alternative service, the only member of the F.A.U. over call-up age who volunteered to do so. Lesly demurred at this decision, since it meant abandoning a very flourishing practice, but he would not be dissuaded.

As he explained to Desmond Wilcox in a BBC television interview: "By that time I was making a good deal of money at the Bar, which didn't seem right with people away at the war, so I did what seemed logical. I threw up my practice and joined the Friends' Ambulance Unit."

BY REASON OF Gerald's service with the Friends' Ambulance Unit during World War II, it has often been assumed that he is a Quaker but the assumption is wrong. He joined it for the same reason as many hundreds of others in every walk of life, from doctors, teachers, clerks and lawyers to actors, scouts, salesmen, engineers and factory workers, who all had one thing in common, a conscientious objection to killing fellow human-beings.

The link between this very mixed lot was not a belief in any particular faith or creed, since the members consisted of Methodists, Protestants, Catholics, Quakers, atheists, agnostics and even Buddhists. The misconception that the F.A.U. was exclusively Quaker in character arose from the fact that it was originally formed in World War I by a small group of Friends traditionally faithful to the declared intention made to King Charles II in 1660: "We certainly know and testify to the World, that the Spirit of Christ which leads us unto all Truth, will never move us to fight and war against any man with outward weapons, neither for the Kingdom of Christ, nor for the Kingdom of the World."

Paul Cadbury, Arnold Rowntree and Philip Noel-Baker (then an M.P., later Lord Noel-Baker were among the earliest moving spirits to put their principles into practice, and were responsible both for the Ambulance Unit coming into existence and for its revival in the Second World War. Philip Noel-Baker's work with the F.A.U. during the years 1914–1945 no doubt inspired his efforts for disarmament during the late fifties and sixties with the C.N.D., finally culminating in his leadership of the World Disarmament Campaign in the eighties – an amazingly consistent record for a remarkable nonagenarian!

In 1940 membership of the F.A.U. was limited simply to men and women who shared the Quaker view on peace and war, no other qualification being necessary. Many lost their lives while serving in Europe and other parts of the world, while those who survived still hold their reunions, F.A.U. bonds of friendship being of the lasting kind. Letters from Friends in widely different countries continue to arrive on Gerald's desk, giving him the latest news of their work and experiences.

Late in 1943, kitted out with four blankets, stout boots, gym shoes, an old suit and a whole set of articles including knife, fork and spoon, Gerald left London for the Friends' Ambulance Unit Training Camp at Manor Farm, Birmingham, where he remained for two months, taking a first aid course under the supervision of the Red Cross and brushing up his knowledge of car maintenance. The intricacies of the combustion engine were not unfamiliar to him, for when he was twenty-one his mother had given him a motor-cycle as a birthday present, but before he was allowed to ride it Robert Septimus, typically thorough, had insisted on sending him to a motoring school to master its mechanics and maintenance. Not having ridden a machine for almost twenty years, Gerald found himself slightly out of practice at Manor Farm, and many months later, on his arrival in France, his performance was still so erratic on the muddy, rutted roads that it caused consternation in his section, and the Dame Colet School subscribed to buy him a truck in which he could sleep if necessary, as well as carry F.A.U. stores.

When his stint at Manor Farm came to an end Gerald was transferred to Hammersmith Hospital to receive his medical training for the next three months. On completing it he could do everything from coping with bedpans and bottles to taking out stitches, and in 1944 he was considered efficient enough to be sent to a camp on the south coast, there to await D-Day.

During the period of waiting and preparation Gerald, senior by some years to his fellow volunteers, whose average age was between twenty and thirty, became head of a Section. A Section consisted of ten persons with a leader always in charge, and by the time he went over to France in the summer he was in charge of all nine Sections in North-Western Europe. Members of the Unit were unpaid, and received only the essentials of life for their service. They wore khaki uniform with a Red Cross on the shoulder, but no other distinguishing mark of rank. All groups who worked under the Red Cross umbrella, however, had officer status and wore ties. This was insisted on (much against the inclination of the F.A.U.), as it was felt that any other arrangement would have caused real confusion with so many groups operating in conjunction with the army. The only exception was the Friends' Relief Service, which followed later on to deal with Displaced Persons from the German labour camps: they wore grey uniform and were a rather independent bunch. Army orders were that no one was allowed to fraternize with the enemy. This order the Friends' Relief Service members refused to obey, whereas the F.A.U. agreed to it but afterwards fraternized whenever they felt like it. The various volunteer groups obviously possessed strong individual traits, which made it all the more commendable that they managed to work together amicably and successfully during the ugly mopping-up operations.

D-Day came and went, and from June 6th, 1944, embarkation of the F.A.U. to France became imminent. Soon after the Allied forces invaded the continent Gerald, in charge of two Sections, received orders to leave. Conveyed across the Channel in tank-landing craft, they went ashore on the beaches at Arromanches, and by the evening of September 6th had proceeded through Normandy with eight of their vehicles to the Red Cross Civilian Hospital, the Château Versainville near Falaise. Because of delays in negotiation, and various hold-ups due to the disorganized conditions prevailing everywhere after the landings, they found they had arrived too late to be of service while the initial battles raged, the troops having just quitted the Falaise area to fight further east. The chaos that existed after they had gone was serious enough to keep the F.A.U. fully stretched for some time. In Calvados, 435 out of 715 villages were razed to the ground, resulting in emergency hospitals being swamped, while it was extremely difficult to distribute relief supplies to the sick and wounded. The Red Cross acted as an intermediary between the F.A.U. and the army, who found that the Ambulance workers were invaluable in the complicated administration of relief stores and accommodation – so much so that the refugee camp ended up largely in the care of the F.A.U., with local assistance from the "Resistance".

By the middle of September the two Sections under Gerald's direct command had been allotted their particular areas: Section 2, led by Len Darling, was sent to Berg Leopold in Belgium, while Section 1, led by Richard Wainwright, remained in Normandy for a few weeks before going into Holland, where the Germans had just pulled out, leaving devastation and great suffering in their wake.

"In the small Dutch town of Heusden some 200 citizens were told by the German forces to take shelter from British shells by crowding into the Town Hall. In the early hours of the morning the retreating Germans exploded a charge under the hall. It caved in, nearly all the shelterers were entombed and the local people who escaped unhurt were only able to dig out about fifteen living people."[*]

Such was the scene that greeted Gerald and Richard Wainwright on

[*] *F.A.U.* by A. Tegla Davies (Allen and Unwin, 1947).

arriving in the town. Hardly able to grasp the enormity of the tragedy, the shocked citizens only began to realize the bitter truth as the dawn light revealed the corpses strewn among the wreckage. An appalling amount of laborious searching among the ruins went on, and those rescued then had to be fed and housed. This meant setting up a temporary kitchen immediately and preparing hot soup as first priority. The local architect investigating the disaster estimated that 150 persons had lost their lives.

Section 2 moved from Belgium into Holland, and after the Arnheim landings set up camps outside Nijmegen. During October about ten thousand refugees, together with their livestock and household goods, were given assistance by the F.A.U. with the help of a Dutch team supervised by Len Darling. Then in November a request came from the Civil Affairs Director, 21st Army Group, for five more F.A.U. Sections, favourable reports having been received of the valuable work done by the first two under Gerald's command. The request having been agreed to, he departed at once for England to arrange for the necessary reinforcements, and on December 31st he returned to the continent with the largest single group the Unit had ever sent overseas. Three of the new Sections went to Antwerp, where, with German rockets and flying-bombs constantly hampering their efforts, their ambulances proceeded to carry to hospitals nearly 500 casualties and others needing medical care. Some of the remaining Sections allocated to Refugee Detachments provided reception bases to which army transport brought growing floods of refugees.

While the Allied forces waited for winter weather conditions to improve before making their spring assault on the Rhineland, Gerald and Richard Wainwright transferred Sections to Brussels in order to set up headquarters for the F.A.U. in North-Western Europe. There they worked in co-operation with the Deputy Commissioner, Lt Colonel Agnew, who had just arrived from England to supervise all the voluntary organizations working under the Red Cross umbrella.

On March 21st British troops forced a crossing over the Rhine and a F.A.U. Section followed two days later to establish a transit centre for Displaced Persons. The rest of the Sections, with the exception of one left in Holland to deal with refugees, pressed on in the wake of the liberating armies. Transit centres, no sooner set up, were invaded, not only by refugees but by thousands of Displaced Persons released from the Nazi camps where they had been employed as forced labour. Required to live and work in appalling conditions, once free they began to seek their revenge on the local population for their sufferings. They resented being put into the sort of camps from which they had recently fled, and the only remedy seemed to be to feed them and then arrange for their return to their own countries as speedily as possible.

One of the F.A.U. Sections, driving into the Rhineland in the wake of the advancing troops, was the first to reach Belsen, the concentration camp of ill-fame. Confronting them as they approached the gates were some lack-lustre Hungarian guards who quickly surrendered and allowed them through. Despite the notice-board warning ACHTUNG! TYPHUS! the F.A.U. contingent followed the army into the compound, only to be stopped short by a sight so horrendous that it paralysed all movement.

Hundreds of corpses piled high in heaps lay rotting on the ground, seemingly ignored by an equal number of ragged, living skeletons feebly dragging their emaciated limbs about as they tried desperately to fend for themselves. Overcome by weakness and disease, many collapsed and died as they struggled to carry on, while others crawled towards the fallen in the hope of salvaging shoes or anything else that might alleviate their suffering.

Since the war, newsreel cameramen have publicized so widely the ghastly conditions existing in Belsen at that time, not to mention the far worse ones in Auschwitz and Buchenwald, that after a lapse of thirty years it seems unnecessary to elaborate further on the state of the inmates. Those who survived have also given first-hand accounts of the horrors they endured inside, so no more will be added here.

Overwhelmed by the totally unexpected enormity of the task facing them, the Section leader immediately contacted Gerald at H.Q. to enlist his help and advice. Arriving that same evening from Brussels and realizing the unprecedented nature of the situation, Gerald attended a meeting called immediately by the army and their medical personnel to discuss what could possibly be done to cope with the hordes of sick and starving prisoners. After much discussion it was decided to move as many as could possibly survive into a tank training school nearby that had been abandoned by the enemy. The question of medical care then arose. The army had only a light field ambulance unit consisting of two doctors and ten Alexandra nurses, hardly adequate to cope with 30,000 men, women and children who were dying like flies. The addition of the F.A.U. ambulance only slightly improved the grim situation.

The army M.O. decided to signal 30 Corps at H.Q. for medical reinforcements. The reply came back that regretfully nothing could be spared, and they would have to make do with their present allotment. Gerald, determined not to give up, left the meeting and drove to 2nd Army H.Q. to consult the General in command there. He stressed the desperate situation at Belsen, and said that what they really needed was a British General Hospital to cope with such an emergency. His request for help, however, met with the same reception as the one from 30 Corps. It was turned down, the reason given being that heavy fighting was still going on everywhere and all medical teams were stretched to their limit and beyond.

Driving back through the night to Brussels, Gerald made up his mind to appeal to the Chief Army Medical H.Q. as a last resort. In the morning, when he arrived and obtained an interview with the authorities, they were considerably taken aback. Gerald was the first person to report to them on the entry into Belsen and the conditions prevailing there. Whether his request for more doctors, nurses and medical supplies ever bore fruit he never discovered. Soon afterwards he left Brussels, responding to a call for his presence in Berlin.

Surprisingly, the local people of Belsen, who had been commandeered by the British troops to help bury the dead, appeared to have been kept in ignorance of what had gone on inside the camp, for when the women started digging the countless graves the tears streamed down their faces. By the time Gerald made a second visit, a week later, the mood had changed, and they seemed by then immune to the horror as they stolidly continued their digging of the graves. The tears had dried up.

Meanwhile, the Germans having surrendered on May 8th, 1945, the war had virtually ended; but two more F.A.U. Sections arrived from England, and in June the Unit moved its headquarters to Vlotho, a small town on the river Weser in Westphalia, where for the next few months they continued dealing with the enormous problem of the Displaced Persons. Detailed to go to Berlin with the intention of renewing contact with a number of Friends whom H.Q. had not been in touch with for six years, Gerald left Vlotho after settling in the Sections. Accompanying him was a F.A.U. member named Cook, who spoke fluent German and was to act as his interpreter.

They set out for the capital but unfortunately, since no reliable map was available, the two men found themselves in trouble within a few miles of it. Although he had studied the route as carefully as possible Gerald, who was driving, strayed into the Russian zone by mistake and was soon in serious difficulties with Soviet armed guards. On being challenged they produced their passes and identity papers, but as the guards were mostly illiterate Mongols misunderstandings arose, and several times they feared they would be shot and bundled into a ditch. Eventually they manoeuvred their way out of the zone and found the road to Berlin, where they arrived several hours overdue.

The next morning Gerald began his mission, and in two days travelled 200 miles or more around the city in his attempt to trace the Friends. He was the first Englishman to renew contact with them. No sooner was this accomplished than he was off to Italy to co-ordinate plans with Lewis Waddilove, who was in charge of F.A.U. Sections in that country. He next crossed back into France, and in Paris went over plans for the future with Michael Cadbury, the leader of other Sections in the capital.

By now the F.A.U. was operating efficiently everywhere in Europe with the help of local communities in each country, but as time went on, and the members in various Sections gradually began to dwindle, H.Q. in London, after much discussion and heart-searching, decided that its work in the Second World War must come to an end. In the following year, on June 30th, 1946, it finally ceased operations.

Gerald, meanwhile, realizing that his financial resources were in serious danger of running out after his two-year absence abroad, and that Lesly and Carol would suffer if he continued any longer in the service, had made preparations for his return home. He eventually flew back to England in September 1945 to face the daunting prospect of exercising his legal expertise again after the interregnum of war, knowing it to be distinctly on the rusty side.

A few days after his return a letter arrived from F.A.U. headquarters in Gordon Square. Tegla Davies, who had received notice of Gerald's resignation, wrote expressing his feelings concerning the decision, which he said "was the biggest blow the Unit had suffered for a long time". After thanking Gerald for all he had done for it, Davies went on:

> You were ideally cast for the difficult if exhilarating job of steering our frail barque through the snags and shallows of NWE: there is obviously no one in the Unit who could have done it as you have. Apart from administrative gifts and experience which few Unit members could touch, your devotion to the Unit "idea", your understanding and championing of the ordinary Unit chap,

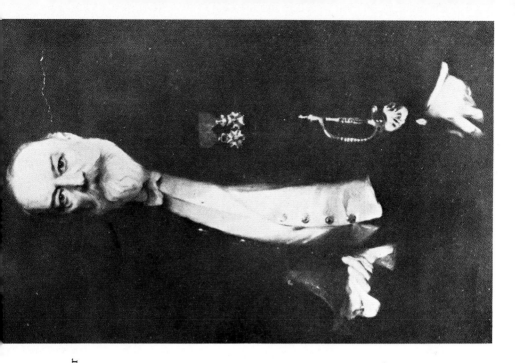

Left:
Alice Gardiner,
Gerald's mother
and grand-daughter
of Dr Dionysius
Lardner.
A painting by
Philip de Lazlo.

Right:
Robert
Septimus Gardiner,
Gerald's father.
a painting by
Philip de Lazlo.

Right:
Susan Lardner (*left*),
Gerald's grandmother,
and her sister Helen
(*right*), daughters of
Dr Dionysius and
Mary Lardner.
Watercolour by an
unknown artist.

Left:
Alice Gardiner's
crayon portrait of her
two sons (*left to
right*) Cyril and Gerald.

Left: Dr Dionysius Lardner, Gerald's great-grandfather. A painting by Alexander Craig, *c.* 1840.

Below: A soirée at Lady Blessington's *c.* 1830–40. Notable guests include Dickens, Thackeray, Leigh Hunt and Dr Dionysius Lardner.

Daniel O'Connell   Leigh Hunt   James Smith
Miss L.E.Landon.   Thomas Moore.   Miss Jane Porter.

M.Thackeray.   Hon Mrs Norton.   Rev Dr Lardner.   Bulwer Lytton.   Count D'Orsay.   D.Maclise RA.   Charles Dickens.
B.Disraeli.   Countess of Blessington.   Lord John Russell.

Right: The Harrow schoolboy, 1918.

Below: Gerald in his early twenties.

Opposite right: Gera playing Horatio in *Hamlet* for the OUI 1924.

Right: The young advocate, 1925.

Left: Detail from a portrait of the Lord High Chancellor, painted by Norman Hepple, R.A., hanging in the Inner Temple hall.

above: Lesly Gardiner at Oxshott.

above right: Gerald with Carol in Tite Street, 1930.

below: Trying out Carol's new toy, Oxshott, 1935.

below right: Carol Gardiner during her visit to Australia, 1965.

Gala matinée at Oxford organized by Gerald for the OUDS. Among the performers are: Irene Vanbrugh, Emlyn Williams, Joyce Grenfell, Barry Jones, Terence Rattigan, Michael Denison, John Gielgud, Anthony Oliver, Richard Goolden, Mary Ellis, Wilson Wiley, Jean Cadell, George Howe, Pamela Brown and Jane Baxter.

and your habit of driving yourself fantastically hard, have all made your loss hard to bear. . . .

The war years had inevitably wrought many changes in the Gardiners' home life. When Gerald joined the F.A.U. the lease on their Oxshott house was not renewed, and it was soon taken over by the army. Lesly moved into a smaller one at Farnham not far away from her daughter, who was then at Frensham Heights, where she was a pupil until the age of eighteen. Like many a grass widow at the time, Lesly offered her services as a driver to the Women's Voluntary Service for the duration. When the war was over she left Farnham to find a more convenient place in London where Gerald, on his return, would be r.earer his chambers. This turned out to be a flat in Jubilee Place, Chelsea.

When he eventually joined her there, adjustment to life at the Bar, after the tumultuous and disturbing years spent in Europe, was not as difficult as he had imagined it would be. Adam, the old chief clerk at his chambers, had just died, and a new one, Goodale, had taken over, who was to prove of very real assistance.

It was Goodale who greeted him one morning in mid-October when he emerged from the underground station to make his way towards Fleet Street. Crossing over, he presently approached Lincoln's Inn Fields, and stopped short on arriving at the door of 3 New Court close by. He went inside, to a welcome which made up for the unfamiliarity of his new quarters – for Hare Court had had to be vacated when the serving barristers returned at the war's end.

Shortly after hostilities in Europe ceased the General Election in Britain, resulting in a great swing to the left, took the country by surprise, for it was thought by many that Churchill would be sure to retain the leadership. After all, who was this man Attlee? Nobody appeared ever to have heard of him.

Gerald reacted with enthusiasm to the first Labour Government to be elected in England with an overwhelming majority, and had high hopes that it would achieve the changes which were vital to the country in the aftermath of war. Meanwhile, for him, politics had to take a second place, since the state of his income urgently required that he should waste no time on extraneous matters but should start coping with the briefs which Goodale steadily guided his way.

As soon as his financial future looked settled, links with the Haldane Society and the Howard League for Penal Reform were renewed. He was to find the former in a state of turmoil and schism, for during his absence it had amended its rules: anyone could now join who was in general sympathy with its aims and not be required, as previously, to be a member of the Labour party. In consequence a number of Communists infiltrated its ranks, and as they gradually increased began to undermine the policies of the Labour party which the society was pledged to support. The Labour lawyers were distinctly worried, and Gerald, who in December 1945 was elected chairman, was also deeply concerned, so much so that he was moved to write a letter to the secretary on the Society's change of character.

> . . . Don't think from all this that I am rabidly anti-Communist. I am no more anti-Communist than the ordinary English Socialist and much less so than Transport House. But there are differences between communism and socialism and this Society professes to be a Society of Socialists and not of Communists.
>
> I do not shut my eyes to the fact that our few Communist or Communist inclined members are about the most active and helpful members we have. I should be the first to oppose any attempt by Transport House to get us to exclude them. . . . But things must be done regularly, and if I am supposed to be persuading people that we are not Communist run, my job must not be made an impossible one.

Despite this warning there seemed no way of bringing matters to a head until a year later, when Gerald called a meeting of all members in an endeavour to get the rules altered back again. To do this a two-thirds majority vote was necessary. On the night of the meeting all the Communist members turned up in full force, whereas when the vote was taken the non-Communists discovered to their chagrin that they had failed to gain the necessary majority. At this point Gerald decided to approach the Secretary of the Labour party, Morgan Phillips, in order to explain their predicament and offer a solution. He suggested a compromise whereby a new group could be formed of those who were against admitting Communists to the Haldane Society, calling itself the Society of Labour Lawyers and limited only to accredited members of the Labour party.

The idea was acceptable to Phillips and eventually led to the Haldane Society being disaffiliated and the Society of Labour Lawyers coming into existence. Both societies have been active in their separate ways ever since. Gerald was chairman of the new society for several years, during which time, with a typical lack of formality, he insisted on all the members calling him by his Christian name. In the late fifties he led a delegation of Labour lawyers to give evidence before the Wolfenden Committee, which had been set up to study the problems of homosexuality. Some of his suggestions were incorporated in its Report, which was eventually to influence legislation passed in 1965. His chairmanship of the society came to an end when Harold Wilson appointed him Lord Chancellor. However, following his six-year term he was elected president in 1970, and remained in that office until he retired in 1980. His speech at the dinner given in his honour received a standing ovation, and was vigorous enough for Peter Archer[*] to comment in a letter to me: "Gerald's speech was like re-reading Blatchford or Arthur Henderson. He made me think again of why I joined the Labour movement."

Zest for reform was the main reason why Gerald in 1947 became a member of the Committee on Supreme Court Practice and Procedure, the second being that only one other representative of the Bar was on it, and he felt there needed to be more in order to overhaul in a balanced manner the workings of the Appeal and High Courts.

Lord Justice Evershed, Master of the Rolls, acted as chairman, and the committee, dealing with a great mass of detail, sat for five years. The effect of attending 330 sittings made such a lasting impression on Gerald that thirty years later he was impelled to write to *The Times* expressing his concern about the criticism that had been levelled at the Williams Report on Obscenity and Film Censorship by people who had never even read it.

House of Lords
November 27th, 1979

Sir,

I write to plead for fair treatment of those who serve on Royal Commissions and Departmental Committees.

I served on one Departmental Committee which sat for five years and I attended all of its 330 meetings. When they were all-day meetings I had, of course, to refuse briefs with its attendant loss of income. For 16 years, successive Lord Chancellors appointed me to their Law Reform Committee and since leaving office I have been Chairman of another Departmental Committee.

[*] Rt Hon. Peter Archer, Q.C., M.P., Solicitor-General in the Labour Government 1974–79.

The Treasury reasonably reimburses the expenses of the members of Royal Commissions but are very niggardly about the expenses of members of Departmental Committees who are invariably out of pocket and who, if they are self-employed, incur further financial loss.

The Williams Committee on Obscenity, consisting of a distinguished Chairman, a Bishop, a former Chief Constable, a headmistress, doctors, lawyers, journalists – including your film critic – and others, sat for two years, and their report, which is said to be unanimous, is due to be published tomorrow.

Is it not intolerable that before the report is published an extremist like Mrs Whitehouse should charge the Committee with moral cowardice and castigate the report as a "pornographer's Charter"?

I should have thought that the least any reasonable person could do is to wait until the report is published, obtain a copy, and then read it, before making any comment upon it.

Yours faithfully,
Gardiner.

Coming back to the Bar and beginning to find himself steadily in demand, Gerald gradually realized, and finally had to admit, that he really loved the work. The theatre had not lost its magic for him, but the courtroom by degrees took over from the stage as a milieu where he could capture an audience and enjoy its reaction. He soon began to be valued for his thoroughness and flair as an advocate, especially in libel actions, appearing in them with considerable success. After the war, however, one of his first cases was of a very different character.

On March 5th, 1946, Dr Alan Nunn May, a young research scientist of thirty-four and a lecturer at King's College, London, was arrested and later charged at Bow Street with having communicated to some persons unknown, for a purpose prejudicial to the safety and interests of the state, certain information which might be useful to an enemy. He pleaded "Not Guilty" and his application for bail was refused.

According to an entry in my personal diary of that year his brother, Ralph Nunn May, was so devastated that he hurried round to Guild House in St Martin's Lane (where my husband, Sydney Box, the film producer, was working) in a state of utter bewilderment.

"Alan would *never* be disloyal to his country. He's innocent, Sydney. I'm convinced of that." His distress was acute. "I just can't believe it!"

From his own point of view Alan Nunn May *was* innocent. He never saw himself as a spy or regarded what he had done as a crime, believing as a scientist that it was his plain duty to share any knowledge he acquired with others engaged on similar research, regardless of where they lived and worked. His solicitor made a round of the Bar in search of a barrister willing to take on the defence but, despite the moral obligation laid down by Lord Erskine, was unable to persuade anyone to do so. All said they were tired of working on so many "spy" cases during the war and had had enough – all, that is, except Gerald, who agreed to represent Nunn May. His trial took place on May 1st in the Central Criminal Court, the prosecution being in the hands of the Attorney-General, Sir Hartley Shawcross, K.C.

When the case was reported in the papers the British public was shocked, the dust having scarcely settled after the atomic bombing of Hiroshima and Nagasaki. Repercussions had set in and nuclear problems were by then an emotive topic. Dr Nunn May, a senior member of the Nuclear Physics Division in Canada, had access to secret reports on uranium and was consulted on nuclear atom energy (not bombs). His researches had been published, as he later explained, "qualitatively but not quantitatively", and he had not benefited financially in any way from his actions.

Before his case came up for trial he admitted having passed on information to a Russian, and therefore proposed to change his plea to "Guilty". The proceedings proved to be brief, for there was little left for Gerald to say in his defence except that he seemed utterly sincere in regarding himself as one of many other scientists holding the view that research information should be shared among nations for the benefit of mankind as a whole.

It should perhaps be remembered that in 1946 the "cold war" had barely set in, and even Churchill had not long since declared that we should share our technological advances and information with our Allies; the Soviet Union was still considered our "gallant ally" at this period. Nunn May made a particular point of this when explaining his position.

Sir Hartley Shawcross, opening the prosecution, said that if certain information had got into the hands of enemy scientists it would have shortened their researches by a considerable period, but there was no kind of suggestion that the Russians were enemies or political enemies. The court had already decided that the offence consisted solely in communicating information to unauthorized persons, which Nunn May had signed an undertaking not to do.

In May 1942 he had been invited to become a member of one of the staffs of scientists set up by the Government to research into atomic energy. In January 1943 he went with other scientists to Canada to continue their researches, and while there occupied a position of considerable responsibility as senior member of his division. Until September 1945 no suspicion had arisen concerning him, but in February 1946 he was interviewed by a member of the Special Branch C.I.D. of military intelligence authorities, and told that it was known he had an appointment with someone near the British Museum which he did not keep. Nunn May agreed that he had not kept it when he returned from Canada because he had decided to "wash his hands of the whole business". He went on to say that a year previously he had been contacted by an individual (whose identity he declined to reveal) who called on him at his private apartment in Montreal, who apparently knew he was employed by the Montreal laboratory and who sought information from him concerning atomic research. After this preliminary meeting, he met the individual on seven subsequent occasions while in Canada.

"I gave the man," he said, "a routine report on atomic research as known to me. This information was mostly of a character which has since been published or is about to be published."

The Attorney-General remarked to the court that this information had by no means been made public.

Nunn May continued: "Before I left Canada it was arranged that on my return to London I was to keep an appointment with someone I didn't know. I did not keep the appointment because I had decided that this clandestine procedure was no longer necessary in view of official release of information. The whole affair was extremely painful to me. I only embarked on it because I thought this was a contribution I could make for the safety of mankind. I certainly did not do it for gain."

Gerald, addressing the Judge, later commented on this attitude: "Doctors take the view that if they discover something of benefit to mankind they are under obligation to see it is used for mankind and not kept for any country or people. There are scientists who take substantially the same view and Dr May held that view strongly."

Nevertheless, Mr Justice Oliver, on passing sentence of ten years' penal servitude, remarked: "I cannot understand how any man in your position could have the crass conceit to arrogate to himself to do what you did knowing it was one of the country's most precious secrets. I find you have acted not as an honourable man but as a dishonourable man. It is a very bad case indeed."

The extremely lengthy sentence imposed was considered in certain quarters to be inordinately savage, and on May 13th the Executive Committee of the Association of Scientific Workers issued a statement in which they called for it to be reduced. "It is noteworthy that the maximum sentence under the proposed Atomic Energy Bill is penal servitude for a period of five years. It is clear that no account was taken of Dr May's contribution to the winning of the war by his scientific work and that the sentence is out of all proportion to the magnitude of the crime committed." On May 17th W. J. Brown, the Independent M.P. for Rugby, asked in the House of Commons whether the Home Secretary would review the sentence passed on Nunn May, but in reply Mr Chuter Ede answered that he was unable to find any grounds on which he could recommend any interference with the sentence that the court had imposed.

Mr Brown persisted: "It was perfectly obvious that this man was no common criminal and was no traitor in the ordinary sense of the word, that he had suffered a much heavier sentence than had been passed on many people who had sold their country for money and that the whole issue of atomic bomb secrecy constituted an extremely doubtful ethical era. Would the Home Secretary look at this case?"

Chuter Ede brushed this aside, saying that it was still open to Nunn May to appeal against his sentence. "I do not accept the implications made by the honourable member. I can understand, although I cannot condone the attitude of a man who said he was willing to make knowledge he had acquired generally available, but this man did sell knowledge he had acquired in the service of this country to a foreign power for their private and particular use."

This was greeted with loud cheers and no one, not even Mr Brown, reminded Ede that the Attorney-General had found no evidence of Nunn May "selling" his knowledge!

For some while Gerald had been debating in his mind whether or not to apply for Silk. During the war years he was too unsettled by events to entertain the idea, and when hostilities ended financial considerations held him back. His income was so depleted after two years' absence that the risk of taking such a step was daunting, especially since his bank manager refused him an overdraft of £1,500 which would have tided him over the next couple of years while fees owing to him dribbled in. Solicitors being notoriously slow in collecting them from clients, it was considered extremely unwise professionally to jog their elbows and remind them that barristers also had to live. He was in a dilemma.

Not knowing which way to turn, Gerald consulted his personal solicitor and had no recourse afterwards but to follow his advice: he borrowed what he needed from a moneylender and set to work. By 1948 he had so far re-established himself in his profession as to be rated one of the most successful Juniors at the Bar, thus lessening the risk involved in making a change. He observed that quite a number of Junior Counsel, after taking Silk, had proved failures in advocacy and in consequence received far fewer briefs. After making his application he devoutly hoped the same fate would not be meted out to him. Silk was granted, and in 1948 he became a K.C. He was never to regret it.

The following year he moved from New Court to 12 King's Bench Walk, and, finding his chambers badly in need of attention, bought himself a boiler suit, paint and brushes, and with characteristic thoroughness set to work to decorate them. It took him a month instead of the week he had estimated, but when finished they were perfect. Among the legal fraternity who frequented the Inner Temple, Number 12, with its illuminated windows shining late into the night, came to be known as The Lighthouse.

The added responsibilities of a Silk did not deter him from continuing to involve himself in social problems, principally with the abolition of the death penalty. An amendment to the Criminal Justice Bill suspending capital punishment for the next five years had just been passed by the Labour Government and had gone through both Houses of Parliament, which seemed to point the way for even further reform.

Christopher Hollis, Conservative M.P. for Devizes from 1945 to 1953, a vigorous campaigner for complete abolition, knowing Gerald's views, persuaded him to contribute a Foreword to his book *The Homicide Act*.* In April 1949, the *Law Quarterly Review* contained an article on *The Judicial Attitude to Penal Reform*, the result of a collaboration between Nigel Curtis-Raleigh and Gerald, which was printed afterwards as a pamphlet dealing mainly with the reactionary pronouncements of judges on capital punishment over the centuries. It showed they had consistently favoured retention from the time a boy of ten could be sentenced to death for secreting notes in a post office to the present

* Victor Gollancz Ltd, 1964.

century, when Ruth Ellis killed her lover and was the last woman to be hanged in this country.

Some time during 1949 Gerald was approached by a gentleman from Transport House to ascertain whether he would be interested in nursing the constituency of West Croydon for the Labour party. An election was a possibility within the next couple of years, and the ground needed to be prepared in readiness.

Gerald, although he had no political ambitions, was nevertheless interested in the proposal, for he had been very impressed by Attlee's Government, which had inherited a bankrupt economy at the end of six years of war, had built a National Health Service and Social Security scheme out of the ruins, and had created jobs for the masses returning to civil life in a remarkably speedy operation. Having suspended the death penalty for five years, perhaps with a little further pressure the Government could be persuaded to abolish it completely? There is no doubt this may have been at the back of Gerald's mind when he decided to consider the nomination and agreed to go before a Selection Committee. The only thing he felt should not be kept under wraps was the fact that he had been a pacifist during the war. He was advised that it would be wise not to volunteer this information unless he was specifically asked for it. On this understanding he survived the Selection Committee interrogation and agreed to become the prospective Labour candidate for Croydon West.

For the next eighteen months he went around the constituency knocking on the doors of its 54,000 electors, and when in August 1951 Attlee decided to go to the country for an increased majority he felt ready to contest the seat, regarded by all as a safe Conservative stronghold.

The letter to his constituents at the time has a strangely *déjà vu* element about it when read thirty years later, but many of his intentions expressed therein are felt as strongly by Gerald now as when he originally wrote them. The main body of the letter reads:

> I am not a professional politician. I have no political ambitions. A man is no better for having initials after his name. It may well be that I should have more money in my own pocket under a Conservative Government. I was brought up as a Conservative but joined the Labour Party in the '30s because of the state to which successive Conservative Governments had reduced the country.
>
> Politics is only a means to an end – to create conditions in which people can live happy and useful lives. What do people want?

International peace, industrial peace, a job, a home, freedom of speech, freedom from fear of unemployment, of an unprovided-for illness, accident or old age and a fair distribution of the national wealth which we all help to create. These are the interests of the Labour Government.

I am profoundly convinced that a Conservative Government would be disastrous and that capitalism in which they believe is an unjust and out-of-date system which cannot and ought not to last. No Government you elect is going to have an easy task until re-armament is finished in two years' time. On your choice of Government depends the welfare of all of us and of our children.

The result of the election was disappointing, for no Conservative seat was won by Labour that year and Gerald's was one of the many casualties.

Thus ended his first political venture at the age of fifty-one. Thirteen years were to elapse before he became involved again, and then it was a slightly different story.

FIVE

DURING HIS UNSUCCESSFUL attempt to win West Croydon Gerald learned that he was required to resign from one of the committees on which he had been sitting for several years.

His chairmanship of the Disciplinary Committee of the Pharmaceutical Society carried with it a remuneration of £50 per annum, and he was advised by the party official to relinquish it or risk being disqualified as a candidate. He discovered that his was a Privy Council appointment to the Society, and it was illegal for him to hold an office under the Crown both as a candidate and if he was elected. It was with some regret that he handed in his resignation, for he had enjoyed advising his pharmaceutical colleagues on several matters during his membership, but was pleased that they regretted his enforced departure as much as he did. In their unanimous opinion he was the best chairman they had ever had, despite the fact that he was the only one on the Committee who was not a chemist!

When he had first been approached by the Pharmaceutical Society Gerald found its members divided in their views, which needed reconciling if its affairs were to run smoothly. One half considered themselves professionals, and for them to advertise was to act improperly. Also they frowned on any alliance between a chemist and a doctor, particularly if the latter wanted a share in the business. The view of the other half was that chemists were virtually shopkeepers who sold fancy goods and toiletries in addition to dispensing medicines, and therefore were not expected to observe professional etiquette. The Disciplinary Committee eventually adopted the first view, for they were concerned about their dispensing powers.

These thorny questions came to a head when a case was considered by the Committee involving the firm of Boots the Chemists. The Society threatened every shop with closure if Boots did not withdraw an advertisement appearing in railway carriages which was so worded as to suggest that they dispensed medicines better than any other chemists. Boots were finally forced to give way.

In another case, where a chemist had been convicted of procuring an abortion on the premises, Gerald managed to persuade the Committee not to strike him off their register. He argued that the young woman concerned happened to be the chemist's fiancée, and they had been in the habit of meeting in the shop after closing time because they had nowhere else to go. The abortion he had performed there had not been done for financial gain or as part of a business, and it would be more humane to let the young man remain on the register during the period of probation that had been ordered by the Judge than to deprive him of his livelihood.

For the next decade or so Gerald divided his time between sitting on committees devoted to a variety of reforms and his legal work, which had noticeably increased since taking Silk. One would have thought that as he became more successful, and his briefs proved more interesting and high-powered, they would have received his undivided attention, but not so; apparently his energy was inexhaustible. The list of committees he sat on over the years concurrently with all his court work is formidable. By coping with both simultaneously and with equal industry, he clearly indicated the way he intended using his talents for the rest of his life. Kenneth Tynan's description of him during the *Lady Chatterley* case certainly confirms that he showed no sign of strain or of taking on too much.

"Gerald Gardiner, possibly the Topmost Dog of the moment, is scrupulously cool in style and obviously finds histrionics distasteful. . . . He's noted in the profession for the beautifully lucid and careful preparation of his cases. He is a certain choice for a judgeship but has said that he will never go to the Bench until the death penalty is abolished."[*] Although this reference to him might suggest an extremely ambitious careerist bent on high, or even the highest, office, Gerald affirms that he has never had desires to become "Topmost Dog" in any profession, but simply wished to make an excellent job of his work at the Bar. As he has a personal antipathy to sending people to prison, he has never wanted to be a judge or "anything grand", as he puts it, and on the only occasion when he stood for Parliament he was very relieved that he failed to capture a seat from the Conservatives.

The number of the committees on which he sat in the forties and fifties shows the extent to which he stretched himself. Asked whether he ever managed to spend a night at home, he laughed: "Not often. I was a very busy fellow in those days." The following are some of the societies in which he was involved, but by no means all:

[*] *Observer*, November 6th, 1960.

Member of Committee on Supreme Court Practice and Procedure
(1947–53)
Chairman of Disciplinary Committee of the Pharmaceutical Society
(1948–51)
Chairman of Society of Labour Lawyers (1948–64)
Member of Legal Committee of the National Marriage Guidance
Council (1951–64)
Member of Executive Council and Hon. Treasurer (1954–64) of the
Howard League for Penal Reform. President in 1969
Member of the National Association for Care and Resettlement of
Offenders (NACRO), for many years until the present day
Member of Lord Chancellor's Law Reform Committee (1952–63)
Member of Committee to reduce costs of litigation in the Supreme
Court, appointed by Lord Chancellor (1952–63)
Chairman of the General Council of the Bar (1958–59)
Founder of the Committee of Young Barristers to initiate Reforms
(1958)
Chairman (with Victor Gollancz) of the National Campaign for the
Abolition of Capital Punishment (1960–64).
Director, later Chairman, of the Board of the *New Statesman and Nation*
(1959–64)
Chairman of Committee to Report on The Younger Generation,
appointed by Hugh Gaitskell (1959)

When he became Chairman of the Bar Council (having defeated Sir
Lionel Heald, Conservative Solicitor-General, at the election), Gerald
felt there was an urgent need to raise the fees paid to barristers, as they
had not been increased since before the war and were very low. For a
long period, ever since he became a member of the Bar Council in the
late thirties and again after taking Silk, he was convinced they needed
upgrading, and now set himself to work to that end. The following
extracts from letters show his concern in the matter and the extent of
some of his efforts to get remuneration improved. Any change involved
a complicated process affecting not only the London and Middlesex
Courts but all those throughout England and Wales. The payment, for
instance, for drafting a divorce petition at that time was £2. 4s. 6d., as it
had been in 1939; for settling an indictment £1. 3s. 6d., and for a legal
conference £1. 5s. 6d. (4s. 6d. of which went to the Clerk as originally it
had been his duty to provide the candles!). Allowing for inflation over

the previous twenty years, the current fees had obviously decreased in value to an absurdly low figure.

December 9th, 1959

To the Editor of *The Times*

Sir,

In the opinion of the Council there are two principal reasons for the fall in the numbers of those commencing practice at the Bar.

The first is the fact that, almost alone now among the professions, the intending barrister receives no income during the years he spends qualifying and commencing practice.

The second is that, in spite of the enormous increase since the war in rents, wages, travelling and hotel expenses, there has been no commensurate increase in fees. The first is a matter for discussion with the Inns of Court. Steps have already been taken, and are still being taken, by the Council to remedy the latter.

In a second letter to *The Times* a week later he took up the case for junior barristers as well as the work done by their clerks which had been criticized:

With regard to payment for "devilling" work, in their annual statement for 1955, the Council said:

"The Council has been considering the increasingly difficult financial position of young members of the Bar. The Council wishes very strongly to stress its views that in these days no barrister can be expected to 'devil' work, without a fair financial return whether in cash or otherwise." The Council believe that there are few chambers where such work is not remunerated, but a sub-committee had already been appointed (in June) "to prepare a draft statement of approved practice for the remuneration of 'devilling work' for the purpose of obtaining a greater measure of uniformity in this particular field. . . ."

Eventually Gerald was instrumental in getting the fees substantially raised during his two-year period as chairman. He declined to continue in that office for a third year, believing that two were quite long enough for anyone to occupy it, but during that short period he made considerable efforts to improve conditions in the Law Courts. He was concerned about the comfort of those who had to work there and critical of the poor way the Courts were furnished. Counsel were expected to sit all day on hard wooden benches devoid of cushions, with nowhere to put their legal documents or books, and to conduct their cases in old-fashioned rooms with bad acoustics. Some of these things he was able to improve, but progress was slow, for Gerald was an impatient man when it came to getting things done. This was even more evident when he was Lord Chancellor. He was anxious that everything should be stream-lined and made as convenient as possible for those concerned. Procedure, he felt, should be simpler, cheaper and less wasteful of solicitors', Counsel's and witnesses' time. This impatience was ex-pressed in his opinion of the Board of Trade and especially of the Home Office, for which he had scarcely a good word. Since they were far too slow in getting things done he was in favour of transferring some of their functions to the Lord Chancellor's office, which he considered was much more efficient. As *Punch* reported in 1969, he was referred to by some as "Gerry and the Pacemakers", when he started on his reforms.

The inclusion of his name on the Committee of Young Barristers is not strictly accurate, since he never actually sat on it. He was the originator of the idea of having a body of young men who could submit new ideas for injecting fresh life into the legal profession and setting in motion much-needed improvements. He urged them at their first meeting in 1958 not to hesitate in being as revolutionary as possible in their notions for reform, but warned them not to be surprised or hurt if the Council turned them down. They consequently went away and came back shortly with the suggestion that all High Court judges should be made to retire at the age of sixty-five, and not allowed to go on working indefinitely as was the custom at that time.

The Bar Council accepted this on the understanding that the retiring age should be put at seventy, and then sent the resolution to the Lord Chancellor for him to consider. He eventually replied that he was in agreement with putting a time limit on the retirement age, but it could not possibly apply to existing judges. He added that he would have to bear in mind the length of time a Parliamentary Bill of this kind might take to get through both Houses (there was always a danger that if it were prolonged this might prove prejudicial to its acceptance), so to be on the safe side he set the age limit at seventy-five. Gerald is still of the opinion that seventy would be a happier medium. Thus it has remained; the only High Court judge sitting in 1982 on the Bench who was over seventy-five was Lord Denning, Master of the Rolls, who resolutely carried on though well into his eighties, and was fond of saying that "he possessed all the Christian virtues except resignation".*

Early in 1959 a commission was appointed by the Rt Hon. Hugh Gaitskell, M.P., on behalf of the Labour party, to report on the younger generation, which Gerald was asked to chair. He agreed to do so, and by April had gathered together a committee to look into the "Problems of young people and the contribution which the Government and Local Authorities and other public or voluntary agencies can make to their solution". The group consisted of a bunch of keen individuals with varied interests and backgrounds who set to work with considerable dedication. They were Elizabeth Pakenham, Ted Willis, Sylvia Sims, Penry Jones, Beatrice Serota, Humphrey Lyttelton, Richard Davies, Jimmy Hill and Eileen Ascroft.

As far back as 1939 a Service to Youth directive had been issued by the Ministry of Education, stating that Local Education Authorities were to be responsible for youth welfare, which was officially declared to be part of the national system of education. Local authorities were advised that they were eligible for grants in order to provide a comprehensive youth service. Although this policy was confirmed in the Education Act of 1944, little was done afterwards to expand it, Whitehall giving scarcely any guidance in the matter and even reducing the grants enabling youth centres to be set up.

The Ministry's spokesman admitted the neglect of the Service, which in 1959 was having *less* spent on it than it had done in 1950. The project, having got off to a good start in 1944, had deteriorated rapidly, the number of youth service leaders declining from 1,000 in 1956 to 700 in 1959. To run it efficiently 5,000 to 6,000 trained personnel were originally estimated to be necessary, plus an intake of 300 a year. There were warnings that "unless an attempt is made quickly to improve the situation the gains since the war in this service may be lost".

No action was taken, and financial aid had actually diminished to a trickle when the commission of inquiry was ordered by Mr Gaitskell. It thoroughly explored every aspect of the young generation's problems, and the resulting improvements it advocated were copious and far reaching.

But although it sat for four months, had fifteen meetings lasting from three to eight hours each and was given the invaluable assistance of a secretary in the youthful person of Mr Peter Shore (at that time head

---

* Francis Bennion. Letter to *The Times*, January 20th, 1981.

of the Research Department at Transport House), the Report, duly presented in August of the same year, was virtually ignored by its sponsors. Aneurin Bevan was practically the only person to express admiration for it, and nothing was ever done to implement its recommendations, except for a pamphlet published by Transport House at 1s. 6d. Eventually it sank without trace – though some of its recommendations are as relevant today as they were twenty years ago, and had they been carried out might have helped to prevent the steady rise in crime and violence among young people.

Gerald's work on the commission was not entirely wasted, and the labours of all who worked on it eventually bore fruit, though not until nine years later and only in regard to one aspect of it. The members had discussed at some length the question of the age of majority, and had come out in favour of reducing it from twenty-one to eighteen. Gerald does not easily relinquish an idea once persuaded something should be done about it, and he therefore resolved to pursue it further at the first opportunity. Five years were to pass before this happened, and by then he had become Lord Chancellor.

A society to which he devoted much time and energy came into existence not long after he had made a trip to South Africa in 1956. This was Justice, later to become the English branch of the International Commission of Jurists.

He had been approached by Canon Collins of Christian Action to go to South Africa as an observer at the Magistrates Court in Johannesburg. One hundred and fifty-one people from all over the country had suddenly been arrested in a dawn swoop on their homes and flown straight to Johannesburg, to be charged with conspiracy to overthrow the Government by force. Christian Action co-operated with the Defence and Aid Society in South Africa, and offered to finance the trip if Gerald would agree to go. Having consented, he discussed the situation with some of his colleagues on the Bar Council, and found that they were in favour of an unbiassed report on the Treason Trials (as they came to be known), and would give him their official support.

When he touched down at Johannesburg airport he was met by a rather hostile press who demanded to know why it was thought necessary for anyone from England to be at the Magistrates Court. On learning he was there simply as an impartial observer, they expressed annoyance, and next morning a leading newspaper article commented that his visit was an insult to South African justice. As Gerald remarked, he could have reminded them that, when Queen Victoria sent one of her ministers to attend the Dreyfus case in the same capacity, no one thought that anything derogatory or exceptional was implied.

That evening, after dining at his hotel, he set out for a stroll around the town, and was a little surprised to find it somewhat deserted – no white people visible and only a few blacks in the streets. Commenting on this when he returned, he was told that no whites ventured out alone after dusk except in their own cars, and if he valued his safety he would be wise to follow their example.

The Magistrates Court, where preliminary proceedings were to be conducted, had been found too small to hold the number of accused, so a large drill hall or gymnasium had been commandeered in the city centre and converted for the purpose. The next morning, when Gerald made his way through a dense crowd of Africans towards the gates, he found them closed and guarded by police, who contended that they couldn't be opened or the crowd would surge through. However, they allowed Gerald to climb over some railings erected outside and, having accomplished this to the accompaniment of shouting and singing from Africans and others who were angrily shaking the railings or parading with posters saying "We stick by our Leaders", he at last managed to squeeze inside. A noisy argument was in full spate about the non-admittance of 300 Africans who had been waiting two hours to claim the public seats allotted to them, which were now being made available only to Europeans. The Sergeant to whom their protests were lodged stood firm, muttering: "Too many Kaffirs would smell out the court."

While the 151 prisoners were led in and seated, Gerald was introduced to their Defending Counsel, Mr Maisels, Q.C., who complained that no amplifiers had been fitted in the makeshift hall and that the defendants would not be able to hear the proceedings. This resulted in a two-hour adjournment while efforts were made to rectify the trouble, without any noticeable improvement. The Magistrate, Mr Wesel, had no recourse but to order a further adjournment till the next morning.

The following day proved to be even more of a shambles, for savage riots broke out early between police and Africans wanting to get into the court. Twice, during the proceedings inside, Mr Wesel had to adjourn, for the situation was getting out of control, the noise of gunfire and fighting outside filtering into the hall. In the adjoining Twist Street hundreds of Africans and squads of police were having a pitched battle, with the Bishop of Johannesburg, the Rt Rev. Ambrose Reeves, a colourful figure in his crimson vestments, vainly endeavouring to stop the firing into the crowds and at the same time trying to pacify his flock. Four Europeans and ten Africans were injured in the baton charge and shooting, and were taken to hospital, before order was restored by the arrival of a senior police officer.

On entering the court that second day Gerald was taken aback by the sight of two enormous steel and wire cages, similar to those seen in zoos, which had been erected overnight and into one of which black defendants had been thrust, while whites had been thrust into the other one. Mr Maisels was having great difficulty in hearing the accused, and eventually, turning to the Magistrate, he announced that if these conditions continued and the cages were not removed forthwith, he would leave the court. This occasioned the first adjournment of the day, while abortive attempts were made to dismantle them. After a couple of hours, and only on condition that the cages would not be there the following morning, Mr Maisels reluctantly agreed to continue, and the case went on with the 151 defendants being charged with using revolutionary methods to overthrow the State, under the Suppression of Communism Act 1950 and the Riotous Assembly Act.

The adjournment of the hearings over Christmas, until January 9th, dictated the return of Gerald to London, where he reported to Christian Action and addressed a crowded meeting of three hundred lawyers and a number of journalists in the Niblett Hall. At this meeting he dealt with the court's proceedings, but not with the trials themselves, since they were sub-judice. All he would say was: "It was a situation which could have been easily handled by a fairly small number of London policemen. The use of the baton was far more prevalent in South Africa than in Britain and the real trouble was an unnecessary baton charge. This led to stone throwing by the crowd, the police got frightened and some opened fire." Apart from the steel cages, which had since been removed, the conduct of the trials was in accordance with the British system. It was nevertheless salutary, he thought, for South Africa to realize that the eyes of the world were focussed on Johannesburg to ensure that justice was being seen to be done in the coming months.

The months dragged on into years, making the Treason Trials the longest in South African history. By dribs and drabs the accused were acquitted, until in the final stages they had dwindled to a mere 28. Halfway through, the trials had been transferred to a court in Pretoria, and it was there, on March 29th, 1961, over four years after they had begun, that they ended with a dramatic suddenness which almost stunned the weary accused. All 28 were acquitted and set free by Judge Rumpff, who announced that the verdict was unanimous and could not be appealed against by the Crown because it was given on a question of fact and not on points of law. He said that there was no evidence of communist infiltration into the South African National Congress (of which several of the accused were members). It was "not proved" that the ANC had become a Communist organization , but "it was working towards a state based on demands set out in the Freedom Charter . . . it did not intend to achieve this new State by violence".

Bishop Reeves was delighted at the result, and declared that without the Treason Trials Defence Fund it would have been quite impossible to provide financial aid for the families of the accused or secure the best legal defence. Back in England the Fund's sponsors – Bertrand Russell, Victor Gollancz, Sir Compton Mackenzie, William Plomer, Max Gluckman, Father Trevor Huddleston and Lord Faringdon – were equally delighted that the £800 they had raised had proved helpful.

Soon after the Trials ended Mr Maisels decided to leave South Africa, to continue his work in Rhodesia, since he feared his successful defence of the accused would preclude him from ever becoming a judge there. He foresaw the Government in future appointing only barristers who were of the same political persuasion as the Nationalist Party. His prediction has since proved substantially correct.

The opinion of some South Africans concerning overseas observers at the Trials was reported in the Nationalist paper *Die Burger* on April 10th, 1960, and reveals the strength of their resentment. "What all red-blooded South Africans would like to do would be to take a bunch of the visiting British correspondents by the scruff of the neck and throw them out of the country, after giving them a hiding with the rhinoceros-hide siamboks which they discovered in such quantities this week."

When Gerald had met colleagues on the Bar Council to seek their views before deciding to accept Canon John Collins' invitation to go to South Africa to observe the Trials, it had been mooted by the Council that an all-party organization, consisting of leading lawyers representing the three main political parties, should be formed to "uphold and strengthen the principles of the Rule of Law in the territories for which the British Parliament is directly or ultimately responsible: in particular, to assist in the administration of justice and in the preservation of the fundamental liberties of the individual". It was also concerned to help the International Commission of Jurists in its efforts to promote observance of the rule of law throughout the world.

As the result of this resolution, and mainly due to the efforts of three men – Sir John Foster, Peter Benenson and Gerald – Justice came into being in the spring of 1957, when the Treason Trials were just getting into their stride. Gerald has worked for the society until the present day (barring his six years as Lord Chancellor), becoming its chairman for three years in 1972. Those who have given it great support are Lord Shawcross, Lord Foot, The Rt Hon. Sam Silkin and many other legal lights. Many have sacrificed their time in travelling to countries all over the world to uphold justice and preserve civil liberties.

But the linchpin of the society was Tom Sargant, its indefatigable secretary for 25 years until his retirement in 1982. He and Gerald had known one another even longer, for Tom recalls that at the General Election of 1951, when he was Labour candidate for South Hendon, Gerald spoke for him at an eve-of-poll meeting, and made the finest political speech he had ever heard, without notes of any kind. Both men had the objectives of Justice very much at heart, and when Gerald became Lord Chancellor he was always accessible if Tom wanted help or advice. Anyone who had been sentenced for contempt of court was an object of concern to Gerald, and once, in the case of a man named Lusty, who had been in prison for eighteen months for contempt, Gerald asked Tom to hire the best lawyer he could find and "get him off". Moreover, he paid for this to be done.

Earlier, when Gerald was chairman of the society, he never waited for Sargant to tell him of things needing attention; he would call in at the office at regular intervals and ask what required to be done – the only Justice chairman, Tom declares, ever to act in this way. While speaking of Gerald he continually stressed his kindness and concern for individuals, and their problems.

SIX

DURING THEIR long-drawn out proceedings the Treason Trials attracted other observers beside Gerald Gardiner, among them Dame Rebecca West, who covered them in a series of articles for the *Sunday Times*.

She had come to be regarded as an authority on the subject of treason, for some years previously she had written a very successful book, *The Meaning of Treason*, and had also been an observer at the trials of Dr Alan Nunn May and Fuchs. In 1956, while making some alterations to a new edition of her book, she included some unfortunate remarks concerning the writer Evelyn Waugh, which he found objectionable and defamatory.

Her comments immediately brought forth an action for libel which Dame Rebecca and Pan Books, her publishers, subsequently lost. Waugh was awarded £3,000 damages and costs, but, on realizing that Pan Books would suffer acute financial loss which might cause them to go out of business, he waived his damages.

He was not so generous where another action was concerned, but in this case he had good reason to be less magnanimous. Besides the Rebecca West case he was suing with considerable relish Miss Nancy Spain and the Beaverbrook press for libel, and had engaged Gerald as his Counsel.

Gerald found Waugh a colourful eccentric, at times awkward and irritating but an amusing customer, who during his sessions in court sported a huge ear-trumpet with elaborate aplomb and who, sartorially, gave the impression of a well-to-do country squire. The origin of the clash between himself and Nancy Spain lay in her visit to his home in Gloucestershire in 1955, when she arrived on the doorstep of Piers Court with Lord Noel Buxton, hoping for an interview with the celebrated author of *Decline and Fall* and other famous books, which as literary critic of the *Daily Express* she wished to include in a series of articles.

Evelyn Waugh refused to see her, and as a result of being turned down sharply Nancy wrote "My Pilgrimage to see Mr Waugh", an article describing her inhospitable brush-off, and handed it over to the

Express to print. Although he wasn't exactly pleased Waugh sensibly ignored it, but a year later he noticed another reference to himself in the same paper to which he took great exception, since it reflected on the sales of his books. He wrote at once to his agent, A. D. Peters:

Dear Pete,

I have long waited to catch the *Express* in libel. I think they have done it this time. Miss Spain's statement that I complain the *Express* sold only 300 copies of my novel is entirely false. I enclose the article she has misread.

Also the figures of my sales are, as you know, wildly wrong.

There should be no difficulty in proving malice.

Will you please take legal opinion and if that is favourable bring in a writ. . . .

Yours ever,
Evelyn.

The article referred to read as follows: "There is a war between Evelyn Waugh and me. He said some weeks ago, in a literary weekly, that the *Express* had no influence on the book trade. The *Express*, he complains, sold only 300 of his novels. He once had a book chosen by the Book Society, so that sold well. But the total first sales of all his other titles are dwarfed by his brother Alec. *Island in the Sun* (Cassells 16s.), foretold by me as this year's run-away Best Seller, has now topped 60,000 copies as a direct result of my *Daily Express* notice, so the publishers told me yesterday."

Faced with an action for libel, Nancy Spain counter-claimed against Waugh for implying that she was an ineffectual literary critic in an article he had recently written for the *Spectator* magazine, in which he said: "An investigation has lately been made in the Book Trade to determine which literary critics have most influence on sales. . . . A good review by Arnold Bennett in the *Evening Standard* was believed to sell an edition in twenty-four hours. . . . The claim was exaggerated as I learned to my disappointment when he kindly noticed my first novel. The ensuing demand was, I think, between two and three hundred, but I wonder whether any critic today has so large an immediate influence. . . . Things have changed. The Beaverbrook Press is no longer listed as having any influence at all."

Thus, on February 20th, 1957, Gerald, with Neville Faulks as his Junior, confronted her Counsel, Sir Hartley Shawcross, and Helenus

Milmo in the High Court. Opening the case, he said that Waugh felt that Miss Spain's comments would lead people to think he was an unsuccessful and embittered writer who had made false and malicious attacks on Miss Spain by reason of personal spite against her, and that he was a writer who carried insignificant weight with the general public, the film rights and options on whose books were not worthy of purchase, and who was not worthy of consideration for the writing of articles.

Referring to Nancy Spain's visit to Piers Court, Gerald stressed the fact that there was a notice on the gate reading "No admittance on business", which showed clearly that visitors like Miss Spain were unwelcome. It was still a free country, so he thought. "In June 1955 the *Daily Express* announced a new series of articles in which its critics would make a new appraisal of such famous people as Sir Malcolm Sargent, Evelyn Waugh and others. The first article was a particularly vicious attack on Sir Laurence Olivier and his wife.

"Miss Spain had been warned over the telephone by Mrs Waugh that her husband did not wish to be interviewed, so that when the lady and Lord Noel Buxton arrived on their doorstep at 7.45 p.m. one evening they were told Mr Waugh would not see them. They persisted in their efforts, whereupon Mr Waugh, hearing a man's truculent voice arguing with his wife, came to the door and ordered them to leave in no uncertain terms. He also wrote to the *Daily Express* that night expressing a hope that the delinquents would be suitably punished. Nancy Spain's article concerning this visit in her paper he ignored, but when, the following March, he read her remarks in another article, 'Does a Good Word from Me Sell a Good Book?' he felt she was unjustifiably attacking him.

"Every sentence in it," said Gerald, "was untrue. There was no war between Mr Waugh and Miss Spain. In his *Spectator* article he had not said the *Daily Express* had no influence on the book trade, nor had he complained that the *Daily Express* had sold only 300 copies of his novels. He was pointing out what the *investigation* had said and that his own experience confirmed it. The article made it look as though Waugh's books only sold about 40,000 copies, when his sales were about 4,280,125, of which over 2,774,000 had been published in this country and the rest in America. First edition sales amounted to 180,000. The article was obviously written recklessly and in a flaming temper and, having no real defence, Miss Spain had counter-claimed. In the twelve months prior to Waugh's article, no less than twenty-two people in addition to Miss Spain had reviewed books in the *Daily Express.*"

Sir Hartley Shawcross, on cross-examining Waugh, remarked that Miss Spain was a friendly, warm-hearted person according to the review of her autobiography by Gilbert Harding in the *Evening Standard.* Sir Hartley paused to ask: "Perhaps you do not approve of him?" No reply. He hurried on: "No. I thought you would not. Do you think it's just possible that, like so many of us, you sometimes tend to take yourself rather seriously?"

"No," said Waugh.

The questions continued inexorably and the cross-examination was proving rather uncomfortable for Waugh when it was suddenly terminated. Sir Hartley abruptly left the Court and the case, never to return. Despite his departure, which was clearly damaging for Nancy Spain, Gerald was gloomy about the result of the case as he had been from the beginning, for he felt they had the wrong judge in Mr Justice Stable. Evelyn Waugh was also conscious of this and Neville Faulks tried to cheer him up by saying that Gerald's pessimistic air was just "an act", and he would present the case with his usual brilliance – "not to worry".

Waugh's own words in a letter to Nancy Mitford when it was all over confirm this: "The Judge was a buffoon who invited the jury to laugh me out of Court. But I had taken the precaution of telling the Dursley Parish Priest that he should have 10 per cent of the damages. His prayers were answered in dramatic Old Testament form. A series of Egyptian plagues fell on Sir Hartley Shawcross from the moment he took up the case, culminating in a well-nigh fatal motor-accident to his mother-in-law at the very moment when he had me under cross-examination and was making me feel rather an ass. He had to chuck the case and leave it to an under-strapper whose heart was in the Court next door, where a Bolivian millionaire was suing Lord Kemsley for saying he buggered his wife (the Bolivian's wife, not Lady Kemsley)."

Gerald, in dealing with Nancy Spain's counter-claim, charged her among other things with inaccuracy which severely damaged her case.

"Miss Spain's counter-claim was not defamatory. It would be difficult to imagine anything more injurious to the reputation of an author than the words of which the plaintiff complained. I am not making any sort of imputation on Miss Spain as a writer. Her articles are most cleverly written and most amusing and it may well be that as a result of this case she will receive a higher post in the Beaverbrook organization. She has certainly followed her master's footsteps. But I do ask you to show by your verdict that newspapers which have these large circulations and great power have some responsibility and ought not to attack a man simply because he exercises his legal right not to have their reporters in his house if he does not want them. They ought not to make a series of damaging statements about him which they have conceded are untrue and about which they made no attempt to ascertain the truth before writing them."

Mr Justice Stable, summing up, was not exactly impressed with either of the contending parties. Commenting on Waugh's *Spectator* article he assured the jury: "If you come to the conclusion that it didn't reflect discreditably on Miss Spain you will dismiss the counter-claim. If on the other hand you think that it did, you will compensate her accordingly. . . . When Miss Spain said that the sale of 60,000 copies of Alec Waugh's book *Island in the Sun* was the direct result of the articles she published, she was rather overstating the case. It seemed that she had scraped through it somewhat rapidly in the cocktail bar of the Ritz, and that rather cursory notice of the book was by no means the most important factor in stepping up the sale of Alec Waugh's book."

In conclusion he indicated clearly his personal attitude: "It may be that members of the jury in this literary atmosphere may recall one of Shakespeare's earlier works, *Much Ado About Nothing*. Whether this expression applies here is exclusively a matter for you to decide."

Nevertheless it took them two hours to return a verdict which resulted in Evelyn Waugh being awarded £2,000 damages and costs, the counter-claim against him being dismissed. He was jubilant in his account of it to his friend Nancy Mitford:

"I had a firm solid jury who were out to fine the *Express* for their impertinence to the Royal Family, quite irrespective of any rights and wrongs. They were not at all amused by the judge. All the £300-a-day barristers rocked with laughter at his sallies. They glowered. That was not what they paid a judge for, they thought. So Father Collins got £200 and a lot of chaps at White's got pop."

While Gerald's success at the Bar increased steadily year by year, he was unable to make much headway in another direction: his campaign for the abolition of the death penalty. Ever since he returned from service with the F.A.U. he had continued to address meetings up and down the country in town and village halls, however poorly attended. Never unduly discouraged by the sight of a meagre half-dozen in the audience, he became, if anything, more determined than ever to pursue his course. Whenever he was lucky enough to have a fair-sized audience he approached it with a definite plan in mind. He would start by taking a vote for or against capital punishment and recording the figures. Those in favour were almost always in the majority, but when his talk and subsequent discussion were over a second vote was asked for and the figures were consistently reversed. He took some comfort from this, feeling that provided people were given the facts on the subject their enlightenment would generally result in a more tolerant approach to it.

Over the years he received so many requests from those who were troubled about the unique deterrent effect of the law, and the fact that there was no alternative, that in 1955 he decided it was time to provide them with some information on the matter by writing a modest book, *Capital Punishment as a Deterrent and the Alternative*, which Victor Gollancz published in the following year.

The zeal with which Gerald pursued his objective was remarkably similar to that of Sir Samuel Romilly, who campaigned unceasingly for like reforms at the beginning of the nineteenth century when punishment for high treason was "that the offender be dragged to the gallows: that he be hanged by the neck and then cut down alive: that his entrails be taken out and burned while he was yet alive: that his head be cut off: that his body be divided into five parts, and his head and quarters be at the King's disposal". Whether they were reserved as a delicacy for his table was not revealed. The Bill to modify this savagery to a punishment of a simple hanging or beheading was defeated in the House of Commons, but Romilly was not dismayed. The penalty for stealing as much as 5 shillings from a shop was death, as it was for some 200 minor offences which he tried to get abolished during his years as an M.P. He repeatedly failed, with the exception of two small crimes, pickpocketing and begging by soldiers and sailors without obtaining a pass to do so. Nevertheless his persistent parliamentary defeats left him unmoved, and before dying in 1818 he still firmly adhered to the views that he expressed during the High Treason Bill, which he lost by twelve votes:

> From the spirit which I have seen I shall not be surprised, and I certainly will not be deterred, by any vote this night. . . . It was my lot to hear in parliament a negative upon that Bill which was intended to deliver this enlightened nation from the reproach of the cruel and disgusting punishment of burning women alive. It was my

lot again and again to witness in this house the defeat of those wise
and humane exertions which were intended to rescue Englishmen
from the disgrace of abetting slavery. But the punishment of burning
is no more, and Africa is free. No resistance, no vote of this night shall
prevent my again appealing to the good sense and good feeling of the
legislature and of the country. If I live another year, I will renew this
Bill, with the Bill for repealing the punishment of death for stealing a
few shillings and, whatever may be my fate, the seed which is
scattered has not fallen on stony ground.

With the same sense of purpose Gerald doggedly pursued his aim, and
in 1955, when the National Campaign for the Abolition of Capital
Punishment was formed by Victor Gollancz, he became his staunch
ally. By 1960 they were joint chairmen, since Gollancz could not give full
time to it owing to pressure of work. Peggy Duff, who assisted Gollancz in
the campaign, described later Gerald's devotion to the cause, which was
launched at the Central Hall, Westminster:

> Very often, in the evening, he would come into the office with a large
> suitcase. He would fill it with the memorials and envelopes, take it off
> home, and late into the night he and his wife would fold and fill. Early
> the next morning, on his way to chambers, he would call in again
> and leave the results of his night's work with us. I have had many
> chairmen over the years, whom I loved, admired, occasionally hated,
> often argued with, but there never was any other chairman who did
> that.

A marked improvement in Gerald's legal reputation, which had
steadily increased since the war, was noticeable after he took Silk in
1948. This was not as predictable as it sounds. It is one thing to be able
to present a case for your leader with thoroughness and expertise, but
quite another to shoulder the entire responsibility and expound it with
eloquence and lucidity in court. A barrister may have a high reputation
as a Junior only to find himself severely out of pocket (or ruined) as a
result of fancying himself in a silk gown. The first year after becoming a
Q.C. he expects to earn very little, as Sir Neville Faulks explains in *No
Mitigating Circumstances*, where he too admits to having been in two
minds about taking the plunge. The fact that a new Silk with heavy
responsibilities is allowed for a year to continue his Junior practice
work whilst still acting as a Q.C., without his clients having to engage

unior counsel, no doubt helped him to make up his mind. But Faulks
vas still doubtful. "I toyed with the idea of taking silk in the hope of
getting the big defamatory work. It is true that Gerald Gardiner was
here and looked as though he would be there forever. He would
obviously be the first choice of any litigant, but I thought that as he
couldn't be on both sides at once, I might be number two."

His conjecture was roughly correct, for as it happened Neville Faulks
collected many of the briefs that Gerald was too busy to take, since he
was careful never to cope with more than one at a time, thus ensuring
that each received his undivided attention. A Q.C. who takes on more
than he can manage often finds himself forced to relinquish a case at the
last moment to another colleague, who may have no chance to become
familiar with it before it comes into court, thus causing much
frustration and disappointment to the client who engaged him.

On May 3rd, 1957, the two barristers found themselves together in
the High Court of Justice engaged on a rather curious case of contempt
involving Mr Eldon Griffiths, the London representative of an
American magazine called *Newsweek*, which was sold in England. This
comparatively young journalist of thirty-two eventually became Conservative M.P. for a Suffolk constituency, and later still Under-
secretary of State to the Department of the Environment, but until his
appearance in what turned out to be something of a *cause célèbre* nothing
much had been heard of him. Prosecuted with him were W. H. Smith &
Sons Ltd and Rolls House Publishing Co. Ltd, who respectively sold
and distributed the magazine in question. A regular feature headed
"BRITAIN" had referred to a certain Dr Bodkin Adams, whose trial for
murder was proceeding at the time in the Central Criminal Court.
Underneath the heading "The Doctor on Trial" were the words: "He
employed three servants and a chauffeur to drive his MG or Rolls
Royce on visits to his elderly patients, a remarkable number of whom
remembered him in their wills when they died. Over a period of 20
years, 17 of Dr Adams' grateful patients bequeathed to him the sum
total of £90,000 – and this is what started the tea-cups rattling in
Eastbourne." The article went on: "Eastbourne's frenzied gossip
pushed Dr Adams' alleged victims as high as 400."

The news item was considered prejudicial to the outcome of the case,
and therefore constituted contempt of court. The words were brought
to the notice of W. H. Smith, who immediately took steps to withdraw
all unsold copies from their bookstalls, and in due course briefed Gerald
and Helenus Milmo to act for them. Neville Faulks defended Eldon

Griffiths, while Rolls House Publishing Co. engaged the services of Percy Grieve.

The Lord Chief Justice (Hilbury) and Mr Justice Donovan, trying the case, were perplexed by its complexity, for no one appeared to be responsible for *Newsweek* in London. The Attorney-General (Sir Reginald Manningham-Buller), prosecuting, was anxious to hear from Eldon Griffiths why he had not acted promptly and withdrawn the magazine when he first saw that it contained references to the Bodkin Adams trial. Speaking for his client, Neville Faulks said: "He sent cables to America telling them not to touch the trial, to play it down. Instead the paper published the article of which complaint is made. Had he attempted to interfere with what was published he would have been reprimanded and might have been dismissed."

The Attorney-General, plainly not satisfied with this, asked Eldon Griffiths: "But you are the person in this country responsible for the Extra European editorial text, are you not?"

"A special person in New York does that," was Griffiths' reply. "Many stories appear in the column 'Britain' of which I know nothing."

Neville Faulks supported him: "It might be expedient to hold my client responsible, but it would not be justice."

The same could equally well be said of W. H. Smith & Sons although they admitted their oversight and tendered a sincere apology for what had happened. Having conveyed this, Gerald went on to emphasize that the firm had done its best to remedy the situation by withdrawing all copies of the magazine the moment they realized their mistake. Apparently this failed to convince the Lord Chief Justice, who was definitely worried about the firm on the grounds of contempt. Gerald put forward mitigating circumstances, for *Newsweek* was only one of a hundred foreign publications handled by W. H. Smith. "After 20 years, during which there had been no complaint, it had no reason to suppose the magazine would contain anything improper. When deciding to sell any new periodical, three of their directors took the trouble to read and examine thoroughly the contents of the first three issues. Thereafter, if nothing was amiss, they could not possibly be expected to go on reading each and every copy they sold, it being quite impractical." The court accepted that on the whole this was reasonable.

Rolls House Publishing Co. were in a similar position in that they could not be expected to read everything they distributed and, if anything, were even less to blame for what had occurred. Since each party denied responsibility, one question remained to be answered, and Justices Hilbury and Donovan put it to Neville Faulks: "What we want to know is, who is managing the business here?"

"Mr Griffiths is the senior employee," Counsel could only repeat. 'He had not written the article and only collected information for the editor in New York."

They were no nearer a solution and, faced with such a problem, Mr Justice Hilbury told the court they needed further time to decide who bore the real responsibility, and that their judgment would be given a week later. The fact of the matter was that a company in Dayton, Ohio, owned *Newsweek*, and the New York office received material from Eldon Griffiths which was edited there before being sent to Amsterdam for printing.

On May 11th the court reassembled, when the Lord Chief Justice was heard to remark to Mr Justice Donovan, albeit *sotto voce*, that he didn't see how they could punish the agent for the crime of his master. This exonerated Eldon Griffiths, but in their judgment the other two respondents were guilty of contempt and bore the real responsibility, and each was fined £50 and ordered to pay half the taxed costs.

It is interesting to note that Dr Bodkin Adams was acquitted of the murder charge against him, but whether the outcome of his trial was affected by the contempt of court proceedings in the High Court of Justice it is impossible to determine. Even though Gerald was to act some time later in a case involving Dr Bodkin Adams, he was never able to find out. One thing is certain, however: someone had to be blamed for the column in *Newsweek*, and as the real culprits were out of this country, and the long arm of the law could not reach them, W. H. Smith and Rolls House Publishing Co. took the rap. As far as one can tell a similar situation could arise today, for international relations serve to protect law-breakers rather than the reverse, and innocent people have to suffer.

In Portugal events under the rule of Dr Salazar impinged on Gerald's life in the middle of 1957, when he visited that country at the behest of the International Commission of Jurists.

Political and economic conditions had been building up over many years, while repression and tyranny had long reigned there since a military clique had seized control in 1926 and had later, in 1932, appointed Dr Salazar (formerly Finance Minister) as their Prime Minister. His power had grown until he became virtual dictator, the serious repercussions of whose leadership were felt not only among his own people, but among those of them who fled as refugees from Portugal to Brazil when the going got really rough. Rumours of torture and illegal imprisonment, with no hope of redress, percolated through to the outside world, despite a strict censorship which decreed that every newspaper had to bear the censor's stamp before it reached the public. So glaring was the arbitrary treatment of political prisoners confined indefinitely without trial, and of defence lawyers who suffered intimidation and threats from the authorities, that the International Commission of Jurists decided it was time an independent inquiry was made into the alleged injustices.

Several political trials were pending there in June 1957, affording the Commission an opportunity not to be missed. Gerald left England on the 11th of that month and arrived in Oporto just in time to watch the end of the trial of 52 students who had been arrested for attempting to organize strikes in the universities. It had begun in December 1956 and had already lasted six months. Prior to that the accused had been in prison awaiting trial since 1955, and had been subjected in many cases to harsh interrogation and the "statue", a form of torture which leaves no physical traces behind and which condemns the prisoners to hold their bodies erect against a wall for several days and nights until they fall asleep standing up. They have no respite from this exhausting posture and interrogation except for short meal breaks, when, having sat down to eat, they find it almost impossible to rise again and have to be prodded by guards to do so. This was similar in some respects to interrogation methods used in

Northern Ireland before they were abolished by Mr Edward Heath in 972 on Gerald's recommendation.

The military court where the students were being tried – without a ury – invited Gerald to sit with the judges. He took his place beside hem on the bench and listened to the defence lawyers complaining that ome of the accused had endured the "statue" for as much as five days nd nights at a stretch, and one of them, Hernani Silva, for seven onsecutive days and nights. The political police (P.I.D.A.), the quivalent to Hitler's Gestapo, were responsible for the arrest of the ouths, the youngest being about seventeen, and for the interrogation hey suffered. All the accused were convicted and sent to prison to serve entences, although they had already been in gaol for long periods. One f them, after the death of Salazar in 1970, became President of Angola; nother, as soon as he was free, graduated in medicine and went to 'rance, where he and others set up the M.P.L.A. which eventually ame to power in Angola. Lopes de Oliveira and Manuel da Silva unior suffered and died at the hands of the P.I.D.A. while in prison, ausing considerable public concern. Two investigations, one called for y 72 jurists of Lisbon and Oporto and another by 33 lawyers from Coimbra, were totally ignored by Dr Salazar, who continued the ersecution of opposition liberals well into the sixties.

The next case to be heard, on Gerald's second day in court, was that f Professor Ruy Luiz Gomez, who had been a candidate for the residency in 1954 and had had his campaign broken up by the police. Ie was charged with four others for sending articles to newspapers (not ublished owing to censorship) which appealed for the restoration of ree elections, the restoration of free speech and the right to form olitical parties. On being arrested he was beaten up by the police and orced to be hospitalised, followed by imprisonment on and off for the ext few years. This was his second trial, and the defence lawyer asked or an adjournment since he had not been allowed to speak to his client or nearly a year. The court generously allowed them one hour ogether! Gerald noted that the prosecuting advocate sitting beside the udges had no shorthand notes or record of evidence to refer to, so that it vas impossible to say on what evidence the accused was convicted. ong sentences were again imposed.

Gerald left Oporto about a week later, scarcely impressed by the ature of the legal process there, and found his opinion confirmed vithin a few days on hearing that a certain lawyer, Dr Manuel Carlos, efending in a political trial in Lisbon, was prevented by the court from continuing the defence of his client and was unwise enough to remark: "Your excellencies judge as you feel like, with or without proof." He was charged the same day, summarily tried and sentenced the following morning to seven months' imprisonment. [*]

The Salazar régime continued its repression and ill-treatment of members of the opposition, though not without comment from abroad. In 1959 an article appeared in the *New Statesman* which accused particular prison governors in Portugal of torturing prisoners under their supervision. The response was a libel action brought against the paper by the prison governors, who denied the accusation. Gerald, who had by now become chairman of the company, was immediately consulted, and advised the *New Statesman* to refute the libel and maintain the truth of the article. However, as the case proceeded he became increasingly uneasy, for when witnesses were required to attend they could not be found. Some had escaped from Portugal to Brazil, while others were held in prison. Nevertheless, the search went on, and eventually the stubborn stand taken by the paper, on Gerald's instruction, bore fruit. The prison governors became nervous and finally abandoned the case, and nothing more was heard of it.

In 1961 news came through that all the lawyers who had been arrested and imprisoned had at last been released, even though Dr Salazar was still in power. However, rumours of repression and persecution continued to appear in the British press as late as 1963, when Salazar invited Lord Russell of Liverpool, with whom he had been on friendly terms for some time, to come over and see for himself that they were groundless. When he returned Russell wrote an article which was published in the *Daily Telegraph* in July, denying charges of ill-treatment and tyranny, and saying there was little truth in them and that such reports had been "made in irresponsible quarters".

Gerald, feeling strongly that this was a travesty of the facts, spent more than six months checking them before sending a reply, "Portugal's Political Prisoners", to the same paper on February 10th, 1964. In his article he pointed out that when, after persistent pressure, the Portuguese Government finally agreed to hold an enquiry into the alleged tortures in October 1957, this was abandoned as soon as the first witness offered to name 26 specific cases in which torture had been used. Things could scarcely be as right as Lord Russell had claimed

---

[*] Gerald's experiences in Portugal appear in *Bulletin No. 7*, published by the International Commission of Jurists, 1957.

when the Bishop of Oporto, on appealing for the P.I.D.A.'s methods to be looked into in 1958, was ignored completely, and who, when he returned from a visit to Rome soon after, was refused readmission to Portugal, and ever since had been forced to live in exile in Valencia, leaving his see vacant.

Furthermore, Gerald added, if people complained of ill-treatment, proceedings were immediately taken against the protesters. He, himself, on applying for the same facilities to visit Portugal as those granted to Lord Russell, was refused them, likewise the International Red Cross, who wished to inspect Portugal's penal establishments. No opposition member of the National Assembly had ever been elected since Salazar came to power in 1932, and, although a member of NATO and a partner in the Anglo-Portuguese alliance, Portugal had never allowed the formation of a United Nations Association, which showed conclusively to him, if not to Lord Russell, that Dr Salazar was not as anxious to have an impartial and objective observer inquire into prison conditions and legal procedure as he appeared to be.

Also, he reminded Russell, towards the end of World War II, when Hitler committed suicide in May 1945, Dr Salazar had flown the national flag at half mast on all public buildings! It was time, Gerald concluded, that we in England woke up to what had been happening in Portugal.

It still went on happening. General Delgado, an opponent of the régime over a long period, was forced to leave the country in 1958 to escape arrest. Seven years later he was lured to Badajos, a town in Spain near the Portuguese border, and shot.

For the next decade Gerald's activities on behalf of political victims were in abeyance, for he was fully occupied not only in the English courts, but later in the House of Lords. In June 1959 he acted in a case that attracted considerable notoriety, in which he was assisted by Mr Neville Faulks, who in the past months had become a Q.C.

The case concerned Liberace, the entertainer, who had sued for libel way back in 1956. Liberace's fame was, and is, world-wide, and the newspaper coverage of the case was lavish, particularly in the *Daily Mirror*, which had printed the libel, and which now visually heightened the interest with countless photographs of the participants. Son of an Italian French-horn player and Polish mother who was a concert pianist, Wladziu Valentino Liberace was born in Milwaukee, Wisconsin, in 1919. Of the three children in the family, only one appeared to have inherited the musical talents of the parents, displaying them at an

early age. Paderewski, visiting the U.S.A. in the twenties, was invited
to hear the small boy of seven play the piano and praised his
performance highly. He was just sixteen when he appeared as guest
soloist with the Chicago Symphony, but two years previously it was
doubtful if he would ever play again. One of his hands had developed
serious trouble, and it was entirely due to the obstinacy of his mother
that it was not amputated. She refused to agree to the medical decision
and made up her mind to doctor the hand herself, which she succeeded
in saving. This was not the first time her son had cause to be grateful to
her, for at the age of nine months, when he caught pneumonia, she
nursed him back to health. Liberace never forgot the debt he owed her
and during his subsequent spectacular career as a pianist references to
"Momma" were constantly made in his public performances.

Liberace began modestly, playing with dance bands and then at
supper-clubs, and it was not until he was in his early thirties that his
career really took off. In 1951 the manager of a TV station in California
spotted him and he was engaged at $1,000 a week to appear in a 13
week series of television films, giving his cabaret act which might be
described as a mixture of concert-playing and humorous chat-show
and which he had made quite popular. A year later he gave a
performance at the Hollywood Bowl dressed in a white evening suit
and took the audience by storm. This was the turning point in his
career, and his success, as he put it, "spread like a prairie wild fire".

By the time he came to England four years later his fame had grown
to such an extent that the rapturous, hysterical welcome he received at
Waterloo Station had not been exceeded by that of any celebrity for
thirty years or more. His debut in London collected a mixed bag of
reviews. "Cassandra" of the *Daily Mirror*, a forthright acerbic critic
known in private life as William Connor, wrote a blistering attack on
his performance which resulted in the libel suit that Liberace brought
against that paper. It was published on September 26th, 1956:

I have to report that Mr Liberace, like *Wunderstarke Fünf*,* is about
the most that man can take. But he is not a drink. He is yearning
wind strength five. He is the summit of sex – the pinnacle of
Masculine, Feminine and Neuter. Everything that He, She or It can
ever want. I spoke to sad but kindly men on this newspaper who have
met every celebrity arriving from the United States for the past 30

*A German drink – the most deadly concoction of alcohol.

years. They all say that this deadly, winking, sniggering, snuggling, chromium-plated, scent-impregnated, luminous, quivering, giggling, fruit-flavoured, mincing, ice-covered heap of mother love has had the biggest reception and impact since Charlie Chaplin arrived at the same station, Waterloo, on September 12th, 1921.

This appalling man – and I use the word appalling in no other than its true sense of "terrifying" – has hit this country in a way that is as violent as Churchill receiving the cheers on V.E. day. He reeks with emetic language that can only make grown men long for a quiet corner, an aspidistra, a handkerchief and the old heave-ho. Without doubt he is the biggest sentimental vomit of all time. Slobbering over his mother, winking at his brother, counting the cash at every second, this superb piece of calculating candy-floss has an answer for every situation . . . .

Nobody since Aimée Semple MacPherson has purveyed a bigger, richer and more varied slag heap of lilac-covered hokum. Nobody anywhere ever made so much money out of high-speed piano playing with the ghost of Chopin gibbering at every note. There must be something wrong with us that our teenagers longing for sex, and our middle-aged matrons fed up with sex, alike should fall for such a sugary mountain of jingling claptraps wrapped up in such a preposterous clown.

Clown he may have been, but hardly in the witness-box, where, on the first day, the forty-year-old charmer withstood the rigours of examination and cross-examination for six hours without batting an eyelid.

Gilbert Beyfus, Q.C., and Helenus Milmo acted for Liberace while Gerald led Neville Faulks for the *Daily Mirror*. After a graphic account of the plaintiff's flamboyant career as a talented performer which brought him £367,000, 27,000 Valentines and twelve proposals of marriage a year and 6,000 to 10,000 letters a week, the first question Gilbert Beyfus asked him was plain and unequivocal:

"Are you a homosexual?"

"No sir," was the reply.

Gerald rose hurriedly to protest: "There is no suggestion, and never has been, of anything of the kind."

This had to be clarified from the start, for the crux of the matter was whether Cassandra's description of Liberace could be regarded as fair comment, or whether the ordinary meaning of the words used in the *Daily Mirror* article implied that he was a homosexual. Liberace

obviously thought they did, and expressed himself strongly on this poin
when Gerald came to cross-examine him.

"This is the most improper article," he declared, "that has ever beer
written about me. It has been widely quoted in all parts of the worlc
and has been reproduced exactly as it appeared in the *Daily Mirror*. I
has been given the interpretation of homosexuality; one paper had th
headline 'Is Liberace a man?'"

Gerald: People must have singularly filthy minds if they think thes
    words imply that you are a homosexual.
Liberace: The expression in the article was "fruit-flavoured" and wa
    one commonly directed to homosexuals.
Gerald: Nonsense. It's just a reference to your sugary manner.
Liberace: The reason I'm in court is that this article has attacked m
    below the belt on a moral issue.

Later he added that it had so seriously upset his mother's healtl
when it was brought to her notice that her doctor advised sending he
home immediately. On being asked by Gerald if he had seen at
London theatre the performance of Semprini, which was similar to hi
own, he looked puzzled.

Liberace: Who?
Gerald: Semprini.
Liberace: No, I haven't. (*Then, smiling*) Evidently he doesn't do it a
    successfully as I do or I should've heard of him.

"I cried all the way to the bank" was, he agreed, one of th
expressions he had coined, but dismissed the biography of himse
published in 1956 as mostly pure invention.

Gerald: But you signed a foreword that it was authentic in every detail
Liberace: That was done by my secretary.
Gerald (*holding up book*): That is a deliberate imitation of you
    signature?
Liberace: Yes. She does it very well. (*Laughter*)

Asked to explain why he gave his birth date as 1920 instead of 191ç
he replied frankly: "We find it desirable to make the birth date a roun
figure. (*Then, engagingly*) I borrowed the idea from Jack Benny."

The laughter that followed was infectious and affected most of the court, including the ten men and two women on the jury. One of them, a shapely middle-aged lady, obviously charmed by Liberace, flashed him a deliberate wink as she returned to the jury-box preparatory to the verdict being announced. His *sang froid* rarely deserted him throughout the case, his humour during the long hours of cross-examination stone-walled everything Gerald and Neville Faulks could aim at him. He was impregnable.

Jimmie Thompson, appearing in 1956 in a late night show "Here and Now", as well as in the revue "For Amusement Only" at the Apollo Theatre, while Liberace was performing at the Palladium, came in for questioning by Gilbert Beyfus about his skit on the American artist, particularly in reference to the song he sang concerning his fan mail. Beyfus quoted lines from the lyric:

> I get more and more
> They propose by the score
> And at least one or two are from girls.

Beyfus: That is about as offensive as anything could be.

Thompson: It is intended to reflect on the persons who make the proposals and not on the person who receives them.

Beyfus (*continuing*): My fans all agree
> That I'm really most me
> When I play the Sugar Plum Fairy.

That was a *double entendre* because the word "fairy" is slang for homosexual.

Thompson: In America, sir. I didn't know it was here.

Beyfus (*concluding*): Quite a frenzy of bliss
> I made two children kiss
> In spite of the fact
> Both were boys.

At this Thompson thought fit to explain that he was not the author of the lyric. He had met Liberace, who came to see him after his show and displayed no signs of being offended by the skit, but took it all in good part.

Unexpectedly, the witness who should have been the most reliable when appearing for the defence proved the most disappointing. William Connor failed lamentably when trying to refute another journalist's statement that he had admitted to her that his Cassandra article on Liberace was indefensible and that the paper only printed it for the sake of the publicity it would bring. After five-and-a-half hours' cross-examination his responses were so weak and ineffectual, to the point where he said he detested Liberace as a performer on TV but not as a man, that the editor of the *Daily Mirror* begged to be allowed to give evidence. Hugh Cudlipp (later to become Lord Cudlipp), when put into the witness box, was smartly put through his paces by both Counsel, an exhilarating exercise which did little to alter the final outcome.

After eight days the case came to an end. Gerald, in the course of his final comments, remarked that after Cudlipp's evidence the *Daily Mirror* could not be said to be a paper that ran away. As to the words complained of in the article, they were ordinary English words. There was nothing whatever to suggest homosexuality at all.

"I suggest the plaintiff has a bee in his bonnet about people charging him with homosexuality. It was fantastic to suppose that any reasonable person, reading the sentence in which 'he, she or it' occurred, would have said: 'Oh, I never knew that Mr Liberace went to bed with men.'"

Mr Justice Salmon, the Judge, hinted in his summing up a similar doubt: "I'm by no means saying that I should have come to the same conclusion of fact – that in law those words in their context are just capable of the meaning which has been attributed to them, and that is my finding."

Nevertheless, the jury thought otherwise, for their verdict was that the words used in Cassandra's article were not true in fact, nor were they fair comment. Liberace was awarded £8,000 damages, £2,000 of which were attributable to the imputations of homosexuality, but other comments by Cassandra in another article of October 18th, 1956, were fair comment, and costs were awarded to the *Daily Mirror* and Cassandra.

The enormous boost to sales received by the *Mirror* far out-weighed the costs of defending the case, and Hugh Cudlipp, though advised to go to Appeal, decided in his wisdom to let the matter rest. Yet he apparently enjoyed his participation in it, for in subsequent years he frequently invited the legal wranglers and their wives, Judge Salmon, Neville Faulks, Bill Connor and Gerald (when he was Lord Chancellor), to a lavish "Liberace" dinner to commemorate the case.

Over twenty years have elapsed, and Liberace's act on TV and music-hall is more glittering and outrageously romantic than ever. No doubt in another twenty he will still be "crying all the way to the bank". "Mr Showmanship" knows and relishes his business!

EIGHT

A POLITICAL FIASCO of the middle fifties had certain repercussions
in one of Gerald's cases which distinguished it from any other
conventional action for slander. This was the disastrous Suez affair of
1956.

For a decade after the invasion of Egypt by English, French and
Israeli military forces in order to seize an international waterway, the
Suez Canal, heated discussions raged and countless articles poured forth
to justify or denounce the aggressive act. Even now, more than 25 years
later, it is hard to discover the truth behind the evasions, lies and denials
which abounded at the time, causing bitter argument among politicians,
historians, journalists and, not least, the bemused British people who
lived through this turbulent time. A dozen or more books have been
written about this notorious episode, and no doubt there will be many
more when the official records are made available in 1986. Unfortunately, precious few documents (if any) exist, as most of the British
Government's deliberations at this period went unrecorded, being
secretly decided in Cabinet.

One well-known journalist and erstwhile M.P., the son of one of our
greatest political figures, was keenly interested in the proceedings, and
allowed several extracts from his book on the subject to be published as a
series of articles in the *Daily Express* in December 1958. The author was
Randolph Churchill, who took the view that Sir Anthony Eden, Prime
Minister at the period of Suez, was ultimately responsible for the
appallingly mistaken policy that had left our country's reputation and
our position in the Middle East in ruins, and that he was no longer fit to be
our Prime Minister.

This view was not shared by the majority of the Conservative party,
despite our ignominious withdrawal from the Suez area only a matter of
days after the invasion had begun. Labour opposition in the Commons,
attacks by the Press, pressure from the U.S.A. and world opinion in
general forced the Government to climb down and alter their disastrous
action, and within a few weeks Eden resigned as Prime Minister on the
grounds of ill-health. Among those who were aghast at the outcome of
the operation but who sympathized with Sir Anthony Eden's policies

was the M.P. for Kidderminster, Mr Gerald Nabarro, a Conservative business-man who had risen from lowly beginnings to a position of some eminence in local politics and a certain notoriety at Westminster.

It would be hard to say who was the more flamboyant, Randolph Churchill or Gerald Nabarro, for both exhibited considerable arrogance and conceit and both were forthright in their manner of speech (if not downright abusive at times), but of the two Randolph may be credited with a sharper sense of humour and a more eloquent brand of wit than his fellow Conservative.

On December 6th, 1958, Nabarro made a speech at the Halesowen Conservative Club in which he rebuked Randolph Churchill for criticizing Sir Anthony Eden's handling of the Suez affair in an article appearing in the *Daily Express* that day. "This is a pernicious, cowardly and uncalled-for attack in the present circumstances," he said. "This should have been a national crusade. Mr Churchill made his attack in the newspapers knowing full well that Sir Anthony could not reply. That is the action of a coward. I grieve that these things should have been done when Sir Anthony like other ministers of that time cannot reveal Cabinet secrets in his lifetime and have remained silent."

Immediately a strong letter from Randolph Churchill demanded an explanation and retraction from Nabarro, which was ignored for ten weeks, thus provoking the slander action brought against him on October 25th, 1960. Gerald, acting for Churchill, opened the case by saying that so long as England was England one imputation which no ordinary Englishman would sit down under was an allegation of cowardice. A retraction called for by Churchill had been refused.

"In earlier times," Gerald pointed out, "Mr Churchill would probably have challenged Mr Nabarro to a duel or gone and knocked him down, but nowadays a jury was the proper forum in a matter of this kind." After describing Churchill's career as author and journalist, he tackled the cowardice issue, which Randolph could hardly be accused of since he had parachuted into the Western Desert during World War II, had been wounded, and when he had recovered had proceeded to parachute into Yugoslavia. "His moral courage," Gerald continued, "was exactly on the same footing. . . He had published a book *What I said about the Press*. No one who had not moral courage and who earned his living in Fleet Street would attack in that way the most powerful men in Fleet Street."

The allegation of cowardice arose out of the Suez adventure, but he stressed to the jury that there was no question of party politics since both men were Conservatives and both had strongly supported the Government's policies prior to the invasion of Egypt, but two views were held on the subject. "One side supported the Government and said it was a good thing to teach Nasser a lesson and show the world that the old lion's tail could not be twisted. The other that it was a mistake for a British government to go to war without consulting the Commonwealth, wrong to antagonize America strongly and wrong to bring down united condemnation on ourselves. Some concluded," he went on, "that militarily it was unsuccessful, adding that it was a pity, having started, that we stopped it when we did, and finally, on what was called the 'collusion' issue, it was alleged that it looked hypocritical for us to be sending an army with the French to stop the fighting when the French had, in fact, known of and assisted Israel in the attack on Egypt."

In June 1956, a month before President Nasser nationalized the Suez Canal, Randolph Churchill had agreed with a publisher to write a life of Sir Anthony Eden, but by the time he came to do so the Suez operation was over, Sir Anthony had retired and the whole political situation had altered. He then saw it in a different light and concluded that the Suez adventure had been a terrible mistake. As to the suggestion, Gerald explained, that Churchill had acted in cowardly fashion by attacking Eden when he was unable to reply, the fact was that Eden *could* reply and was now doing so in his autobiography, for which he was receiving £100,000. Both books had subsequently been published, Randolph Churchill's, *The Rise and Fall of Sir Anthony Eden* in 1959 and Eden's, *Full Circle*, in 1960.

In a second attempt to obtain a retraction from Mr Nabarro, Churchill had written to him saying: "It is now ten weeks since the Press Association attributed these words to you. If what you say in your statement of defence is true, will you please issue a statement to the Association to this effect and ask them to circulate your denial, so that the injury done me may be at least partly undone?"

"That was a straightforward letter," Gerald stated, "but the reply from Nabarro's solicitors was, 'Our client asks us to say that he does not buy expensive dogs and bark himself', and evaded the question altogether. In reply Mr Churchill expressed regret that the 'dogs you hire to bark for you are so expensive but they would become more expensive as time goes on', and again asked for an answer to his question." The answer received from Mr Nabarro's solicitors was read carefully twice over by Gerald to the jury:

"'As you are well aware, the fact that our client in his defence statement does not admit that he spoke the words attributed to him in the Statement of Claim does not mean that he denies having made adverse criticism of your client or that he has in any way altered the opinions which he expressed.' That meant," Gerald suggested, "I don't say that I called you a coward. I don't deny that I called you a coward. I don't say what I did say. I still say what I said before."

It was impressed on the jury that they had to decide whether Churchill's *Daily Express* article was based on fact and, if so, whether his criticism was fair comment.

Questioned by Mr Geoffrey Lawrence, Q.C. (for Mr Nabarro), as to his motives in bringing the action, Churchill replied: "I didn't want a lot of paperwork settled by expensive dogs. I hate getting involved in that sort of thing." (This was not the only time he threw the "expensive dogs" phrase slyly back at Nabarro. He was to refer to it again, and when the case was settled it was to have an amusing consequence.) "I always think that two gentlemen ought to be able to settle things without that. But Mr Nabarro wouldn't answer my letters."

For two days Churchill repeatedly crossed swords with Geoffrey Lawrence, their exchanges being acrimonious from start to finish. Several times he remarked to Mr Justice Gormley, who was trying the case, that Counsel was continuously putting words into his mouth. A sample of dialogue between them clearly shows his attitude in court:

Lawrence: Is it clear from that article that you were saying Sir Anthony was unfit to be Prime Minister of Great Britain?

Churchill: Yes. I'm grateful to you for having revived my recollections of this article. I am astounded at the knowledge it shows and also the prescience.

Lawrence: So the article was a very severe attack on Sir Anthony?

Churchill: No, it was a warning to the nation of the troubles we were likely to get into if the nation went on being governed in that way.

Lawrence: Don't fence with words, please.

Churchill: Don't accuse me of fencing with words. I don't go back on a word of it.

Lawrence: And you described Sir Anthony Eden as a man of exceptional vanity?

Churchill: I was attacking his public life – which is the only thing I ever do attack.

Lawrence: You were saying not only has this man laid our policy in the Middle East in ruins but that he is so exceptionally vain that he has tried to evade looking facts in the face?

Churchill: I think I expressed it better than that. Why recast my words in less precise words?

Lawrence: Do you agree with my interpretation of what you wrote?

Churchill: No. I agree with what I wrote . . . every word of it. (*Turning to the Judge he complained of Counsel putting words into his mouth that were not true.*) I was setting out to write the truth as God has given me to see it, which is not what happens to every lawyer.

Lawrence: Was that meant to be offensive to me, Mr Churchill?

Churchill: I was thinking of the profession in general. Lawyers, after all, are expensive dogs, as your client describes it, paid to answer a case in which they have no personal stake. That is perfectly fair comment on a matter of public interest.

Later, when Lawrence asked Churchill if he would accept the proposition that his articles in the *Daily Express* constituted an attack on Sir Anthony, his reply was hardly conciliatory.

Churchill: I am not paid to accept propositions put by expensive dogs – your client's phrase, not mine.

Lawrence: You adopted it to be personally offensive to me?

Churchill: No. To be personally offensive to Mr Nabarro, who has called me a coward, and that is why we are here. I have not called him anything yet.

The rest of his cross-examination continued in this vein, including a sarcastic dig at Lawrence's sense of humour when he was questioning Churchill on conversations in Cabinet meetings over Suez. Churchill mentioned a politician as saying at a meeting: "We did not know we were at war."[*]

Lawrence: You don't report that there was any laughter in the Cabinet at that. You say: "There was a ghastly hush."

Churchill: Yes. Like someone shouting in church.

* Iain Macleod, M.P.

Lawrence: Where is the joke?
Churchill: I can't give you a sense of humour. If you don't see the joke it is
   beyond me.

Shortly after, Churchill's evidence having been concluded, Gerald
brought in the editor of *The Observer*, David Astor, and the editor of the
Daily Herald, Francis Williams, who both agreed that the comments by
Nabarro were damaging to the reputation of a journalist like Churchill.

Mr Nabarro's defence was something of an anti-climax after what had
been heard during the last two days, but it is noticeable that in contrast to
Churchill he treated both Counsel with pointed deference, addressing
them always as "sir".

His main contention was that comments he made in his Halesowen
speech should not rest on the interpretation of a single word; "coward"
should be linked with "action", for what he meant was that Churchill's
attack on Eden, in the circumstances, was a cowardly action. He was not
suggesting he was a coward personally. The quibble over this legal point
continued for hours but found no sympathy with the Judge, who in his
summing up said that it was not the intentions of the man who spoke a
slander that mattered, it was the meaning of the words. In effect the jury
had to decide whether Churchill's statement: "He called me a coward"
was justified, and if so whether Nabarro's words were fair comment or
not. The jury responded by debating this point for two-and-a-half hours
and decided they were not, and Churchill was awarded £1,500 damages.

Some time after the case was over Gerald received a package in his
morning mail which contained a leather collar from Churchill.
Suspended from it was a gold coin on which were inscribed the words
"Good Dog"!

Had the case gone the other way he would no doubt have held himself
partly responsible for its failure, since he had been absent from court
during the last two days, unable to deliver his final speech for the
plaintiff, which was given by his Junior, Colin Duncan.

Gerald was neither ill nor far away but busily engaged in a criminal
court at the Old Bailey defending another action which was to make legal
history: the *Lady Chatterley* case or Regina *v.* Penguin Books Ltd. Despite
frantic efforts by solicitors' clerks to arrange things differently the two
cases overlapped, a common hazard in the courts, where actions listed
for trial unexpectedly come forward, resulting in great difficulty and
confusion for the contending parties, who have to sort out the problem of
their Counsel being required in two places at once.

Lady Chatterley had begun on October 20th, before the slander action, which was set for October 25th. Randolph Churchill was agreeable to Gerald leaving his case providing he departed after his cross-examination of Nabarro and not before. To make this manoeuvre possible, the Judge at the Old Bailey proved accommodating, for he sent the members of the jury away for several days to read the Chatterley novel, during which time Gerald was able to cope with Nabarro as promised. He returned to the Old Bailey on October 27th and resumed his defence of *Lady Chatterley*.

The events leading to this trial began, as did those of Suez, in the fifties. The Obscene Publications Act, a bill with a chequered history going back several years and eventually passed in 1959, set the scene for the action which followed a year later.

Penguin Books, which had been publishing D. H. Lawrence's novels for a decade, wanted to bring out *Women in Love* and *Lady Chatterley's Lover* in the summer of 1960 to mark the anniversary of his death, to be followed by other major works of his which hitherto had not been published in paperback. Deciding not to have an expurgated edition of the book, since they considered the probability of a prosecution of *Lady Chatterley* quite remote, Penguin went ahead with their plans, only to be delayed by their printer, who informed them that the venture was too risky for him to undertake. This set-back was overcome by the book being offered to another printer, who accepted it. Penguin, however, had to inform the trade of the postponed publication date. The details in the press announcement came to the ears of the Director of Public Prosecutions who, thus alerted, ordered a copy of *Lady Chatterley* from a bookseller in the Charing Cross Road.

To avoid involving an innocent bookseller in what now seemed to be developing into a dangerous situation, Penguin notified the police that they could have a dozen copies of the book free if they collected them from their offices in Holborn. This the police did, and it was with considerable surprise that the publishing world learned a short while later that *Lady Chatterley's Lover* was to be the subject of a prosecution for obscenity.

C. H. Rolph, in his excellent book on the trial,* says there was "no reason why *Lady Chatterley's Lover*, 32 years after its first publication, should have been brought to trial under a new Statute expressly designed to inhibit prosecutions of this very kind. It does, however,

* *The Trial of Lady Chatterley* (Penguin Books, 1961).

suggest the only negative reason: there was nothing and no one in the legal machine able or willing to stop it. And the best illustration of this process in operation happens also to have been a recent turning point in the moral censorship of books by the law of England." The new act of 1959 required the Court to consider the book "as a whole", and publication would be justified if it was proved to be "for the public good on the grounds that it is in the interests of science, literature, art, or learning, or of other objects of general concern". Sir Allen Lane of Penguin presumably regarded *Lady Chatterley* as a test case under the new Act, and those who followed the trial throughout with intense interest obviously thought likewise.

From the moment Gerald was engaged on it he started preparatory work by enlisting the aid of literary experts to give evidence. In this context it should be said that Gerald always reckoned to know more about any case he was working on than his opposite number. This involved an enormous amount of preparatory work, often calling for the most precise and detailed knowledge of all aspects of everyday life, such as the working of the internal combustion engine, the finer points of navigation, and medical issues. By the time the case opened on October 20th he had lined up 35 professional leading lights of both sexes, whereas the prosecution, in the hands of the Senior Treasury Counsel at the Old Bailey, Mr Griffith-Jones, had been able to produce only one. D. H. Lawrence, it seemed, inspired loyal support from a considerable number of experts who were ready to defend the quality of his work.

Gerald made up his mind that an all-male jury was undesirable in a case of this kind, and as the prospective jurors filed in one by one he rejected two men, one of whom he replaced with a woman. The jury in the end consisted of nine men and three women. British law does not require Counsel to give any reason for challenging jury members, and it is possible to do so seven times in succession before an explanation is required.

Mr Rolph's blow-by-blow account of the famous case can be read for pleasure and profit in the Penguin paperback edition by those wishing to examine it in depth. Twenty years after the trial Gerald was invited to a private showing of the television version prior to its public showing, and was intrigued by the reactions of the audience to the views and moral attitudes expressed in the film. During the actual hearing of the case everyone in court was quietly attentive to all arguments of Counsel and witnesses – in fact, laughter was minimal. However, at the private show there were bursts of hilarity at what appeared to be the quaint sentiments and old-fashioned pronouncements on the sexual morality and mores of the time.

A colleague of Gerald's told him, not long after the case ended, of meeting a member of the jury who mentioned that when they had finished reading the book and were ready to return to court, they had already made up their minds that it was not obscene, but had to wait patiently for another five days before being allowed to give their verdict. The case of *Lady Chatterley* was worthwhile if only to show the marked change in thought and views of people. During the thirty years since the book had first been banned public opinion had begun to alter considerably; by 1980, after the lapse of another twenty years, it had changed out of all recognition.

The distinguished number of witnesses for the defence were immensely helpful to Gerald, consisting as they did of so many eminent literary figures: Miss Helen Gardner, Dame Rebecca West, Stephen Potter, Richard Hoggart, C. Day Lewis, C. V. Wedgwood and E. M. Forster. There were also well-known politicians, Roy Jenkins, M.P., and Norman St John-Stevas; two leading publishers, Sir Allen Lane and Sir Stanley Unwin; and churchmen of various denominations: the Bishop of Woolwich, Prebendary A. Stephan Hopkinson, Canon Milford and the Rev. Donald Tytler. Then there were the prominent editors Alastair Hetherington and Francis Williams, the literary editor J. W. Lambert, and journalists Dilys Powell, Anne Scott-James, John Connell and Kenneth Young – academics and professionals young and old whose views and education carried weight.

It says much that of all the witnesses examined during the trial only half were cross-examined by Griffith-Jones. It almost seemed as though he was reluctant to embroil in argument authors of the standing of E. M. Forster or of such academic quality as Noel Annan (Provost of King's College, Cambridge) or Sir Stanley Unwin, a Fellow of the Royal Society of Literature and a publisher of repute for 56 years.

A curious aspect of the case was the spectacle of the jury trying it without anyone in the dock, which was empty throughout. The accused, Sir Allen Lane and Hans Schmoller of Penguin, were seated at the solicitors' table in the well of the court. Gerald in his opening speech commented on this rather pointedly to the jury:

"It is not for us to inquire whether in this particular case the Prosecution thought the jury might give a verdict of 'Guilty' rather more readily if the dock were empty than if they saw an individual director sitting there; there is nothing to stop them doing that."

This deeply offended the feelings of Mr Griffith-Jones, who referred to it many days later in his closing speech for the prosecution:

"As in this particular case you have a firm of the highest repute, whose directors one and all have acted from the moment their attention was drawn to these possible proceedings with the utmost propriety, who have withheld the release of this book, who in order to save proceedings being taken against their retailers afforded the Prosecution evidence in order that the matter should be tested, do you think that it would be right to put Sir Allen Lane in the dock, to charge him personally? Can you imagine the comments which my learned friend would have had to make if that had been done? Members of the Jury, nobody – and he, I hope, knows it – is held at the Bar in higher respect than he, and nobody at the Bar holds him in higher respect than I. I leave that matter, I hope without presumption, by saying it was a comment which was wholly unworthy of him."

C. H. Rolph, reporting on this, puts it in a different perspective in his book. "Mr Gardiner's comment had, in fact, offended the Prosecution rather badly. But in all the 1954 prosecutions except one, the publishers, authors, and printers had looked so very respectable sitting in the dock, that it *might* have been harder for the Jury to think of them as depravers and corrupters. The exception was Mr Frederick Warburg in the *Philanderer* case: he looked equally respectable, but Mr Justice Stable brought him out of the dock and gave him a seat at the solicitors' table."

Unexpected moments of comedy during the examination of witnesses brought smiles to the faces of those in court. Mr Griffith-Jones, referring to the Lawrence book, asked Graham Hough: "Where do you get good relations?"

"In the relationship between Connie and Mellors, who really love one another," was the reply.

This intrigued Mr Justice Byrne. "It took them a long time before they really did love one another, didn't it?"

"Yes," answered Hough, mildly. "It often does, my Lord."

Smiles erupted into explosive laughter on another occasion. Griffith-Jones, cross-examining Professor Pinto of Nottingham University, a Lawrence expert, and trying to pin him down on the quality of the writing, said: "Look at page 185, halfway down: 'Th'art good cunt, though, aren't ter? Best bit o' cunt left on earth. When ter likes! When h'art willin'!', and so on and so on. We get 'cunt', 'cunt', and 'fuck', fuck'."

"I think this should be read," answered the witness, "in Nottingham dialect to get the . . ." The rest of his words were drowned in spontaneous merriment issuing, not only from the jury, but from many others, quickly stifled by Mr Justice Byrne's sharp reprimand: "If people cannot restrain their laughter the Court will be cleared!"

Mr Griffith-Jones, when examining a witness, showed that he was somewhat out of touch with contemporary social life, for the reaction of the jury was hardly what he expected. He asked: "Would you approve of your young sons, young daughters – *because young girls can read as well as boys* [my italics] – reading this book? Is it a book that you would have lying around in your own house? Is it a book that you would even wish *your wife* or your servants to read?"

Obviously he couldn't envisage any of the jurors with servantless homes. Mr Rolph, in his eye-witness account of the scene, observed that this reference to "servants" caused an amused flutter among them and "may well have been the first nail in the prosecution's coffin".

Gerald's final speech for the Defence started on Tuesday, November 1st, and continued all day. According to C. R. Rolph it "was unique in legal and literary history. Recollecting how such an opportunity would have seduced some of the Old Bailey ranters of past years, it will be of interest to study Mr Gardiner's cogency and his freedom from empty rhetoric," he wrote.

Although Gerald's many witnesses could not be faulted in their approval of Lawrence's book, given firmly and independently (none was allowed in court while another was giving evidence), he was doubtful about the likelihood of obtaining a favourable result, thinking the jury might be divided in their opinions, perhaps unconsciously influenced by Mr Justice Byrne, who was a Catholic (Lady Byrne also), and who therefore could not have been exactly enthusiastic about Penguin's publishing what his Church regarded as an immoral book, despite the fact that superficially he showed impartiality in his judgement. Gerald instinctively felt that Byrne was against him throughout the case.

Possibly his fears stemmed from an action in which he had participated several years earlier at a quarter sessions where the same Mr Justice Byrne had presided. Four farmers had been charged with fiddling agricultural subsidies and were coming up for trial before the Easter weekend. Gerald was defending one of them. Byrne, just prior to the hearing, sent a message to the barristers' clerks concerned, warning them that anyone not pleading guilty by Wednesday, when the case was to be decided, would go to prison if convicted, meaning that those who *did* plead guilty would only be fined. A rumour also quickly circulated that the moment it was over Sir Lawrence and Lady Byrne were flying to Dublin for their Easter holiday and were anxious not to miss their plane, therefore time was of the essence. Privately worried by the unethical situation, Gerald went to his client and apprised him of the circumstances,[*] only to be met with immediate opposition. The man maintained his innocence, and persisted in declaring he would in no way plead guilty to the charge, although he was made aware that the other three farmers had agreed to do so.

The case was duly tried by Byrne, who behaved with complete rectitude the entire time. The result was odd: the three who pleaded guilty were fined heavily, but Gerald's client was happily acquitted, although the evidence against all four men was pretty much the same!

On November 2nd, the sixth day of the *Lady Chatterley* trial, three hours after the Judge's summing up, the jury returned with a verdict of "Not Guilty". Penguin were acquitted of publishing an obscene article, and what sounded suspiciously like cheers issued from the rear of the court. Lesly Gardiner, who had attended the proceedings throughout, was amused to hear Lady Byrne, seated next to her, exclaim indignantly: "I call that an absolutely disgusting verdict!"

Although acquitted, Penguin were not granted costs by Mr Justice Byrne, nor were they offered the courtesy of an explanation as to why not. It should be pointed out that, although *Lady Chatterley's Lover* at that time had not sold a single copy, its eventual sales as a result of the case would obviously be large, yet that seems no reason why Penguin should have had to pay £13,000 in costs simply to satisfy the Director of Public Prosecutions that he was wrong in bringing the

---

[*] This instance of "plea-bargaining", which had not been initiated by the accused, but by the judge, worried Gerald because it was not strictly in accordance with the conditions laid down by the Lord Chief Justice. When the rules are adhered to time is often saved in the court. A judge cannot see Counsel either for the Defence or for the Prosecution without both being present, and if he is asked whether he has formed a view of the sentence he would impose should the accused be convicted, he is not bound to give any. The judge may, if he thinks fit, say that, having read the depositions, the case is not one in which he would impose a prison sentence. Counsel for the Defence is then entitled to tell his client what the judge has said.

ase against them. Ought not the boot to have been on the other foot?

Some time during the following year Gerald, apparently thinking that he could use some of his abundant leisure more profitably, decided to participate in an entirely different sphere of activity. The initial idea came, not from him, but as the result of an approach by a Labour Member of Parliament, Hugh Jenkins, who wished to know if he would care to become an Alderman of the London County Council. Realizing this would give him a chance to discover how local authorities function and how advantage is taken of the special opportunities the capital offers by reason of its size and complexity, Gerald found it difficult to resist. Having accepted the offer, from then on until he resigned on being created a peer, he attended every Council meeting, including two all-night sittings. He thus became conversant with the peculiar intricacies of local government with a Conservative party in power and a Labour-controlled London County Council.

At the time he became an Alderman the Chairman of the L.C.C. was a formidable character by the name of Sir Isaac Hayward, LL.D., J.P., with 30 years' trade union experience behind him and ten years as General Secretary of his union. He had a long string of public appointments listed in *Who's Who*, and under education: non-provided elementary school. Gerald found him a strong-minded gentleman with definite views on policy which he usually managed to bulldoze through meetings on nearly every occasion. He succeeded in this manoeuvre by arranging a discussion on the agenda at the Labour party meeting in the morning just before the Council meeting which followed. The distinct advantage this gave him enabled him to prepare the ground thoroughly beforehand. He had a streak of obstinacy in his character which led indirectly, so Gerald thought, to the Labour party finally losing control of the L.C.C., because the Conservative members became totally frustrated and conveyed this to their Government, who set up a commission of inquiry into the whole question of the areas then controlled by the L.C.C. The time happened to be ripe for a reappraisal, since the capital had expanded vastly in area over the years and needed realignment; but at the commission of inquiry attended by Sir Isaac the slightest alteration to any area divisions suggested by the Commissioners was firmly and obstinately opposed by him. If he had been a little more flexible and had compromised fractionally, the result might have been beneficial to his party, for when the rearrangement later passed through Parliament some of the newly-drawn areas tended to favour the Conservatives rather than Labour, and led to the latter eventually losing control of the Council.

Quite apart from finding the work fascinating and infinitely varied, Gerald scarcely realized how invaluable his experience as an Alderman was to prove until a year or two later, when he took his place in Cabinet meetings at 10 Downing Street in the newly formed Labour Government of 1964.

NINE

BEFORE LEAVING THE fifties and dealing with the many outstanding
legal actions in which Gerald was involved during the next crowded
decade, mention should be made of a decision taken in 1959 not
unrelated to one previously taken in 1919. Anti-war feeling among
those suffering from serious unemployment, and the aftermath of a
bitter military struggle, mainly determined them that war must never
happen again. On quitting the Coldstream Guards, and before going
up to Oxford, Gerald took the unusual step, for a young man from a
wealthy Conservative family, of joining the Peace Pledge Union. Forty
years later he was to find himself in sympathy once more with a similar
movement, the Campaign for Nuclear Disarmament, becoming one of
its earliest members.

Although gathering considerable momentum here as well as in many
other countries, C.N.D. lost much of its original impetus during the
sixties, but Gerald, in company with the faithful few, continued to
support its efforts to curb the insane arms race. Being still of the same
mind in 1980, he joined the World Disarmament Campaign, acting as
its chairman for the opening meeting at the Central Hall, Westminster, on April 12th, when several thousand anxious and caring people
gathered together to oppose nuclear war. His worst enemy could
scarcely charge Gerald with inconsistency.

During the years following his decision to join C.N.D. he figured in so
many court cases that it is a mystery how he ever found time for his
varied interests, particularly the theatre, for which his devotion never
waned; he missed practically no shows of merit during this period of
almost excessive legal work. It is said a really busy man is the most
likely person to approach if extra work is needed to be done: Gerald was
that kind of man and, what is more, enjoyed being so.

One of the most intriguing and complex cases occurring in the new
decade was that which achieved fame throughout these islands and
became known as the E.T.U. [Electrical Trades Union] Trial and, as
Gerald described it, "the biggest fraud in the history of British Trade
Unionism". The seeds of the dispute were sown several years previous
to the Court hearing in 1961 and were slow to germinate, but when they

came to fruition the consequences were widespread and the harvest extremely salutary.

The domination of some trade unions by Communists had for long been strongly suspected, and in 1956 this situation was brought to the notice of the public by Mr Woodrow Wyatt, Labour M.P. for the Bosworth Division of Leicester, in his book *The Peril in our Midst*. So far as the E.T.U. was concerned, after careful study of the results of an election in 1948 Wyatt decided that it had been definitely rigged in favour of the Communist party members of the union, though in actual fact the posts up for election had been won by Labour party members. Wyatt wrote to Sir Vincent Tewson, then General Secretary of the T.U.C., saying he had evidence of malpractices in the E.T.U. and could produce it if required. The answer he received was evasive and procrastinating, and nothing ever came of this offer.

Later, trouble started brewing seriously on the closure in 1957 of the E.T.U. College of Education, run by Mr Leslie Cannon, who had served the union for over seventeen years, and whose consequent dismissal as its head robbed him of his seat on the Executive Council of the Union as well as of his right to be a delegate to the T.U.C. conferences. Cannon's resignation from the Communist party in 1956, in disgust at the Russian invasion of Hungary, and his switch to the Labour party, was frowned on by the E.T.U. General President, Frank Foulkes, and the General Secretary, Frank Haxell, both dedicated Communists, who from then on persecuted Cannon unmercifully.

His subsequent defeat as a candidate for the Executive Council in the union election of September 1957 was caused by the votes being rigged in favour of the sitting Communist on the Executive Council, but every attempt which he made to air his grievances to the E.T.U. or the T.U.C. was consistently baulked. All criticism was stifled by the Council, who skilfully made the E.T.U. rules to suit themselves, and who were clever enough to prevent the rank-and-file members from altering them. The great difficulty was to *prove* the vote-rigging that everyone knew was going on, but after his patently engineered defeat Cannon was determined to do so. He devoted all his spare time and energy to the purpose, at great sacrifice to himself, his wife and his family; and when the union deliberately delayed publishing election figures, because they said inquiries were being made into the way the ballot was conducted, he was at last able to convince two journalists from the *Daily Mirror* and the *News Chronicle* that the situation was intolerable and urgently needed airing.

Both wrote reports for their newspapers, which again alerted Woodrow Wyatt to action. He prepared and appeared in a television programme on Panorama, where interviews were conducted by John Freeman (later editor of the *New Statesman* and British Ambassador to India and the U.S.A.) with top members of the E.T.U. which highlighted brilliantly what Cannon claimed was going on. A campaign followed by the E.T.U. denouncing what it called the "capitalist press" for persecuting trade unions and discrediting them, and this was kept up for several months. Many branches of this 20,000-strong union, however, had been unhappy about the vote-rigging, so Leslie Cannon, who had by then exhausted all his personal resources in the fight, accepted sufficient cash from Woodrow Wyatt to make a "grand tour" of the branches, investigating their grievances, which had been ignored by head office, and seeking to find ways of dealing with them.

By the time the re-election of Mr Haxell, the General Secretary, became due in December 1959, valuable information had been collected which proved helpful in the trial of 1961. The election of Mr Haxell by a suspiciously slim majority over the Labour candidate, Mr John Byrne, was followed by such an outcry of anger from the many branches which had been disqualified because they had, they were told, sent in their votes "late" – which they vociferously denied – that the General Council of the T.U.C., which had long been importuned to take action against irregularities in the E.T.U.'s conduct and had delayed doing so, issued an ultimatum on May 8th: the union must either agree to an official inquiry or proceed against their accusers for libel. Failure to do so would mean suspension from the T.U.C.

They were too late. Leslie Cannon had found one good friend on the Executive Council of the E.T.U., Frank Chapple, who was in sympathy with his efforts to rid the body of its corruptive elements. He was persuaded to join forces with the defeated candidate, the popular John Byrne, in issuing a joint statement on May 9th:

We have decided to institute proceedings in an attempt to redress the very serious grievances of the members of the union. We are mindful of the difficulties of the General Council of the T.U.C. in the protracted exchanges with the E.T.U., and appreciate that in the light of the lack of co-operation from the leaders of the E.T.U. they might have no alternative but to suspend the union, leading to disaffiliation from the T.U.C. in September.

Unfortunately, this would deprive our members of the prestige and privileges of affiliation to Congress and would still leave all questions unresolved. We are proceeding at this stage because we believe that the very considerable and important issues involved can only be resolved in the High Court. We feel that the membership will understand that we are left with no alternative but to act in this way.

On May 10th, 1960, the writ was issued and the High Court action (Byrne and Chapple *v.* Foulkes and Others, 1961) against the E.T.U and its officers for ballot rigging in the election of union officials was set in motion.

The decision to proceed against the union was not as precipitate as it sounds. For three months consultations had been taking place with Chapple's and Byrne's solicitor, Ben Hooberman, who had to convince his clients that the only solution was an action for conspiracy. The final step was decided on after a meeting at Gerald's chambers on April 8th. The fact that he was strongly in favour of it tipped the scales and put courage into the faint-hearted to go ahead. They were, in fact, not so much faint-hearted as worried, for financial reasons. Woodrow Wyatt again came to the rescue, and not only produced funds to obtain further evidence but also paid their solicitor until legal aid was granted to them.

A slightly condensed record of the famous trial by C. H. Rolph, *All Those in Favour?*, was published by André Deutsch in 1962. It is a taut dramatic account of a civil case heard without a jury which lasted for 42 days and was defended by Neil Lawson, Q.C. Ninety-seven witnesses were called by Gerald, and the case was tried by Mr Justice Winn (brother of journalist Godfrey Winn), whose verdict and summing up ran to 40,000 words or more.

The background of events leading up to the trial, described in the fine biography of Leslie Cannon by his wife Olga and J. R. L. Anderson,* I found as fascinating as the record of the trial itself; *The Road from Wigan Pier* was written more than ten years after the event, and when read in conjunction with *All Those in Favour?* combines a super-detective thriller concerning complicated in-fighting among union officials with a human story of those fighting for justice and for the rooting out of corruption. Little mention is made of Leslie Cannon in the Rolph book or of the important rôle played by him in the preparation of the case. The full story of his heroic effort to reform the union and clean it up is to

* *The Road from Wigan Pier* (Victor Gollancz Ltd, 1973).

be found in his biography; this clearly shows him as the prime mover in the affair, which would never have been successfully resolved but for his tenacity of purpose.

Although the writ was issued in May 1960, nearly a year was to elapse before the case came on, the E.T.U. having been charged with contempt of court in December for circulating to all their members the instruction that no information of union affairs was to be given to Byrne's and Chapple's solicitors. Punishment for such an attempt to intimidate witnesses should have been imprisonment, but this Foulkes and Haxell just managed to escape since the court felt it would have seriously delayed the trial, which had already been fixed for October and had been held up by the contempt case; so the date was re-set for February 27th, 1961. A fortnight before the hearing the E.T.U. appealed for yet a further postponement till June, pleading they could not possibly be ready in time, but were granted only until April 17th. Their delaying tactics were even continued to the first day of the trial, when they announced that during the past months they had discovered "certain irregularities" in the Byrne/Haxell election which meant a fresh one might have to be held, and therefore the case would be better heard after it took place; but Gerald opposed the ruse and protested to Mr Justice Winn, who upheld his objections, so the trial went on.

The first of a long string of branch secretaries began giving evidence concerning voting during the union elections. Precise details of the time of posting and of the rules and procedure of voting were revealed and all the branch secretaries emphatically denied that their envelopes could possibly have arrived late – i.e. five days after the quarterly meeting was held (one of the election rules). On protesting at their disqualification each branch secretary had been summoned to head office to examine the branch's envelope and its date stamp, which appeared to prove him wrong. The witnesses' stories all had a ring of authenticity about them which was obvious to the court, including Mr Justice Winn, but no one could offer any reason as to how or why the "late" envelopes told a different story.

Behind the scenes Leslie Cannon had come up with a cunning guess. Having been engaged by Ben Hooberman as his assistant on the case, by reason of his special knowledge and experience of union rules and regulations, he came into possession one evening of some of the "discovered" documents* which had been sent to the solicitors, at their

* The documents in legal cases which have to be shown by each party to the other side before the case comes to trial.

request, by the E.T.U. They proved to be the disputed batch of disqualified envelopes. As he examined them something odd nagged at him, prodding him to pore over them for two solid days before he suddenly hit on the key to the puzzle. Olga Cannon describes his whoop of triumph as he woke her in the middle of the night, shouting: "*I know how they did it!*"

By setting out a sample of the voting envelopes geographically a strange fact emerged. The dates given by the branch secretaries for posting the envelopes, and the dates of those later examined at head office, differed in one important respect: the former varied considerably over a period of nine days, whereas the latter (the disqualified ones) had all been posted on two consecutive days and formed a pattern. Set out they appeared thus:

Branch Secretary Postal Dates	Place	E.T.U.'s Postal Dates	Place
Dec. 23	Peterborough	Dec. 30	Peterborough
Dec. 24	Boston	Dec. 30	Boston
Dec. 19	Spilsby	Dec. 30	Spilsby
Dec. 20	Brigg	Dec. 30	Brigg
Dec. 23	Doncaster	Dec. 30	Doncaster
Dec. 26	Barnsley	Dec. 31	Barnsley
Dec. 18	Huddersfield	Dec. 31	Huddersfield
Dec. 21	Whitby	Dec. 31	Whitby
Dec. 23	Darlington	Dec. 31	Darlington
Dec. 24	Bishop Auckland	Dec. 31	Bishop Auckland

Envelopes posted in other towns showed the same pattern.

As he reflected on the curious pattern of the E.T.U. postal dating, a picture gradually formed in Cannon's mind. When the votes arrived at head office over Christmas they must have given Frank Foulkes a decided jolt, for they showed John Byrne easily the victor over Frank Haxell for the post of General Secretary. This did not suit the E.T.U.'s book at all; something had to be done about it, and that most speedily. So the votes favouring John Byrne were extracted from their envelopes, placed in new ones bearing the printed address of the union (similar to those used by the branches), sealed, and given to either Haxell or another henchman to post. By making a round trip of certain designated towns the drive could just be completed in two days, and the envelopes would arrive back at head office "too late" to meet the required date, but bearing the fake postal date in proof of late posting.

Leslie Cannon consulted Ben Hooberman, who agreed that the plot was neat and ingenious, but not until the trial had run for thirteen days was it introduced into the case.

The ninetieth witness had just completed his evidence when a Mr William Cobbett, private enquiry agent, was called to the stand. The court then heard how he had been engaged by Mr Hooberman to make a tour of the towns where the disqualified votes had been posted to show how the vote-rigging was carried out by the E.T.U. He described leaving Croydon on January 18th, 1960, and driving to Doncaster, taking in Peterborough and three other towns in one day. At each town he checked collection times, then posted a letter back to Mr Hooberman. The next day he covered five more towns, posting similar envelopes and finishing up at Bishop Auckland.

Several other tours followed, where the same routine was carried out, until all towns from which the "late" envelopes had been posted were covered. The Judge interrupted Mr Cobbett while he was describing his drive through Cumberland.

"That's a remarkably good run, is it not? You went in a maximum of 70 minutes, 52 miles, and some of us know the country between Kendal and Blackburn."

"I agree I had to move, in parts, my Lord."

"I'm not sure that the whole inquiry was not contrary to public policy. You covered a good deal of ground at high speed, didn't you?"

"I did, my Lord."

Although Mr Cobbett's story was revealing, Mr Justice Winn regarded it more as an interesting theory than cast-iron evidence. When finally summing up the case he was more convinced by the evidence of the branch secretaries and the fact that under examination Foulkes, Haxell and other Communist executives repeatedly exposed themselves as blatant liars. He obviously preferred to rely on their statements for making sure the case never went to appeal.

"I regard the whole lot of them with the greatest suspicion, personally," he said, and later, in his judgment, stated: "The purported election of the defendant Haxell as the General Secretary of the E.T.U. was contrary to the rules of the union, was and is void, and was brought about by fraudulent and unlawful devices by the defendants Foulkes, Haxell and others."

Among the "fraudulent and unlawful devices" that swayed him were the 26,000 spare ballot papers ordered by head office which nobody could account for and which could not be produced at Gerald's request.

"Their history must be accounted for, must it not?" Mr Justice Winn remarked benignly. "It may be they disappeared. Some unfortunate

sneak thief thought they were Bank of England notes. We will see wha
the explanation is in due course."

And in due course they did, though only partially.

Many branches dominated by a Communist secretary ordered from
head office several hundred forms more than their membership
warranted. Any further explanation as to what happened to them was
not forthcoming. There was also the strange return of some ballot forms
to a branch secretary on the day *before* he had sent out the official
voting forms to the members, which showed they must have been
illegally obtained. Again no explanation.

One of the main issues was whether the union was dominated by the
Communist party or not, and a vast amount of evidence about the
union's Advisory Committees pointed clearly to the fact that it was.

Only by searching through and verifying 30,000 documents was
Gerald able to make some sense of the ramifications the E.T.U. had
built up. The 1,400,000 words spoken in the trial largely came from the
97 witnesses whom he examined to clarify issues and rules of the union
which on many occasions bedevilled even Mr Justice Winn.

One of the last witnesses, Frank Foulkes, came out with the most
astonishing statement at the end of a gruelling session with Gerald
When challenged as to why he did not ask the T.U.C. to investigate the
allegations against the E.T.U. he gave a long-winded explanation
concluding: "I don't think the T.U.C. were either capable of or would
have given us a fair deal if they'd had an inquiry." Then he offered the
incredible suggestion that "the election was being rigged by somebody".

Gerald for the moment was dumbfounded, unable to speak. Silence
was broken by Mr Justice Winn asking gently: "Do you care to say by
whom?"

"I can't prove it, my Lord."

"Do you care to say whom you *suspect* of having rigged your election,
and if you like by what method?"

"I couldn't say the method. But I would say it has been rigged by
Cannon and those people associated with him throughout the
country."

"Rigged so as to produce a Haxell victory?"

"Rigged to produce a null and void election. My theory is that
Cannon and the other plaintiffs didn't want Byrne as the General
Secretary. . . . What they want to do is to continue the atmosphere that
has been prevalent in our organization from four years ago, when

Cannon was discharged from the college, because we had to close the college down for financial reasons. I have had reports from various parts of the country, from people who don't trust each other, that Cannon made statements that he would spend every penny he had to smash Haxell. . . . I personally think," he added, "that somebody other than my colleagues has been guilty of late posting, in order to create a tremendous number of votes that were not valid in order to keep this atmosphere going. And they are my honest feelings. Only feelings – I can't prove a thing." Not content with throwing this outrageous red herring before the court, he went on to say, regarding the person who posted the bogus envelopes: "I don't know – it may have been him [the inquiry agent, Mr Cobbett] that did it. If they employ him once they can employ him again, and he can do it – he has proved he could do it."

Needless to say, neither Gerald nor Foulkes' own Counsel, Mr Lawson, Q.C., thought it wise to continue on this line of reasoning, since it was so obviously fabricated, and after their final speeches for their respective clients the case ended and the Judge announced he would reserve judgment. About a fortnight later the court resumed to hear it.

Apart from the disqualification of Haxell in the election, Mr Justice Winn found that not only was the E.T.U. managed and controlled by Communists but: "In my judgment in 1959 the Communist party controlled the E.T.U. . . . through the allegiance of Mr Haxell and of other Communists in the union, whom he directed. . . . None of the defendants was frank or truthful, all of them incurred discredit by their evidence about it." (In this context, it is interesting to note that in his final speech for the plaintiffs Gerald had said that the trial must have been a record one for the number of witnesses who, like Mr Haxell, gave their evidence unsworn. "It may be some people think that if they don't take an oath they needn't tell the truth.")

Mr Justice Winn found that Foulkes and Haxell had conspired to prevent the election of John Byrne in the E.T.U. ballot, causing him monetary loss for which he was to be compensated, and he was to be recognized as the General Secretary of the union in the December 1959 election.

The most important outcome of the trial was that it led to a change in the voting procedure in future elections. As Gerald pointed out: "With regard to the forthcoming election, there has been immense activity by the defendants in procuring their own re-nomination by large numbers

of branches. . . . There are two spheres of fraud in these elections. On
is at the branches and one is at headquarters. The arrangement
proposed do not, in my submission, preclude fraud in the branches
The first and vital thing is to secure that the branch secretary sends to
every member entitled to vote a ballot paper, and that he doesn't take
one out of six out of its envelope and keep them in reserve, so that he can
then pass it on to himself. . . . What is really important is that the
member should be certain of receiving his ballot paper, which can be
done only by his being sent it by some independent person, and that he
should be then entitled to send it by post *direct* to that independent
person."

Gerald's suggestion was that the forthcoming election "should be
conducted by the Electoral Reform Society, which conducts elections on
some of the largest trade unions in the country". Mr Lawson protested
that E.T.U. rules did not provide for this, and Mr Justice Winn
commented: "I will say no more about this matter, than that I would
prefer to do that which Mr Gardiner had asked me to do. If I had been a
caliph under a palm tree, I should have done precisely what he has asked
me to do. I am not. In my judgment I should be acting illegally, and
therefore should produce no effective result."

An alternative proposition by Mr Lawson, similar to Gerald's in
many respects, was accepted, making it essential that chartered
accountants should supervise the union's elections, particularly the
balloting routine.

The satisfaction this gave Leslie Cannon and Frank Chapple, not to
mention John Byrne, can well be imagined, and in due process of time
they were able to see these recommendations carried out successfully.

Several years later Chapple was voted in as General Secretary of the
E.T.U., and he has played an important rôle in its affairs ever since
while Cannon later became its President. In 1970 Cannon received a
knighthood, but unfortunately did not live long to enjoy the fruits of his
unremitting efforts to clean up the union. In the same year that he was
honoured he died of cancer at the age of fifty.

─────── ᘉᘉ TEN ᘉᘉ ───────

JULY 21ST, 1961. Battle for Bizerta!

Tunisia, a far cry from London, appeared an odd place for a barrister to find himself following the E.T.U. affair; nevertheless, a few weeks afterwards Gerald was there on a mission of inquiry organized by the International Commission of Jurists.

The French had made a savage attack on the port of Bizerta, using 8,000 troops to crush a force of young, ill-armed and confused guerrillas, mostly last-minute volunteers, who resented the French presence on their land, which had won its independence five years earlier. A commentator at the time observed that it was like "taking a hammer to swat a fly". The onslaught was immediately condemned by several countries which supported Tunisia in her appeal to the United Nations for help in stopping the dispute. The United Nations voted ten to nil for a cease-fire, and sent Mr Hammarskjöld over from New York to achieve it. This he succeeded in doing on July 25th, and a truce was effected between the warring parties.

A month after the cease-fire the Tunisian Government approached the Swedish Government to ask the French to agree to an inquiry by the International Red Cross into certain atrocities, torture and suffering inflicted on Tunisian forces and civilians by French troops during the Battle for Bizerta. No reply having been received to this request, the Tunisian Government invited the International Commission of Jurists to hold an inquiry instead, and this they agreed to do.

The mission investigating the alleged violation of human rights consisted of Rolf Christopherson, Secretary-General of the Norwegian Bar Association and Secretary-General of the International Legal Aid Association, Professor Felix Ermacora, Professor of Constitutional Law at Innsbruck University and Vice-Chairman of the United Nations Commission on Human Rights, and Gerald, former chairman of the Bar Council of England and Wales. They arrived in Tunis on September 5th, and next day Gerald (who had been elected chairman) invited the French to the inquiry. They declined on the grounds that discussions were taking place between Governments. He also asked Vice-Admiral Amman, Commander of the French forces in Tunisia, for permission to take evidence of witnesses in Bizerta, but again the request was refused with the same excuse.

The inquiry opened on September 6th, continuing until September 9th, with 26 witnesses revealing a horrifying story of atrocities carried out by French forces not only on young Tunisian volunteers but on many women and children. The troops used napalm, grenades, automatic rifles, guns from naval forces, low-flying aircraft and parachutists during the attack, and captured about 65 young civilian "volunteers" aged fourteen and upwards. Their bodies, dressed in blue overalls and trousers, were found in a quarry; all had been shot with their hands tied behind their backs. Many others were discovered in different places not far from Bizerta, with stab wounds and mutilated limbs, one with his head cut off, another with his throat cut. As the inquiry proceeded no evidence was produced which implicated French troops ordinarily stationed in Bizerta, only those who parachuted into the country after July 19th, following the Tunisian Government's prohibition of flights over its territory.

The 26 witnesses who gave evidence and produced photographs (later included in the Commission's report) were American, British, Finnish and Yugoslav press correspondents, a Belgian doctor and a Norwegian pastor. All voluntarily testified to the mutilation of civilians: a pregnant woman, disembowelled with the foetus also killed, had been bayoneted, other youths and a girl had stab wounds and many soldiers both ears and hands cut off, some had been buried while still alive and some severely burned.

Although the battle lasted only a few days, ending on July 23rd, casualties were heavy, the Tunisians bearing much the greater loss. It cost them 700 dead, 1,250 wounded and 639 taken prisoner, while the French suffered only 25 dead and 100 wounded. The unanimous report* by Gerald and his fellow Commissioners was completed on September 18th, and printed copies were in the hands of the press on October 12th, roughly a month after the request was made to the International Commission of Jurists – a fairly speedy operation! How much bitterness and sorrow the Tunisians nursed as a result of the attack seems never to have come to light.

No sooner was Gerald back in England than he was obliged to devote his attention to what must have seemed to him a minor dispute after the Tunisian/French fracas and its bloody consequences. He had been

* Report of the Commission of Inquiry into Events in Bizerta between 18 and 24 July 1961, published by International Commission of Jurists, Geneva.

briefed during 1960 to appear for the Association of Ciné and Television Technicians, who were being sued by producer/directors Roy and John Boulting, the twin brothers responsible for such celebrated films as *Seven Days to Noon, Fame is the Spur, Brighton Rock* and *I'm All Right, Jack.*

Although the writ was issued on March 4th, 1960, the action was not tried until more than a year later, by Mr Justice Salmon, with Mr Parker, Q.C., acting for the Boultings, who claimed they were not eligible for membership of the A.C.T.T. and could not become members while exercising their function as employers (they managed their own company, Charter Films Ltd). They were in an equivocal position, wearing two hats simultaneously, one as employee-director/producers, working as technicians in the studio with members of the union, and one as Managing Directors of Charter, the employers financing the film while in production. This made the settlement of any disputes which might arise during the shooting of a picture very difficult, and for this reason their original membership of the union had been suspended for seven years to avoid clashes on the studio floor. Its renewal was now the core of the dispute.

The A.C.T.T., under its Rule 7a, claimed that all employees working on the technical side of film production, including film directors, employee-producers, scriptwriters, etc., should belong to the union. The Boultings had refused to renew their membership, and this had caused a shop steward to call a strike on a picture they had been engaged on, resulting in a stoppage of some two hours and a half before work was resumed. It was to avoid this kind of thing happening in future that a clarification of the position was needed.

Mr Justice Salmon, while appreciating the dilemma the Boultings were often in, concluded that they were employed by Charter as film producers and directors within the meaning of Rule 7a, and were therefore eligible for membership of the union. He dismissed their case, adding that it was not a question of what reason and justice suggested the A.C.T.T. should do, but of what the law said they could do.

This judgment did not satisfy the Boulting brothers at all. Their appeal against it was heard a year later when Lord Denning, Master of the Rolls, and Lords Justices Diplock and Upjohn presided in the Court of Appeal. The result, unfortunately for Roy and John, was the same, although it was not a unanimous decision, Lord Denning dissenting. Lord Justice Upjohn drew the most sensible conclusion when he said: "There seems no reason why a combination of masters and workmen together should not be formed for the purpose of regulating their relations, and this has been done many times; it has been so interpreted for many years and many examples were given to us. I will quote only two. Every band leader, who normally employs the other members of the band, is compelled by the all-powerful Musicians' Union to be a member of it unless he is content, in the most literal sense, to be a one-man band. Actor managers belong to Equity. It seems to me clear that there is nothing illegal in a rule which makes both employer and employee eligible for election."

A success for Gerald and the A.C.T.T. but a disappointment for the Boultings. It made little difference to their future operations, however, for they continued to produce and direct some excellent films as members of the union without apparently rocking the boat. Having directed pictures myself for many years wearing the same two hats as Roy and John (film director and Company Director combined), and remembering the conditions when no union existed in the film industry to protect technicians from exploitation where working hours were concerned and no overtime was paid, I feel that, while some of their rules are extremely vexatious and frustrating to directors, the technicians have a far more humane deal now than they did in the twenties.

Union members, originally meant to be supportive of their comrades, from time to time find themselves in conflict with one another as well as with their employers. When this happens, as in the E.T.U. action, some rather ugly aspects appear and the issues become extremely complicated. Rookes v. Barnard was a case in point. It was the third union dispute in which Gerald was embroiled, and it eventually led to a change in the law when he was appointed Lord Chancellor a few years later.

Of the nine judges who gave their views on it in the Courts and the House of Lords, six took one view and three the opposite, thus proving its complexity. The events leading up to it started in 1955, when a Mr Rookes, an employee of British Overseas Airways Corporation, resigned from his union, the Association of Engineering and Shipbuilding Draughtsmen, in protest at "insufficient action" being taken by it to improve drawing-office accommodation.

This caused an upset in the union and a threat to Mr Rookes that, if he didn't rejoin, the whole operations of B.O.A.C. would be brought to a standstill. He refused, and since there was a 100 per cent closed shop the union handed a resolution to B.O.A.C. to the effect that if they did ot dismiss him from his post all members would strike, despite the fact hat they were breaking an agreement with the firm not to strike but to leal with any disputes by negotiation.

With the threat of a stoppage on their hands B.O.A.C. gave way and ent Rookes home on paid leave in January 1956, dismissing him two nonths later.

Time went by and Rookes, unable to find work that suited him (he efused a job with English Electric because he was a pacifist and would >e required to work on military aircraft), was denied unemployment >enefit and forced to depend on his savings to keep afloat. In lesperation he approached a firm of solicitors, Lewis Silkin and ²artners, in the hope of obtaining some redress for his dismissal in lefiance of the union's agreement with B.O.A.C. He could not have nade a wiser choice, since Lord Silkin (who was previously a minister in Mr Attlee's Government) considered he had a good case and managed to .ecure funds from legal aid, thus enabling him to engage Neville Faulks, Q.C., as his Counsel.

Colin Duncan was briefed on behalf of the three defendants, who vere being sued for conspiracy: Barnard (chairman of the union's ²eltham branch), Silverthorne (a London Divisional organizer) and ²istal, the shop steward in the drawing-office when Rookes was lismissed. Ironically, Rookes had himself been a shop steward in the >ast, since he was a long-standing member of the union!

The case was heard before Mr Justice Sachs on May 19th, 1961, and ifter listening to arguments from both sides he reduced them to the nain bone of contention, an interpretation of the Trades Union Disputes Act 1906, which held that its Section 3 did not apply where the ıct was unlawful (i.e. the dismissal of Rookes by the Corporation after a hreat of strike action unless he was sacked, thus constituting a "tort" of ntimidation and therefore in itself unlawful). He found for Rookes, and he jury awarded him £7,500 for loss of office. Naturally the three lefendants were disgusted with the verdict and determined to appeal ıgainst what they considered excess damages.

It was at this point that Gerald entered the case, and a year later led Colin Duncan in the Court of Appeal to plead the defendants' cause >efore Lords Justices Sellers, Donovan and Pearson, who sat in udgment on Mr Justice Sachs' ruling which reflected so unfavourably >n the union. Having given it serious thought and carried out a thorough 'esearch of trade union rules and practices Gerald came to the Court, as ısual, well prepared. In his autobiography *A Law unto Myself* Sir Neville

Faulks' description of him, starting off at a cracking speed, is most amusing:

Gardiner opened the case at a tremendous rate of knots, so that he had finished quoting one case and passed on to the next before I had found my place in the first one. How the Court of Appeal kept up with him, I don't know. I certainly couldn't. It was all very dramatic to start with, when he told their Lordships that Mr Justice Sachs had driven a coach and four through the Trades Disputes Act, 1906. He seemed to suggest that the trade unions could do anything they liked, however abominably they behaved, because of the protection of Sections 1 and 3 of the 1906 Act.

Gerald pointed out that if the judgment of Mr Justice Sachs was right he had removed from union members a protection they had enjoyed for many years if, *and only if, there was in existence a trade dispute.* He emphasised that he had found there had been at all material times in the case a trade dispute. The three judges presiding concurred and proceeded to base their final decision on the grounds that a threat from the T.U.C. was not actionable by a third party (Rookes) as a tort, with the result that the three defendants won their appeal.

However, this was not the end of the affair, for Rookes, having the resources of legal aid behind him, was able to go to the House of Lords, where his appeal was heard on July 2nd, 1963, by Lords Reid. Evershed, Hodson, Devlin and Pierce.

The complexity of the case, and the labyrinthine rules governing trade unions, discussed by their Lordships, occupied over 50 pages in the published Law Report, which illustrates the difficulties all five of them were up against in debating the issues. The conclusion they reached was that Rookes should be allowed his appeal, but that a further case should be heard on the question of damages, where eventually he was forced to accept a much lower figure than the £7,500 first awarded.

As a result of the Rookes *v.* Barnard case, in 1965 the Labour Government was approached by the trade unions to clarify the law, since diverse opinions on the justice of the case had been expressed, the existing situation being described as vague and incomprehensible to the layman. Gerald, then Lord Chancellor, commenting on the need for a new Bill to restore the law to the state it was in before the Rookes case, explained: "The difficulty of Rookes *v.* Barnard has been that nobody quite knows what it was that it decided. I have read – and I have no doubt a number of your Lordships have read – a larger number of opinions by different learned Counsel on this subject than on any other I can remember, and hardly two that agree." Later he went on to say: "So long as the law remains as it is now, so far as it is certain at all, it is bound, I suggest, to provoke an increase in unofficial strikes." The Bill (Trades Disputes Bill) was passed quickly and helped to satisfy the trades unions, while a Royal Commission (chaired by Lord Donovan), which had been appointed two months earlier, on April 8th, 1965, took somewhat longer to report on Trades Unions and Employers' Associations. It was presented to Parliament in June 1968!

When Mr Rookes took the simple step of resigning from his union in 1955, he would have been astonished had he been able to foresee the legal repercussions during the next thirteen years!

ELEVEN

THE IMPROVEMENT IN Gerald's financial position over the years enabled Lesly to indulge in her favourite pastime, changing houses.

From the Chelsea flat which they had occupied since the end of the war the Gardiners had moved not long after to a larger one in Montpelier Square; by 1950 they had bought a house in Stanhope Terrace on the north side of Hyde Park. Here they stayed two or three years until they were forced to leave in order to meet an unexpected revenue demand, the amount of which took Gerald by surprise. His run of successful cases as a result of taking Silk in 1948 had reached a high peak in the following two years, giving him a deceptively reassuring impression that he was wealthier than he actually was, and well able to afford the luxury of a house of his own. His tax assessment, when it finally caught up with him, came as a shock, completely shattering the illusion.

There was nothing for it but to sell the Stanhope Terrace house. Lesly, never at a loss, soon found and leased a flat in Onslow Square, which remained their home until she discovered it would be more advantageous to move to one on the opposite side of the Square, where some modern conversions were being made, which offered better and pleasanter accommodation. This flat contented Lesly until late 1964, when they left it to move into the Lord Chancellor's residence at the top of the Victoria Tower in the House of Lords.

Meanwhile Carol, having finished schooling at Frensham Heights in 1947, decided on the career of social worker, and for the next three years read political economy at Reading University, where she eventually took her B.A. degree. Having completed a post-graduate course in social work at Barnet House, Oxford, she became active for five years with the Family Service Unit in Stepney, dealing with problem families. By then, feeling the need of change, she considered that a spell in America might open up her horizons and give her fresh opportunities. Although a great deal of determination and heart-searching was needed to make the break with family and friends, the wish to escape from her mother's domination finally gave her strength to strike out on her own. The parting came as a severe blow to Lesly and to Gerald, but was harder for the former to bear, since Lesly's main interest in life was running her home and her daughter, whereas Gerald could always bury himself in work to the exclusion of any personal sorrow, and take the loss philosophically. It was a long time before Lesly could do the same, if she ever did.

Carol, at twenty-eight, set out for Canada, where she stayed for a few months before finding a job and settling down in New York. There she lived and worked for the next 21 years, but spent many of her vacations in Europe travelling with Lesly and Gerald.

The family holidays were anticipated with some excitement, for Gerald always planned them in detail beforehand, studying maps and routes with meticulous care. In the early days, when he and Lesly decided to visit Italy on one occasion, and he was still a struggling young barrister with precious little money, he discovered from reading an *Orario Generale* that one could buy a railway ticket at the Franco–Italian frontier, enabling one to travel all through Northern Italy and out at the Austrian frontier for a very cheap rate. He decided to try it, and, with Lesly, set out for the continent. When they reached the Italian frontier their train stopped and waited, and Gerald jumped out to purchase the special tickets from the booking office. The clerk, mystified by his unusual request (the scheme being entirely new), was hesitant, but when Gerald showed him the details in the *Orario Generale* he searched files, found the appropriate forms and eventually issued a long string of tickets. This had taken time and Lesly, impatiently holding the carriage door open, was intensely relieved to see Gerald tear up at the last minute with the tickets clutched firmly in his hand. Jumping into the train as it steamed slowly out, he slumped on the seat beside her and triumphantly showed the tickets, numbered 0001 and 0002, the first ever issued in that country! Train conductors who subsequently came along studied them curiously and were most intrigued, their like never having been seen before.

When Carol began to accompany them on their travels abroad after the war, customs officials were on the alert for voyagers returning, intoxicated with the many good things they could buy after their years of austerity, and pounced on the smugglers. Lesly delighted in jokes at the expense of officialdom, sometimes at Gerald's expense too. At one inspection, when she was well ahead of him in the queue, she told the customs official that she believed "the tall man in the line behind her" was smuggling in something in a small box. Gerald presently found himself the object of deep suspicion, and despite his protestations of innocence had to submit to the box being opened and examined. It contained a friend's hearing aid which he had promised to bring back! Carol thought this hilarious and moments later, when they were reunited, all three joined in her infectious laughter, Gerald relishing the joke as much as anyone.

Whichever country they explored each year (the Gardiners covered a great many during these holidays) Gerald never went anywhere without his camera. Judging by the pictures he obtained, there is no doubt he was a fine amateur photographer with a natural talent for selecting good subject matter. Nearly all his pictures were in colour and were afterwards stored neatly away in wooden cases, each one sorted and numbered according to time and place. Many years later, when he finally found photography too much of an effort, he gave his heart to gardening with the same enthusiasm. Like a small boy he delighted in bonfires, and could scarcely be lured away from them once they were ablaze.

In the early sixties, when he had been serving for over a decade on the Lord Chancellor's Law Reform Committee, Gerald was approached to bring out a book on the subject that not only would be a worthy successor to *The Reform of the Law*, edited by Dr Glanville Williams and published twelve years previously, but would incorporate all the legal changes which had taken place since then. The idea was to have a collection of about a dozen different views and aspects of law reform written by experts in their particular fields.

Dr Andrew Martin, Ph.D., secretary of the Society of Labour Lawyers and an old colleague of Gerald's, was the moving spirit in the enterprise, and, since he was a practising barrister, became an invaluable help in jointly editing the book. It eventually consisted of twelve sections written by those variously erudite in the law, among them Elwyn Jones, Q.C. (later to be Lord Chancellor), Lord Chorley, Q.C., a professor at the University of London, Gerald Dworkin, lecturer in law at the London School of Economics, and Otto Kahn-Freund, Professor of Law, London University. Others who contributed were C. H. Rolph (author of two books on Gerald's most important cases), Andrew Martin and Gerald himself, who wrote the articles on "The Machinery of Law Reform", "Legal Education" and (with Elwyn Jones) "The Administration of Justice".

On the back of the jacket is outlined Gerald's new scheme for keeping law reform up to date. It should be noted that at this period barristers only spared time for the discussion of law reform once a month, when they met for a couple of hours or so after the courts closed at four-thirty in the afternoon, which left precious little time to devote to the subject. Gerald advocated the "strengthening of the Lord Chancellor's Office by the appointment of a Vice-Chancellor of ministerial rank and of not less than five full-time Law Commissioners who would not be ordinary civil servants but enjoy a considerable degree of independence. It would be their sole responsibility to keep 'the general law' under constant review and, with the help of a highly skilled secretariat, prepare legislation for its reform. The Government would be required, by statute, to make parliamentary time available for the consideration of these legislative proposals." That, in a nutshell, is the structure of the Law Commission today. It has now been operating for more than seventeen years and has proved itself an undoubted success with which Gerald feels justly proud to be associated, as well as gratified that he was instrumental in seeing his idea become a reality.

When Victor Gollancz had successfully launched the book,* an invitation came for Gerald to dine with one of the most highly regarded solicitors in London. Mr Arnold Goodman,† besides professing a very real interest in the arts, had a wide circle of friends, many of whom played significant rôles in politics, which gave him the reputation of a man with considerable influence in that sphere.

So Gerald went along one evening in 1963 to his Portland Place flat to find only two other guests present beside himself. He was greeted cordially by Harold Wilson, then Leader of the Opposition in the House of Commons, and a close friend of Wilson, George Wigg. By the time they sat down to dinner Gerald was naturally intrigued as to why Arnold had chosen to include him in this particular quartet. As the meal progressed the object gradually became apparent, culminating in Harold Wilson asking Gerald if he would be at all interested in going to the House of Lords.

The scene that follows, while not a verbatim report of the conversation which took place that night, is roughly as Gerald recalls it after nearly twenty years. The response to Harold's proposal was typically cautious.

"You must have some reason for asking me. What is it?"

"A simple one. We're desperately short of good lawyers in the House. And there's a mass of work to be dealt with."

"But you have . . ."

* *Law Reform Now* (Victor Gollancz Ltd, 1963).
† Created Lord Goodman in 1965.

"Oh yes, I know we've got Silkin," Harold interjected quickly, "but he's getting on – well into his seventies. We need someone younger and more vigorous to cope with the legal stuff – especially with a possible election looming some time next year."

The others agreed. Gerald, for the moment, could only voice a practical objection in order to give himself time while the idea sank in. "I really don't think I should prove of much use to you in the circumstances." They wanted to know what those particular circumstances were. "Well, I rarely have the chance to leave the Courts much before four-thirty in the afternoon. This would mean my arriving late at the House, which would hardly allow me to give full time to the job in hand."

Harold brushed this smoothly aside, saying there were several others in the same boat – the Master of the Rolls and the Law Lords. Despite their late arrival from the Courts it did not seem to prevent them from doing very useful work in the House. Nevertheless, Gerald had reservations and his manner showed it. Harold, glancing at the others, decided to be more explicit and turned back to him.

"Of course, at a later stage, in the event of my having to form a future Government, I would no doubt want you as Lord Chancellor."

Gerald drew in a deep breath. "That is a very high office, and I'm sure there are several others, far more experienced than I, to take it on."

"Who?"

He thought for a moment. "Frank Soskice, for one."

Harold smiled, and then said with a hint of relief in his voice: "Oh, you needn't worry about Frank. I've something important lined up for him already."

No one ventured to inquire what that was, but when the next Labour Government's appointments were announced Frank Soskice was down for the Home Office.

Harold waited, then, as Gerald was silent: "Anyone else?"

"There's Donovan. Have you thought of him?" He was Labour M.P. for Leicester, a Q.C., and a lawyer for whom Gerald had the greatest respect. His vast experience in revenue work was well known, and his record as a judge in the Criminal Court could scarcely be faulted, whereas Gerald had no experience as a judge.

Harold shook his head. "I'm afraid he's not up to it. His health is far from good at the moment. Didn't you know?"

There was an awkward pause as Gerald still appeared reluctant to make up his mind. At length he remarked: "I'm a pacifist, you know," thinking this would finally settle the matter.

The three men exchanged glances but Harold's reply was unworried. "I shouldn't imagine that need be a hindrance. We've always had a number of pacifists in the Party, haven't we?"

George Wigg and Arnold Goodman were of the same opinion. Gerald, however, would not commit himself. "I should like a little time, if I may, to make up my mind. It's a pretty big decision, which of course I shall have to discuss with Lesly."

Harold had to accept this, which he did with good grace, whereupon the talk drifted into other channels.

The lights in 105 Onslow Square shone later than usual that evening while Lesly learned of the turn events had taken earlier during dinner. As they talked she gradually realized that the decision Gerald had to make was not as simple as it appeared on the surface.

Although he was attracted by the opportunity to become more seriously involved with legal processes in the House of Lords, and be able to influence progressive Bills while they were going through Parliament, instead of having to hang around in the lobbies in the hope of catching the ears of politicians, there were snags which he pointed out clearly to Lesly.

His present work at the Bar, and with other organizations, already left very little leisure to spend with her at home; her life would become even lonelier than it was at the moment if he had to spend long hours several nights a week in the House. This was something Lesly realized only too well and to her cost, yet she knew how much Gerald would enjoy the work and the fresh opportunities it implied. This was important as far as she was concerned, for if he refused the offer he might come to regret it afterwards and both of them would ultimately be unhappy.

There was one further matter to be considered, though the possibility that it would arise seemed quite remote at the time. Wilson had mentioned there would be an election within the next eighteen months or so, and, if the Labour party by some miracle won it, then the question of Gerald becoming Lord Chancellor had to be faced. By going to the Woolsack he would be forced to relinquish all his work at the Bar at a time when he was at the peak of his career as a Q.C.

"But you could resume it later when the Government changes," Lesly reminded him.

"That's just it. You can never resume it. You're pensioned off. Even if the Government only lasts six weeks or six months – and some have in the past – the moment it falls the legal profession is barred to you for the rest of your life."

Lesly saw the point and sought to reassure him. "I don't think we need be unduly worried about it. As things are, the chances of Labour winning the next election seem absurdly remote to me. Anyway, I don't imagine it would happen for the next ten years or so."

They had had a similar discussion in the past when Gerald received the offer of a judgeship, which his clerk, Goodale, urged him to accept, saying he would be mad if he did not. She had listened to Gerald explaining then that perhaps he ought to accept, despite his disinclination to do so. When she asked if it was because he would be involved in death penalty decisions he said, "No. They knew I would never accept one in the Queen's Bench Division where that problem arises, so they offered me one in Probate, Divorce and Admiralty. But I should get thoroughly bored dealing with divorce the whole time. Wouldn't feel I'd done a real day's work."

"Then don't accept."

"But there's the future to think of. Financial security – a decent pension – and that concerns us both. My practice may decline; I may fall ill. A pension is certainly not to be sneezed at."

"You've always enjoyed the Bar so much, what's the point of doing something you won't enjoy?"

Her advice had been followed, and Gerald's opportunity to sit on the Bench slipped away.

Now once again the problem of their future had arisen, and eventually they came to the conclusion that it was early days yet to be speculating about something that might never happen. After all, there was no certainty Gerald would ever be made a peer, let alone be appointed to the prestigious position of Lord Chancellor. If in the event, they argued, he entered the Lords, he could still carry on his legal work at the Bar, and should he find it not satisfactory he could easily cut down on one or the other. It might also give him the chance to initiate some law reform. This last thought, more than anything said hitherto, nudged him to make his decision.

Next day he wasted no time in communicating it to Harold Wilson. Having done so he put it out of his mind, and for the rest of the year his life style as a barrister continued unchanged, his presence in the Law Courts as frequent as ever.

As 1963 drew to a close, any doubts about the future were suddenly swept away. The announcement of his peerage appeared in the New Year's Honours List, and though he was aware that his life was inevitably going to alter from then on he could not possibly have envisaged in how many ways and to what degree.

Anyone who has business to conduct with the College of Arms deals with Garter King of Arms, as Gerald was to learn on entering the House of Lords. He also has to have a sense of humour when deciding what form his title should take. Fortunately Gerald found that he did not need to register a coat of arms with the College since his father had already done so on being knighted, which saved him a fee of £200–£300. He did, however, purchase for a modest sum a copy of the family tree which had been traced many years previously for Robert Septimus.

A suggestion was then made that if he wished to have supporters, i.e. animals to hold up the shield or coat of arms, an extra £70 would be required. Gerald, obediently handing over the fee, could not help remarking that it seemed rather unnecessary since he was, after all, only a *life* peer, to which Garter replied with a touch of hauteur: "Of course, I don't decide. I only advise."

Whom he advised he did not reveal, but later Gerald discovered it to be the Earl Marshal (the Earl of Norfolk), whose decision carried with it a right of appeal to the Queen. But this was not disclosed at the time. The fees varied considerably, there being no fixed scale, each Garter charging what he thought proper or what he could get.

When it came to the question of his name Gerald was somewhat taken aback to be met with: "You cannot be Lord Gardiner, you know." Which, of course, he didn't know; he was to learn that this was because there was a dormant *Gardner* peerage. Apparently this had lapsed in 1883, as Gerald, who had done a little research on the matter, found out. It seemed a long while ago, he said to Garter, explaining that the last Lord Gardner had gone to India, where he took to wife one or more Indian begums. After that his line had become slightly confused, and nothing more had been heard of it. "In any case," he said, "I'm a *life* peer and I don't think I'll live very long. In addition, my name is spelled differently."

Garter solemnly shook his head. "It doesn't matter how it's spelled, but how it's pronounced."

"Nobody who speaks properly pronounces *Gardiner* in the same way as *Gardner*," Gerald protested mildly.

No effect. "There's already been enough trouble over Lord Robens and Lord Robbins. It won't happen again."

"Can't I be Lord Gerald-Gardiner – like Lord Ritchie-Calder?" he asked.

The plea fell on deaf ears. "Not the same thing at all. Exceptional case – can't be repeated. Anyway, Ritchie was his mother's name."

"But if I don't keep my own name it will be very awkward for me as a practising barrister. Solicitors won't know whom to brief."

Even this cut no ice. "You don't in the least appreciate the difficulties. How do I know that a claimant to the Gardner title has not been working on it with his solicitor for the past five years? By first post tomorrow I may get a claim."

Only after long discussion did Garter King of Arms relent and eventually suggest a compromise. "You can be Lord Gardiner as long as your geographical appendage is part of your title."

Gerald's thoughts flew at once to Somerset, to Langford Budville and Kittisford, the little villages of his ancestors. He plumped for the former as it sounded like one of those railway stations Lord Beeching had abolished, but the Herald commented that "Gardiner of Langford Budville" would be rather a lengthy signature to write on a cheque each time, so he chose Kittisford and thus it was settled.

On January 17th, 1964, Gerald was introduced into the House of Lords and on February 14th made his maiden speech on the Legal Aid Bill as Lord Gardiner of Kittisford.

TWELVE

ANY IDEA THAT during the following months Gerald could devote any spare time to the business of the House of Lords and to familiarizing himself with its political techniques, quaint vocabulary and etiquette was soon dispelled by a legal action which demanded his undivided attention. To hear of torture and degradation of human beings in wartime is tragic enough; in peacetime – even in retrospect – it appears even more grotesque and obscene. This action concerned a libel case whose horrifying details, when disclosed in court and reported in the press, appalled and shocked the civilized world.

Back in 1959 Leon Uris, an American author, wrote a best-selling novel, *Exodus*, published in England by William Kimber & Co., in which a certain paragraph contained a short description of medical practices in Auschwitz concentration camp during World War II. This passage was brought to the attention of Dr Alexander Dering, a physician of Finchley, North London. The paragraph read: "Here in Block X Dr Wirths used women as guinea-pigs and Dr Schumann sterilized by castration and X-ray and Clauberg removed ovaries and Dr Dehring performed 17,000 'experiments' in surgery without anaesthetics."

Dr Dering (he had dropped the 'h' in his name after the war), feeling that his reputation was in danger, saw just cause to sue Leon Uris and the publishers for defamation and set about procuring the services of Colin Duncan, Q.C., and Brian Neil to act for him in the case. For the defence Leon Uris briefed Gerald, David Hirst and Louis Blom-Cooper, and came over from America for the hearings. The outcome being of intense interest he sat for many weeks in court, anxiously watching every move and absorbing a mass of detail, which when the case was over gave him enough local colour and material to write a fictionalized account of the whole affair, *QBVII* (short for Queen's Bench Division Court VII), a novel which received considerable acclaim six years later.

On April 13th, 1964, the first day in court, Mr Justice Lawton, who was trying the case, suggested that it might be advisable to ask the jury if any of them had had a relative in Auschwitz concentration camp during World War II. Colin Duncan agreed but Gerald objected saying that a jury in this country was chosen completely at random so as to provide a cross-section of the whole community. Once one started seeking to exclude people who had feelings one way one might include people with feelings the other way. This was accepted and Colin Duncan proceeded to make his opening speech.

He gave a full account of Dr Dering's activities since he qualified at Warsaw University in 1928. When war broke out in 1939 he had joined the Polish Resistance, but in 1940, when Germany invaded his country he had been arrested by the Gestapo, with 1500 others, and transferred to Auschwitz as a prisoner of war, where he worked as a labourer, later being promoted to an orderly in its hospital. The following year, on learning of his medical experience, they made him prison doctor and then surgeon, in order to carry out operations on prisoners (male and female), including those who had received irradiation, for the removal of sexual organs by senior Nazi doctors. His superiors were experimenting in the sterilization of human beings, mostly Jews, and Dr Dering asserted that he was forced to assist them, since a refusal to do so would have meant his own death, and almost certain death for prisoners if they were operated on by less competent or unqualified surgeons.

Colin Duncan explained that the Defence now pleaded that, while still alleging that Dr Dering had performed the operations described in the "particulars",* they did not extend to the precise figure of 17,000 as at first claimed, but to between 120 and 130. The Defence also conceded that an anaesthetic was used in some cases, but the operations were mostly done brutally with a single spinal injection, causing great pain to the prisoners, who remained conscious throughout. Thirdly, they agreed all these took place in Block 21, not Block 10, as had been stated.

Colin Duncan hoped the jury would fully appreciate the three retractions, as well as the fact that, while Dr Dering admitted to carrying out 17,000 operations, he declared they were proper and necessary ones on suffering fellow prisoners. The 130 or so alleged by the Defence as "not ordinary operations" were recorded and described in the hospital register at the time, signed by Dr Dering himself, and not on a single occasion was one of them performed without an anaesthetic properly administered. One of the patients he refused to operate on was a girl who as a result was sent to the gas chambers.

*The details and facts set out when a case is presented.

When called on to give evidence Dr Dering told the court that he was Roman Catholic, and while he was imprisoned in camp had joined the underground movement, of which he was second-in-command, had a hidden wireless receiver, and had daily risked his life trying to obtain extra medical supplies and food for the other prisoners. Also, when trying to hide those who had been intended for the gas chambers he had been in great danger.

As the war came to an end the Russians advanced into Auschwitz and he was imprisoned for about a week before being released. For a time he joined General Anders' army in Italy, then returned to Warsaw to work there, until complaints against him made life too difficult and he was allowed to go to England. Here he obtained employment as a doctor at the Polish General Hospital. This did not last long, for a request came from Poland for his extradition as a war criminal. He was imprisoned for $19\frac{1}{2}$ months in Brixton while the Home Office investigated his case. They concluded that there was insufficient evidence against him and he was released with an apology, and later helped to a colonial appointment in Somaliland, where he used his medical skill for the next ten years.

In 1960, on returning to England, he was awarded the O.B.E. for his services, and since then had been in general practice in Finsbury Park. Answering questions on Auschwitz, he stated that he had personally seen a German doctor or his assistant going round the wards at ten-day intervals, on each occasion selecting 100–150 prisoners, including those still recovering from operations or illnesses. They were all sent to the gas chambers. On this macabre note the first day's hearings ended.

Next morning the court was advised that several threats of physical violence had been made against Dr Dering overnight, which immediately prompted the Judge to denounce them as an outrage. If they were substantiated, he said severely, the perpetrators would be punished with the full rigour of the law. They did not recur.

Continuing his evidence, Dr Dering described his efforts to save 30–40 prisoners who were destined to be liquidated, by ordering his dressers to wash the identity numbers off intended victims' bodies and transfer them to patients already dead, but the Germans discovered this ruse and resorted to tattooing the numbers instead. He himself had been subjected to this, but when Mr Justice Lawton asked if he still had the tattooed number he replied that he had excised it in 1945 while being persecuted in Poland. He added that on refusing to perform some of the operations demanded of him by Dr Schumann, his superior, he met with sharp rebuke: "Don't you think I can do with prisoners wha I like?" followed by an abrupt exit from the theatre. Later on, when h discussed the difficult situation with other prisoner-doctors, the came to the conclusion that if they refused to obey their Nazi master the gas chambers would be their fate, and in addition they would pu the prisoners' lives at risk by leaving them to be operated on b unqualified surgeons. They decided to carry out orders.

Several months earlier, when Gerald began preparation of the case the solicitors working on it with him had experienced great difficult in obtaining evidence and witnesses supporting Leon Uris' allegation for not only had 21 years elapsed since the events had taken place, bu any survivors of Nazi persecution had dispersed all over the world anc were almost impossible to trace. The first set of particulars therefor lacked many important details to justify the damning figures men tioned in *Exodus* and the result of the case looked, to say the least, ir some doubt. Jewish organizations everywhere, when alerted, mad painstaking searches for any living Auschwitz victims, but this prove a long and baffling business. Then, out of the blue, a heaven-sen letter arrived one day, shedding light on the distant past. D Klodzinski, a Polish medical student during the war, who had bee arrested by the Nazis and transferred to Auschwitz at the time D Dering was working there, offered to give evidence. He also cam forward with an invaluable piece of information, namely, that the medical register kept in Block 21 by Dr Dering, recording all operations and daily signed by him, was preserved in the Auschwitz museum.

The Defence solicitors, Kaufman and Siegal, together with Rubin stein and Nash, at once made urgent requests for the loan of the register, but only after lengthy negotiation between the two countries was the historic document permitted to travel to London at the end of May 1963 in the care of an embassy official. The Defence was given permission to make photostat copies of its pages but was not allowed possession of the actual register. However, the copies enabled them to trace many of the Nazi victims they had been seeking. Throughout the trial the register remained always in the custody of the Polish representative, who produced it when required. Dr Dering, when examined by the Home Office in 1947, had bemoaned the lack of the hospital registers – they had not been found by then – which he declared would have exonerated him as a war criminal. Their discovery just prior to the case must have been a severe shock!

When Colin Duncan asked whether he had ever carried out experimental operations on Auschwitz prisoners or performed them without an anaesthetic he answered "No", and on being confronted with the register during subsequent questioning he proceeded to justify each of the many cases listed there with seemingly valid explanations. The operation had been necessary because the patient suffered from an hereditary disease or had been previously operated on and needed a second treatment, had received radiation, or had been ordered by a Nazi court to have his or her sexual organs removed for testing in cancer research or as a punishment for criminal activities. He protested that some of the allegations against him were completely untrue, including statements made by Dr Klodzinski concerning a testicle operation he was supposed to have witnessed.

Counsel finally concluded Dr Dering's examination on the morning of April 14th, having presented his client as a man who had done his utmost, under the most terrible circumstances, to alleviate the tragic condition of fellow prisoners, irrespective of creed or race. He had been in the witness box for well over five hours.

Gerald then rose to cross-examine and kept him there for another seven. His cool, detached style was in complete contrast to that of Colin Duncan, who had been called by the Judge, "the Homer of that section of the English Bar as concerning itself with libel". A description of Gerald by a fellow barrister who was present at the time gives a more accurate picture than any I could give twenty years after the event:

"Tall, thin, pale and austere, he had no histrionic tricks. He speaks quietly and quickly, his voice scarcely seeming to alter in tone or inflection, but it is a delicate and skilful instrument, and his art is that of understatement, not declamation. He stands upright and looks directly at the person he is addressing. His only idiosyncrasy is the slow rolling up and unrolling of the 'fee-bag' string which hangs down the front of his gown. His speech in this trial was both quiet and effective, but he also resorted to colloquial expressions such as 'That was anti-Semitism, that was', and 'Hoicking out their ovaries', which caught the attention in a case of such grave import."*

Dr Dering's air of self-confidence and rectitude had remained constant during his long session with Colin Duncan. He was sixty-one years old and he answered Gerald's questions about the keeping of the register and his methods of work without a flicker of nervousness, in

* *Auschwitz in England* by M. Hill and L. N. Williams (MacGibbon & Kee, 1965).

English which was not very fluent. Only when asked about the meaning of an entry reading "*casus explorativus*" did he appear slightly embarrassed, and was called to be more explicit by the judge when he gave evasive answers.

"Is it done," asked Gerald for the third time, "in order to assist in diagnosis?"

"Yes."

"That is not the nature of any operations in the last ten lines of this page, is it?"

"Not of this kind."

"It was a false description?"

"False?"

"That is right, is it not?"

"It was false in your meaning, but we had to put some diagnosis. Proper diagnosis would be 'X-rayed testicle'."

Gerald corrected him. "The proper diagnosis would have been 'for one of Dr Schumann's experiments', would it not?"

Dr Dering paused and considered carefully before admitting that he couldn't put that because he would have been in trouble with Dr Schumann. Referring to other entries in the register Gerald queried whether one operation had been carried out without the prisoner's consent.

"It was done under a German court order."

"Was it done against his will?"

"I did not ask him."

"Did you know that no German court had any legal right to make such an order merely because a man was a homosexual?"

The doctor looked a little worried. "I do not know what is German right. I was a prisoner. I could not argue or discuss with Germans any question and problems."

"Did you ask to see the court order?"

"No."

"Why did you carry it out? As a doctor you had taken the Hippocratic oath and you were being asked to castrate a potent man against his will. That requires, does it not, some justification by a doctor?"

"I would like to answer your question exactly. Since I entered Auschwitz all law, normal, human and God's law, were finished and there was only German law. I could not refuse. It would be done, if not by me, by unskilled S.S. corporal."

"You feel that it is a good excuse, do you, for doing what you did – hat if you had not done it somebody else probably would?"

"Some unskilled people would do," answered Dr Dering, "and the people would suffer much more than done in proper way."

"Unless, of course, they were doctors. And I suggest that there were ,ome in Auschwitz, whom I shall be calling, who refused to carry out German orders."

On this the case was adjourned and Gerald left the doctor to brood overnight on his last words. They could not have given him pleasant dreams.

Next morning the interrogation continued but on a somewhat ,harper note as Gerald faced the plaintiff in the witness box. "I would ike to refer to Case No. 2 in the register – a potent male who had not been radiated. Was the operation done with or without his consent?"

"It was done on court order."

"With or without his consent?"

"He was not asked for his consent."

"Was there any medical reason for it?"

"The diagnosis and sentence were based on his mental disability."

"If the S.S. surgeon, Dr Entress, had said to you: 'I am going to sterilize this man. There is no court order at all but that is what I am going to do and you are going to assist me', what would you have done?"

"I would have assisted him whether there was a court order or not."

"You started as a labourer, being beaten with the others, did you not?"

"Yes."

"Then you became a medical orderly?"

"Yes."

"Then you became a prisoner-surgeon in control of the whole hospital?"

"Yes."

"The Germans must have trusted you a good deal before they gave you that position, must they not?"

"I did not discuss the matter with the Germans. Simply I was appointed and I had to accept this post against my will and wish."

Gerald, after asking questions implying that Dering was working his passage, which the doctor denied, referred to another entry in the register. "Look at May 6th. On that day fifteen men had their left testicles removed – seven by you and eight by Dr Grabczynski [his

assistant in surgery.] These were not operations being performed fo
medical reasons, were they?"

Dr Dering hesitated. "All were X-rayed cases." Then, as Gerald
repeated the question: "It depends. It could be done in norma
circumstances."

Mr Justice Lawton considered this scarcely answered the question
"Well, Dr Dering, who wanted these operations performed? D
Schumann or the patient?"

"Dr Schumann."

Gerald was quick to follow this up. "And you knew that D
Schumann wanted them for his experiments?"

The doctor, reluctantly: "Yes."

"If you knew he wanted them for his experiments, they wer
experimental operations, were they not?"

"The experiments had been done before by X-ray. That was th
first step; and this was, if you like, the second step of his experiments."

"And so it was an experimental operation?" persisted Gerald.

"In a way, yes."

"Were they all young Jews?"

"Yes."

"The night before they were done, did they have a piece of wooc
put up their rectum in order to induce an ejaculation, to see that they
were still potent?"

Dr Dering shook his head vaguely: "I don't know." Then, on th
excuse of faulty memory, he again avoided answering Gerald.

"Do you remember one of them saying to you: 'What am I here for?
I am quite well. Why should I be operated on?' And your saying: 'If I
don't take out yours, they will take out mine'?"

"No," the doctor replied. "I don't remember such a conversation
It seems to me unlikely."

He was then subjected to rigorous interrogation on the methods
and technique of castration at Auschwitz, but reiterated that he did
the operations under duress and that in most cases the prisoners
sexual organs had already been destroyed by X-ray when they came
to him.

Gerald conceded that spinal anaesthesis was quite customary on
the continent; nevertheless, since the young men were having a
testicle removed against their will it would have been kinder if a
general anaesthetic had been used, so that they were unaware of what
was going on during the operation.

"Lord Gardiner, I had not always in abundance any kind of anaesthetics," said the doctor, "and I had no anaesthetist." He added that, although he had argued with Dr Schumann, he was told the young men were needed for work in the interest of the great German Reich, otherwise they would be sent to the gas chambers.

He was reminded that the previous day he had said he had had only one personal encounter with Dr Schumann, but this was not true. He was forced to admit he had seen him later on several occasions when discussing the right strength of X-ray for sterilizing testicles. He also agreed that two of the cases for *castratio* had been wrongly written up by him in the register. Then followed a string of questions concerning the plaintiff's early period in Warsaw, when he admitted that in the twenties non-Jewish students insisted on Jewish medical students sitting in a different part of the class-room. And, after much pressure from Gerald and Mr Justice Lawton, he agreed that the doctors working with him at Auschwitz and named in the register were all officer-type non-Jewish Poles. He had no knowledge, he said, of the "cancer-research" experiments that were made by Dr Wirths on hundreds of women in Block 10, even though he agreed that he was kept fully informed by the underground movement of all that went on in the camp.

Dr Dering was surprised at the suggestion he was "friendly" with his superior, Dr Clauberg, but he had heard about the sterilization experiments Clauberg was conducting in collaboration with Dr Schumann. Gerald then informed him that when hostilities ceased both men had been indicted as war criminals; Dr Schumann made his escape to Ghana and disappeared, while Dr Clauberg committed suicide prior to his trial.

At this point Gerald brought two very important documents to light, not as evidence against Dr Dering, for they had been included by him in the documents* he listed as concerning the trial, but because, had they not been revealed, in addition to the register, the case would largely depend on whether he or an important witness for the Defence, Dr Brewda, was telling the truth. How the doctor came by them, and why he preserved them, never emerged. One can only assume he was making sure that if the Allies won the war the letters would incriminate the Nazis and exonerate him, whereas if the Germans won they were evidence of his loyalty in assisting Dr Clauberg in his experiments. In either eventuality he was covering himself.

*After the war, following his trial and imprisonment at Brixton by the Home Secretary, Dr Dering preserved these letters.

The first letter Gerald read was headed:

HEADQUARTERS OF THE FUEHRER
July, 1942
Secret Reich's Matters
Single Copy.

On 7.7.42 a conference was held . . . object of the discussions being the sterilization of Jewesses. Himmler confirmed to . . Professor Doctor Klauberg [Clauberg] that the concentration camp Auschwitz is at his disposal for his experiments on human beings and animals. On the basis of some fundamental experiments a method is to be found for causing sterilization without the person concerned noticing it. As soon as the result of these experiments is known [Himmler] wants a report transmitted to him in order that the sterilization of Jewesses can virtually be started. Moreover it should be tested preferably under consultation of Professor Dr Hohlfelder, who is an expert on X-rays in Germany, in what way a sterilization of male persons can be achieved by application of X-rays. [Himmler] stressed to all those present that the most secret matters are involved which can only be discussed internally, and whereby, in each case, all those participating in the experiments or discussions must be pledged to secrecy.

The second document read:

To [Himmler] . . . As far as the question is concerned which you put to me a year ago, i.e. time is required to carry out sterilization of 1,000 women in that way I am able to predict today the following: If the experiments which I have been carrying out continue to come off as well as hitherto – and there is no reason to suppose that they will not – the time is not very far off when I will be able to tell you, "by a properly trained doctor, in a properly fitted place (with assistant personnel of perhaps ten – the number of assistants depending upon the desired speed of the proceedings) most probably several hundred, if not thousand in one day . . ." Heil Hitler . . .

Dr Clauberg.

THIRTEEN

THE LETTERS PASSING between the Fuehrer's Headquarters and Dr Clauberg at Auschwitz clearly established that it was the Nazis' definite intention to practise genocide on all Jews. It was also proof that the orders Dr Dering received came from the highest authority.

The moral question raised many times by Gerald and emphasized throughout the case, however, was whether an individual should be held guilty for carrying out orders against his conscience in the circumstances prevailing at Auschwitz. Examining Dr Grabczynski, who had come from Poland, Gerald referred him to an operation on a potent man who had had his testicles removed on Dr Schumann's orders.

"If Dr Dering had said: 'I am not going to do this. I have disobeyed an order before and nothing much happened to me.* I shall disobey again.' Would you have done the operation?"

"No, I would not," replied Dr Grabczynski. He also agreed that other prisoner-doctors might have refused to do likewise in the circumstances.

It became increasingly obvious that without the hospital register Defence would have had little hope of justifying the libel. Medical experts called on both sides cancelled each other out, as well as prisoner-doctors from Auschwitz who had worked with Dr Dering, some attesting that he had obtained hospital supplies and extra food for the inmates and had been generally kind and helpful to them, while others said the exact reverse. Mr Justice Lawton reminded the jury that the Defence was not implying Dr Dering had been brutal or insensitive to all the patients he attended, but only to those belonging to the Jewish race. It was necessary at this stage to clarify the issue, since the doctor was beginning to appear in the rôle of a guilty man defending himself against accusations of criminality, when actually he was the plaintiff in the case accusing others of libelling him.

It was an odd development, and even the *Guardian* newspaper, reporting the first day in court, used the words WAR CRIMES TRIAL when it was nothing of the sort.

---

* He had refused to give a lethal injection to a Jew, and his only punishment had been confinement to the camp for two weeks.

Dr Alina Brewda was now called upon to give evidence. In 1926 she had been a student in Warsaw, and it was here that Dr Dering had first met her. She had been arrested in 1943 and sent as a prisoner-doctor to Auschwitz. Dering admitted that he had encountered her there, but denied that she had ever been present when he operated. Dr Brewda's allegations, previously made to the Home Office in 1947 during Dering's investigation as a war criminal, were reiterated, the most damning being those concerning ovariectomies performed by him on a number of young Jewesses from Salonika, which but for the register would never have come to light.

The whole of Dr Brewda's criticism of Dr Dering's surgical methods – not washing his hands between operations, giving spinal injections without general anaesthetic to girls screaming in protest, performing on some who already had bad radiation burns and neglecting to give proper after-care – was stoutly denied by Dr Dering. He suggested that she was acting out of malice towards him: it was her duty, not his, to give morphine to patients before operations, and she could not possibly have witnessed any of his surgery since she was never allowed to be present in the theatre while he worked.

Gerald reminded him of the case of two girls with bad irradiation burns about to have ovariectomies. Dr Brewda had said to him: "Leave them alone. They have suffered enough already." "You replied," Gerald went on, "'Shut up. I have my orders. They will kill me. I have to do it.'"

"No, no, no," Dr Dering protested vehemently. "I could be strict but was never rude, especially to women. Remember, I had no anaesthetist."

Gerald glanced at a page in the register. "But, Dr Dering, there are hundreds and hundreds and hundreds of cases showing you giving a general anaesthetic. I suggest it is not true that you were short of anaesthetists, because the register shows that a large number of abdominal operations were done under a general anaesthetic."

As the doctor started what purported to be a dissertation on the subject, the Judge interrupted.

"Never mind what the type of operation was. I understood you to say earlier today that one of the reasons you gave these amputations of testicles a spinal anaesthetic was that you hadn't the services of an anaesthetist. Lord Gardiner is pointing out that in the register, in your handwriting, time and time again, there are cases where a general anaesthetic was given."

Gerald listened to Dering explaining his various reasons for pre-
rring a spinal to a general anaesthetic, and then suggested: "If
1ese girls were struggling and screaming, it might have been kinder
ɔ give them a general anaesthetic?"

"General anaesthetic takes time," said Dr Dering. "It takes at
:ast twenty minutes. We had not the time. We worked from six in
1e morning till six at night in very great rush, so I could not wait
ny time for operations I did not want."

"But you had time to give the others on this page a general
naesthetic?"

He was silent. Then followed various questions concerning the
urgical methods the doctor employed on one of the young girls
·hose spinal anaesthetic appeared to be wearing off, for she had
10ved on the operating table and complained of pain. He could not
ecollect this but said that something should have been done about
:.

"I suggest you did do something," Gerald retorted, "that when
he last girl but one moved you hit her and said: 'You damned
ewess, keep still until I have finished.'"

"I strongly deny these allegations." Dering's indignation rose per-
eptibly. "It is a conspiracy against me. If I may prove Dr Brewda's
·uthfulness . . ."

"This is another of Dr Brewda's inventions, is it?" queried Gerald
n his most dulcet tones.

"Yes."

"Why do you think that?"

"Dr Brewda as medical officer of Secret Police in Warsaw pro-
luced horrible accusations against me . . . sent them to London
eventeen years ago as proof I was a Gestapo officer . . ."

"You are not suggesting that Dr Brewda has said to anyone that
·ou hit the girl and called her 'damned Jewess'? Why do you say it
vas an invention of Dr Brewda's?" As the doctor seemed at a loss for
he moment, Gerald turned and surveyed the court. "I think it only
air to say this girl is alive and has been found, and it is *she* who says
vhat you did to her, and that while Dr Brewda was sitting there on
he stool you hit the girl."

"You have Dr Brewda's word –" he protested.

"No. I am not relying on Dr Brewda's word, but on the word of
he girl who has been found and is alive and is here. Is it true or
10t?"

"It is untrue."

Gerald tried another tack. "Did Dr Brewda complain to you that she had only paper bandages?"

The doctor denied this categorically. "At that time no one had paper bandages."

"But she knew you had proper bandages."

"If *she* had not, it was her fault."

Gerald persisted: "But she knew *you* had proper bandages and was pointing out to you that she had only paper bandages. She asked if you could give her something for the girls."

"On my visit to Block 10 I was surrounded by these six young pleasant girls, who were very friendly, including Dr Brewda herself and they just joked with me. I looked at the patients. Everything all right. No temperature. No dirty or septic wounds. What should I do more? I was satisfied and left the Block."

Gerald continued to probe about his movements in 1945 when he returned to Warsaw, and learned that Dr Brewda and other Poles had survived the destruction of Auschwitz and were determined to denounce him as a war criminal. This caused him to flee to Italy. The doctor repudiated this, saying a friend had warned him that Dr Brewda was chief deputy medical officer to the Secret Police and that he had seen her name on the door of the Secret Police office. This had "simply' shocked him.

For the first time his tone became self-pitying and showed some distress. "I worked hard for my people, but just through the ambition of one bad woman who wanted to cover up her own experience in Block 10 . . ." He faltered and could not go on.

"I do appreciate that some of the things I have put to you may be painful to you," said Gerald, "but you *do* realize that it is *you* who have brought this action for damages against a novelist whose whole Auschwitz episode in his novel occupies one page?"

Dr Dering's composure by this time was badly shaken.

In 1948, when Poland had asked for his extradition from England as a war criminal, the Home Office had received a statement from his Counsel, putting his case for the cancellation of his deportation order Gerald now passed this to the doctor to examine, asking whether he considered it to be fair and cautioning him to look at it very carefully After studying the document for several minutes, Dr Dering accepted its accuracy. Gerald picked on one phrase.

"Then it was right to describe you as 'an admitted anti-Semite'?"

With the evasiveness which typified so many of his replies, Dering answered: "I was called by some people – rather a small group – anti-semitic, but I can say I have still today very sincerely Jewish friends."

Gerald did not allow him to leave it at that. "His Lordship asked you to say whether there was anything else which did not represent your views. It was *your* document; and it says: 'The victims in Block 10 were Jewesses, as were the doctors, whereas Dr Dering, by contrast, was an admitted anti-Semite.'"

The doctor made no response. A few minutes later Gerald ended his cross-examination and sat down.

The second week in court saw him make the opening speech for the Defence, followed by the examination of several Greek Jewesses and some male Jews, all prisoners at the camp in 1943. Dr Klodzinski was also called on to give evidence, answering questions by Mr Hirst, junior Counsel for the Defence, as to how he came to be present in Block 21 at Auschwitz, since he was in another ward. He replied that he often watched operations there but as "a student of medicine. Dr Dering was allowing him to enter the theatre." He admitted that the rule against doing so was simply "theoretical". There were also infectious diseases in Block 21 where "asepsis was not very strictly kept".

He went on to describe how one day he had come across a queue of young men in the corridor outside Block 21. They appeared not to have had morphia injections before going into the theatre for operations. He went inside himself and saw Dr Dering making a surgical incision on a male prisoner for the removal of a testicle which he took out and placed in a kidney-shaped dish.

All who had been subjected to "experimental" operations remained anonymous throughout the case and were provided with interpreters, since none spoke English. On giving evidence each displayed the number tattooed on his or her arm, a gesture which never failed to affect those in court, while several broke down and wept uncontrollably on being reminded of the horrors of Auschwitz.

Of the eight women appearing for the Defence in the witness box, who had come from different parts of the world, the seventh, a middle-aged woman named Marta, gave the most graphic and typical account of her sufferings in the camp. Born in 1923, Marta had married a man in Salonika during the war, was arrested by the Germans in 1943, and went to Birkenau, the factory town near Auschwitz, where she worked until she was taken to the hospital for irradiation treatment, together

with several others. Her resulting burns became infected and too
roughly a month to heal, and on recovering she was sent with fou
others to Block 10 and later to the camp hospital, where she an
another girl called Bella were operated on by a Dr Samuel, who wa
carrying out orders from Dr Schumann. Complications from thi
operation kept her in bed for three months, at the end of which she wa
marched on foot, with ten other girls, to the theatre in Block 21. One b
one they went inside, Marta being the last to enter the annexe wher
she was injected by a male nurse, who bent her body over and pushe
her head down between the knees of another male nurse and the
despatched her to the operating table.

Mr Hirst, examining the witness, wanted further details. "Was th
moment of injection painless or painful?"

"Certainly it hurt. I screamed at the moment of injection. I did no
want to be operated on twice." She added that her friend Bella had als
screamed, and the memory of it suddenly overwhelmed her. Sh
became extremely agitated, and several minutes passed befor
Mr Hirst could resume his questioning.

"What effect did the injection have on the lower part of your body?"

"It was not dead. I had only pains."

"Was your brain clear or clouded?"

"I was clear, and I spoke."

"When you got on to the operating table, what happened?"

"I saw the lamp over me and it was full of red," said Marta. "
screamed for very strong pains. Dr Brewda told me always: 'Don't b
afraid. It will finish soon.'"

"Did you yourself have any conversation with either of the men i
white?" asked Mr Hirst.

"Yes."

"Will you tell us what was said?"

"I asked them to finish with me because I could not stand the pai
longer, and he told me: 'Let me finish my work, *verflüchte Judin*' – tha
means 'damned Jewess' – and he gave me a blow on my breast. Th
doctoress stroked my hair. I was crying and sweating."

"Did you see with your own eyes what was removed from you
body?"

"I heard they cut inside and I saw that they took out something."
She assured Mr Hirst that she had received no morphia before th
operation and that the following morning all her "wound was open"
and later, when it eventually healed, she had a scar in the shape of

cross, from the two incisions, which was still evident and could be seen. She had seen a man come round the ward about a week after her ordeal but he did not examine the girls who were lying in their bunks.

"Can you tell us whether the man who came round . . . was the same man or a different one from the one who called you a damned Jewess?"

"I recognized him from the front," she told Mr Hirst. Asked about her general health since then she explained that she had no periods. "They made of me a beast." Although she had remarried after the war she had no children of her own and had adopted some.

Mr Duncan in cross-examination suggested that she might have been confused in her recollection of the two operations since they happened twenty years ago, but she remained firm.

"I know what happened at the first and second operations. I know." In answer to further questions about them and the other girls she said: "All of them cried, but I cried more because I did not want to enter the second time. . . . We went one after the other, within one hour, as guinea-pigs." The memory swept over her and she broke down, weeping.

When she had fully recovered the Judge was interested in how she came to learn German in the camp and suggested giving her a little test. "Perhaps the witness will now say in German 'Let me finish my work'."

"*Lass mich fertig mein Arbeit*," said Marta, "*verflüchte Judin.*"

Mr Justice Lawton appeared satisfied.

The sufferings of the six male victims from radiation and castration were as cruel as those of the women who lost their ovaries. They received the same treatment before and after Dr Dering's surgery and all were rendered childless except one, who, being allowed to keep a single testicle, had produced two children.

Three women prisoner-doctors, Dr Brewda, Dr Lorska and Dr Hautval, were then called on to give evidence concerning the conditions and sterilizing programmes being carried out at Auschwitz. Each one testified that she had never taken part in an "experimental" operation, having found ways and means of avoiding participation, though Dr Hautval had openly refused several times and was prepared to face the consequences.

Dr Lorska arrived at the camp in August 1943 from Poland and was put in Block 10, which was adjacent to Block 11, the execution block. Dr Hautval, a French Protestant, had already been there for six months. On learning of the work being done by the S.S. doctors, and considering it unethical, Dr Lorska seized the opportunity to go to the "institute of hygiene", where she examined blood and sputum in the laboratory. The Judge showed interest in her account of what went on in Blocks 10 and 21 and asked how often executions took place in Block 11.

"During the first weeks of my stay in Block 10," she said, "two or three times a week." She had heard not just one shot but the mass execution of scores of people, both women and children. When firing was heard in Block 10 everyone knew what was going on.

Mr Duncan and the Judge plied her with questions about the penalties for not obeying orders in the camp. Did those who disobeyed suffer torture by flogging or hanging up by the wrists or feet?

"I know that one could by-pass the orders of the S.S. men in such a way as to avoid punishment," she answered firmly.

When Gerald came to re-examine her he asked: "If you had been ordered to take part in experimental operations, would you have done so?"

There was a pause as Dr Lorska intimated to Mr Justice Lawton that she wished to explain something. This she was allowed to do. "In the first days of my stay in Block 10," she said, "one evening I spoke with Dr Hautval. This conversation took place in the operating theatre. She explained to me as a doctor what was happening in Block 10. At the end of that conversation she told me that it was impossible that we should ever get out of the camp alive. 'The Germans will not allow people who know what is happening here to get into touch with the outside world,' Dr Hautval said, 'so the only thing that is left to us is to behave, for the rest of the short time that remains to us, as human beings.' I have never forgotten that conversation, and in all the difficult moments of my life I have remembered what she said to me."

Mr Justice Lawton was still a little doubtful. "If Professor Clauberg – who was an S.S. General, was he not? – had said to you, 'Tomorrow morning you will take that girl's left ovary out,' I gather that you would have refused?"

"I think I should have committed suicide," she said.

The second important prisoner-doctor to give evidence was Dr Alina Brewda, who in 1926 had studied with Dr Dering at medical school in Warsaw and had been sent by the Nazis in September 1943 to Auschwitz. On arriving there she had been ill with pneumonia, but soon learned from Dr Lorska the nature of the experiments being carried out by the S.S. doctors and the sufferings of male and female Jewish prisoners. Some of the latter were young adolescents who had caustic fluid injected into their wombs in order to sterilize them and were then left to bleed from their wounds. She had been greatly surprised on meeting Dr Dering in the hospital to find he was the senior doctor, and asked for drugs and extra medical supplies to help alleviate the pain of the girls under her care, but received the minimum of help from him.

The crux of her evidence came in her account of what happened in Block 21 on a November morning when ovariectomies were performed on ten Jewesses. She had been summoned by Dr Schumann to go there and calm the girls, who were creating a violent disturbance by screaming and protesting at being given spinal injections. It was her first appearance in Block 21, and she had to watch Dr Dering carry out his surgery on the struggling and raving girls and try to keep them quiet. Standing at the head of the operating table she comforted each one in turn as he worked, for since they had not received any morphine they were conscious throughout and struggled desperately to release themselves from being strapped to the table.

Asked about Marta and Bella, the youngest of the girls, she described their unhealed irradiation burns and the fact that Marta had had an ovary removed. If the other one was taken away, she told Dr Dering, she would be like a eunuch, but he took no notice and went on at great speed to perform his operations. She described the after-effects as "terrible". Bella died from internal haemorrhage during the night and shortly after another, Buena, died from operational shock, while the wounds of most of the girls started to open and they had nothing but paper bandages to cope with them. She appealed to Dr Dering for help, but only on the fifth day did he make an appearance in the ward. She reported the deaths of two of the patients, but after a cursory inspection of the ward with her he said nothing about the girls' condition and did not visit them again, although many remained there for several months. The drugs and bandages she asked for never came, and altogether her evidence was severely critical of Dr Dering's surgery, which she felt, as a doctor herself, she was competent to judge. It was an uncaring and insensitive picture which she painted, and it confirmed most of what Dr Lorska had described.

The last prisoner-doctor was Dr Adelaide Hautval, who had been arrested by the Nazis while trying to visit her mother in the French-occupied zone. On complaining of their treatment of the Jews she was promptly labelled "*Amie des Juifs*" and despatched to Auschwitz to be imprisoned with them, although she was a French Protestant. During her stay there she was in conflict with the S.S. doctors about sterilization and ovariectomies, to which she strongly objected, and this resulted in her being denounced to Dr Wirths. He asked her why she had not carried out his order to co-operate, to which she had replied that it was contrary to her conception of how a doctor should act.

Gerald wished to know how he responded. Dr Hautval's answer struck the Judge as "devastating" and would, he said, live in the jury's memory for many years. "He asked me," she said, "'Cannot you see that these people are different from you?' And I answered him that there were several other people different from me, starting with him."

Questioned by Counsel about her hiding patients with typhus on the top floor of the Block to stop them from being sent to the gas chambers, she agreed she would have been in serious trouble had this been discovered.

"It was an everyday occurrence for people to be punished, was it not?" Counsel asked.

"Yes. It was sufficient to smoke a cigarette."

In describing further her talk with Dr Wirths about the Jewish question, she mentioned she had said that no one had the right to dispose of the life and destiny of others.

"Did you ever take part in any of Clauberg's experiments?" Gerald asked quietly.

"No."

"As a result, were you shot?"

Before she could reply, laughter surged through the quiet court as the point of the question went home.

"*Non*," she replied, with a smile.

"Were you punished in any way?"

"No. Not in any way."

Another doctor whom she had refused to assist in peculiarly cruel and revolting operations on Jewish twins was a Dr Mengele, and the only result had been her Nazi superiors saying: "We cannot force her to do what she does not want to do." She was sent back to Birkenau and advised not to show herself too much so that she would not arouse their fury.

So ended the evidence of the three doctors who refused to participate in the atrocities at Auschwitz, the ones who, Gerald had warned Dr Dering, would say they had refused to obey orders. They were all of the "weaker" sex!

The following morning Gerald began his final speech for the Defence in a case which he said history would no doubt describe as showing what the Christians did to the Jews in Western Europe in the middle of the twentieth century, and nowhere in all history was there a blacker picture than this. That was anti-Semitism, that was! He reminded the jury that the day on which you knew that, whatever else happened in life, you would never have any children was a day you were not likely to forget, and none of the witnesses remembered having any injections of morphia to help them to forget.

In the whole of Dr Dering's evidence concerning the terrible operations which he performed on the young men and women there was not a single act of compassion, not one single word said to them such as, "I am sorry to have to do this", or, "It will be better for you if I do this". Nor, after the operations, "Of course, I was terribly distressed to have to do these operations. My heart bled for them." In the witness box there was no word of regret, only the excuse that if he had not performed the operations he might have been sent to the gas chambers and they would have been done instead by an unqualified S.S. corporal. Yet Dr Hautval had shown what happened to Christian doctors who deliberately defied an order. She had done it four times running and escaped punishment. When Dr Dering was ordered by an S.S. doctor to give a lethal injection to a prisoner he had refused, and, as we have seen, the only punishment he had received was the rather absurd one of not being allowed outside the grounds in his free time for a fortnight.

There had been a good deal of evidence from a good many witnesses of doctors disobeying orders, but after the "Save the doctors" order went out in 1941 there was no evidence that any Christian or even Jewish doctor was ever punished for declining to obey an order contrary to medical ethics.

Maybe Dr Dering would not have got his release if he had refused. Very few people were ever released from Auschwitz. Some bribed their way out, but from 1941 only two prisoner-doctors were released: they were Dr Dering and Dr Grabczynski – the two doctors who had helped the Germans by doing the operations. Was that just a coincidence?

What damages had the plaintiff suffered from the fact that people had read this book (*Exodus*)? What sort of damages should a man have who "hoicked out" the ovaries of those wretched girls without a proper anaesthetic? The register showed that ether was administered by two doctors 188 times in November 1943. What nonsense it was to say he had not got any anaesthetists. The plaintiff's last excuse was that he was not going to waste his time because a general anaesthetic took time.

There was a considerable conflict of evidence between Dr Dering
and Dr Brewda, and also between many of the Jewish witnesses, both
male and female, who came to give evidence, but it was up to the jury to
decide who was telling the truth. They might think that a person who
tended not to do anything which might cost him his release should just
have lived with his conscience and not have raked it all up after twenty
years, in support of a claim for damages. It would be an outrage if this
man, who had done these unnecessarily cruel things, were to be
awarded anything other than purely nominal damages.

Colin Duncan followed with a speech eloquent on behalf of his client
but mainly concerned with refuting many of the statements made
against Dering by Dr Brewda, which he mostly attributed to malice.
He pointed out that the evidence of all the witnesses was somewhat
unreliable, since it was based on memories of what had happened
twenty years previously.

Mr Justice Lawton then began his summing up. It was May 5th, the
seventeenth day of the hearings, and his speech carried on to the
following day when he finished at 11.55 a.m., having spoken for nearly
five hours. Meticulously fair in everything he said, and sifting every
scrap of evidence in order to arrive at the truth, he finally turned to the
jury, saying they had to make up their minds whether this case came
where Lord Gardiner said – a near miss – or where Mr Duncan said, an
outrageous attack on a man who did his best. The truth must be
somewhere between those limits. Warning the jury to take as long as
they liked as it was a very difficult problem, he ended: "Members of the
jury, will you now retire and consider your verdict?"

Whereupon Gerald rose from his seat: "May I remind your Lordship
to direct the jury as to the specific question?"

The Judge was quick to see his lapse, and told them first to find
whether the verdict was for the plaintiff or the defendants, and if for the
plaintiff, then how much the damages should be. The jury rose, and at
the end of two-and-a-half hours returned and found for Dr Dering
awarding him the sum of one ha'penny.*

---

* If a jury is of the opinion that on all the "evidence in the case"
the action ought not to have been brought, they are entitled to find for the plaintiff
but only for the smallest coin in the realm. In this particular case the jury could
not find for the defendants because they had greatly exaggerated the number of
operations which they claimed Dr Dering had performed, and said that he had done
them without anaesthetics, whereas he had used a local anaesthetic. However
what he had done was so appalling that he was not deserving of anything except the
smallest damages.

Lord Denning, commenting later on the case, said: "Many are the reports of State Trials or Famous Trials. None will have greater interest or importance than this trial of the libel action of *Dering v. Uris and Others*."*

* *Auschwitz in England* (MacGibbon & Kee, 1965), from the Foreword by Lord Denning.

FOURTEEN

As THE SUMMER of 1964 drew to a close the political scene in the country changed significantly, though the change was not unexpected. The Conservative Government, whose five-year term was shortly to run out, decided to set the date for a general election in early October. Before the House rose for the summer recess Gerald, who had been a member of the committee working on Lord Longford's report on Crime and Punishment, was asked by the Chief Whip, Lord Shepherd, to initiate a debate on the subject in the House of Lords, which he did on a Wednesday in June.

During the two months' vacation he devoted a considerable amount of time to speaking at public meetings all over the country at the request of Transport House. It never occurred to him to take a rest after the rigours of the Auschwitz trial or the intricacies of a highly complex shipping case for which he had been briefed. His seemingly inexhaustible energy was expended recklessly until his legal commitments were resumed in the High Court.

The Conservatives, led first by Prime Minister Macmillan and then by Sir Alec Douglas-Home, had been in office continuously for the past thirteen years. It was the end of the "you never had it so good" period, but it was doubtful whether the great British public appreciated the fact. When polling day, October 15th, 1964, was over and the results began pouring in, the fate of the contending parties was by no means clear and excitement grew as voting announcements swayed crazily during the night from one side to the other, finally narrowing between Labour and Conservative to a cliff-hanging conclusion.

By mid-afternoon the following day Gerald was informed by the court usher that Labour had been elected to govern with a majority of four. Not exactly a resounding victory! When the Court's proceedings were concluded for the day he returned to chambers to be met by his clerk with a message that his presence was required by the Prime Minister at six o'clock at No. 10 Downing Street. The subsequent interview was brief and to the point: the office of Lord Chancellor, offered by Harold Wilson to Gerald several months earlier, was firmly repeated. After obtaining the Prime Minister's assurance that he was confident he was really the man for the job, Gerald finally accepted and was sent on his way with the heady prospect of a new career opening for him at the advanced age of sixty-four.

The next day he repaired to Buckingham Palace to receive his seals of office from the Queen. The ceremony for handing them over is slightly different from the one experienced by Ministers of State, who accept them from her hand. On a certain occasion in the past the Great Seal fell and injured the Chancellor's foot as it was passed to him by the sovereign; thereafter the Queen and her new Chancellor simply laid their hands, one after the other, on the seal and that was all.

From the palace he went to the House of Lords, where he proceeded upwards to the Chancellor's office in the Victoria Tower. On the way a Lobby correspondent prophesied in passing that the new Government could not possibly last longer than three months, for, as he cheerfully explained to Gerald, when the Speaker was elected Labour's majority would shrink to a mere three!

Sir George Coldstream, the Permanent Secretary, was waiting to introduce his new chief to the staff and to the intricacies of his work, for as well as being the occupant of the Woolsack the Lord Chancellor is also the Speaker of the House of Lords. Coldstream was to prove of inestimable help in the years to come, which Gerald especially appreciated because, as a "reforming Chancellor", he put a very great deal of work on the shoulders of his Permanent Secretary. The two men were not unknown to each other, having been on friendly terms during the past few months, dining together and discussing ideas for legal reform which Gerald felt was urgently needed. The idea of establishing a Law Commission to keep the law continually under review was mulled over at these early meetings, and the names of Commissioners suitable to act on it, Leslie (later Lord) Scarman being mentioned even then as the appropriate person to run it.

Another individual familiar with the routine of the House, who took great trouble to explain its rules and guide-lines to Gerald, was an old-timer, Lord Silkin, Minister of Town and Country Planning in Attlee's Government after the war. By the time he had been coached in all the quaint rituals and the mode of speech considered requisite by Her Majesty's peers, Gerald felt he would just about have mastered them by the time the Government fell and he was out of office, unable to return to the Bar!

Almost immediately after taking over his duties he was confronted with a problem for which he was totally unprepared, despite his careful tuition. Within hours George Coldstream informed him that he had to decide whether the Burmese royal regalia should, or should not, be returned to Burma.

"Where is it now?" Gerald asked, somewhat puzzled.

"It's been on show in a glass case for many years outside the gentlemen's toilet in the British Museum."

"But what on earth has this to do with me?"

George explained apologetically: "Well, you see, if two Ministers fail to agree on a course of action, and they don't want the dispute to go to Cabinet, they ask the Lord Chancellor to act as arbitrator and decide for them." He then went on to explain that the Commonwealth Office was about to receive an important visit from a Burmese general from whom they wanted a certain valuable concession. In exchange it was thought diplomatic to offer him the return of the royal regalia. The Foreign Office, however, said that all the books concerning it were housed in the India Office Library, and if the regalia went back to Burma the Burmese Government would naturally expect the books to go with it. Several other countries, including India, also had many of their books here in museums, and if Burma were to recover hers they would insist on being treated likewise and we should lose them all.

Gerald, after giving the matter the deep and serious thought it merited, decided the Foreign Office fears were probably exaggerated and that the Commonwealth Office should be free to offer the regalia to the Burmese general. No adverse result followed this momentous judgment and no more was ever heard of the "Burmese Affair"!

The wide range of people for whom the Lord Chancellor is responsible was brought home to him a short while later in the House where a peer of the realm was proving somewhat of a nuisance. He lived in a mental asylum, and whenever he exercised his right to take part in a debate arranged in the Lords became so wildly excited that he made an obstreperous nuisance of himself by shouting and gesticulating at his fellow peers.

Lunacy, unfortunately, is no disqualification for being a member of their Lordships' House (there have been several insane peers over the years), and after many unsuccessful attempts to persuade the mad peer not to attend, the staff could think of no other solution than to make excuses whenever he applied for his Writ of Summons, without which he could not enter the Chamber or vote, on penalty of a fine of £500.

This ruse worked for a time, but as the months passed and the Writ of Summons never appeared, the peer became thoroughly incensed and created such a fuss that it eventually reached Gerald's ears. He investigated, discovered what had been going on and told his staff they had been acting illegally and that they must issue the madman with his Writ at once. Whereupon the gentleman started coming to the House again and thoroughly disturbing it with his antics. Everyone became frantic. Gerald made some inquiries of his own and discovered that when the peer did not attend the Lords on his free days he played golf, of which he was inordinately fond, on a Surrey course near his mental asylum. A little research was then conducted quietly, and Gerald found that there existed in the Midlands a pleasant mental hospital with its own golf course. The peer was diplomatically approached and asked if he would like to transfer there and enjoy its amenities, providing a vacancy occurred. He agreed, and as soon as one came along he went and settled down in the Midlands asylum and thenceforth never returned to bother the House.

Having, as Gerald later explained to me, "to live over the shop" in the House of Lords, the Gardiners found they had to uproot themselves from Onslow Square. The flat was immediately relinquished and its contents transferred to the Lord Chancellor's residence in the Victoria Tower, a floor above his spacious office overlooking the Thames on one side and Victoria Gardens on the other. Lesly felt rather isolated in this eyrie, and was never entirely happy living there.

All links with the numerous societies and associations to which Gerald belonged had to come to an abrupt end for the time being as he shouldered his new duties. He was advised to refrain from driving his own car in future, since a chauffeur-driven one would be made available to him. Apparently Lord Chancellors are not encouraged to run the same risks on the road as ordinary folk! He could never leave the country without first notifying the Queen in order that the Great Seal could be affixed to documents by two or three Commissioners in his absence.* If Parliament was in recess, he also signed a document recalling it if necessary while he was away. This actually happened when he was on holiday in Norway and Parliament had to be recalled on the occasion of the invasion of Czechoslovakia.

During the previous nine months he had prudently made use of his time in the House of Lords on the few occasions when his legal work

* Macaulay describes the terrible commotion caused by King James II running off with the Great Seal in the middle of the night and deliberately dropping it in the Thames. No single order, either to the armed forces or to anyone else, could be carried out and frightful confusion reigned in Parliament.

permitted him to attend, not only in learning the etiquette and niceties of its rules, but in familiarizing himself with the political style of debate. While sitting in the Chamber he carefully studied the "form", the way the Lord Chancellor coped with the conduct of the House and its business and at the same time carried out his responsibilities as Speaker. How much Gerald absorbed in that short space of time is shown by his comments on the office of Lord Chancellor in his speech during the debate on Law Reform which took place on June 11th, 1964, four months before he himself was appointed to that office. Of it he said:

"He [the Lord Chancellor] is, after all, a member of the Cabinet who has to read the Cabinet papers like any other member. He is, in effect, the Speaker of your Lordships' House. He has to appoint all the High Court judges and all the county court judges. He is responsible for the administration of that dreadful building in the Strand, and the salaries and wages bill of the inhabitants, apart from the judges, comes to over £500,000 a year. He has to deal with the whole of the administration of the county courts. He has to appoint all the justices of the peace. He is, incidentally, having to appoint clergy to new benefices; indeed, he has five times as much ecclesiastical patronage as the Archbishops of Canterbury and York put together. He has supervising duties in lunacy. I think I am right in saying that every lunatic has a statutory right to write to the Lord Chancellor – and most of them do.

"My Lords, this is the man who, in his spare time, is supposed to be thinking about whether English law is working properly or not, and of course he cannot."

He went on: "It has never been anybody's job to see that our law is kept up-to-date and in good working order. Theoretically it is the job of the Lord Chancellor with, I think, in criminal matters, some responsibility on the part of the Home Secretary. The line is not clear, because again, when as a Junior Counsel at the Bar I found some obviously defective criminal law, I wrote to the Lord Chancellor about it and he said it was a matter for the Home Secretary. I wrote to the Home Secretary and he said it was a matter for the Lord Chancellor. . . . Somewhere between the Lord Chancellor's office and the Home Office is a large hole where projects for the reform of our criminal law lie deeply interred. . . .

"There are, I think, 4,000 extant statutes, and if you took down those volumes of the statute which contained Acts which are still in force I think you would have to take down something like 358 volumes –

though a firm of law publishers that we all know has kindly already done the job for us and reduced it to 33 volumes. Then there are 99 volumes of delegated legislation and about 350,000 reported cases. What sort of system of law is this? . . . On almost any subject, to find the law on some particular point one may have to look at twenty different Acts of Parliament all dealing with the same subject matter. It is not just that this all takes up lawyers' time that has to be paid for – and of course, from the point of view of the community, the less spent on lawyers the better – but that here we are coming up to the scientific revolution and we are all saying, I am afraid, lawyers included, that industrialists and commercial people have to be a good deal more efficient than they are at present . . .*

"If you contemplate a major overhaul, and it is of importance to our people, what is holding up law reform? . . . The Code Napoléon was drafted and enacted in ten months and has stood the test of time. . . . Personally, when I talk about law reform, I am envisaging a major overhaul of the whole of our law. I think it is in a state where it can no longer be allowed to remain."

However, Lord Dilhorne, who was then Lord Chancellor, entirely disagreed, saying: "I do not believe for one moment that that case is made out," thus revealing the opposition Gerald was likely to expect when he introduced the Law Commission Bill in the House a year later.

During his first few months in office Gerald wasted no time in starting to carry out the major reforms which he believed to be essential. He began by appointing a committee to report on the age of majority, which was set up on July 30th, 1965, under the chairmanship of Mr Justice Latey.

Geoffrey Howe, Q.C., Robert MacLennan, M.P., Mrs B. Serota, J.P., Dick Taverne, Q.C., M.P., Katharine Whitehorn and half-a-dozen others were members of the committee, which sat for two years. Its report was presented to Parliament in July 1967, with the same verdict as had been given in 1959 to the Commission which Gaitskell initiated, in favour of reducing to eighteen the age at which young people could marry without parental consent, be free to make contracts and to own and dispose of their own property. It was another three months before the report was introduced into the House

* Some idea of the immense variety of the subjects on which a Lord Chancellor may have to address the House can be gauged from the Appendix.

of Lords, and a further twelve months before it was debated as a part of the Family Law Reform Bill on November 26th, 1968.

Presenting the Bill, Baroness Serota (as she now was) said: "Thanks to the typical generosity and kindness of the noble and learned Lord, the Lord Chancellor, who really is the father of the Bill, it is certainly a great privilege for me personally to be associated with the first Family Law Reform Bill ever to be introduced into either House." Later she added: "I hope I shall be forgiven, therefore, for cherishing a rather maternal feeling for it, although like all good parents (to use the words of the Latey Report), I shall try to 'hold tight with loose hands'."

It was the first time that anybody who had been on such a committee had had the experience of introducing a Bill to implement its report, and it must have afforded Lady Serota, as it did Gerald, great satisfaction that, after the Committee members' assiduous work on the Younger Generation and the Age of Majority Reports over the previous nine years, their efforts had been rewarded with success. At that time countries in Europe maintained the age of majority at twenty-one, and it is interesting to note that the ten years which followed witnessed a change of law not only in all the West European democracies but also in the U.S.A. – which emulated the English example and brought it down to eighteen.

How had it come to be twenty-one in the first place? This was a question which Gerald found extremely difficult to answer, and only after a good deal of tortuous research into the obscure past was some light shed on it.

It seems that before the Norman Conquest all young men came of age at fifteen, by which time they were able to carry arms. During the next three centuries, as armour became heavier and heavier and horses bigger, it was decided they did not have enough strength or ability to bear arms until they were twenty-one. But this only applied to the knights: the feudal tenant's son still came of age at fifteen, as soon as he was capable of husbandry, and the burgess's son when he could count pence, measure cloth and conduct his father's business. This continued to be roughly the rule until the military tenure of land ceased and Charles II signed a statute in 1660 which caused the age to be set at twenty-one, in order to prevent all young persons under the old rule from achieving majority at fifteen, when they might have squandered the family inheritance.

Before presenting the Law Commission Bill in April 1965, Gerald had been responsible for an Administration of Justice Bill and a series

of routine measures dealing with agriculture, immigration and hous-
ing, none of which excited or absorbed him as much as the reform of our
out-dated law. He had just four months in which to prepare this
extremely important and historic Bill, and to select those whom he
needed to run the Commission, an extraordinarily difficult choice that
would be closely examined and challenged by the Opposition.

The Law Commission Bill was the first which Gerald personally
introduced in the Lords after he became Lord Chancellor. He opened
the proceedings on April 1st, warning the House that when his
distinguished predecessor, Lord Brougham, made his famous speech
on law reform on February 27th, 1828, it lasted six hours, and that if he
were to explain everything that was wrong with English law he would
take rather longer than that! Actually he spoke for nearly 50 minutes.
Much of the substance of his speech reiterated points made in the
earlier Law Reform Bill of the previous June, but was extended by
stressing the cumbersome nature of some of our laws, for instance on
marriage. To elucidate this, he said, before one could understand the
precise situation it was necessary to consult 40 different Acts of
Parliament from 1540 to 1949!

Explaining why it was impossible for the Lord Chancellor's department to make any real progress as far as law reform was concerned, he
shed some light on the way its work is carried out, particularly in
relation to his own efforts. "On the occasions on which I have to leave
the Woolsack," he said, "your Lordships may think I am going to have
a drink at the bar. This would perhaps be excusable, because while
your Lordships' Chamber has many amenities, oxygen does not seem
to be one of them; and without wanting to reform everything, perhaps
that is a reform which we may make at some time. But yesterday, for
example, I had, I'm afraid, to miss quite a large part of the very
interesting debate on agriculture. This was because I had first to see a
judge about a particular matter. Then I had to see the Lord Chief
Justice of Northern Ireland. Then I had to see the Commonwealth
Secretary on an urgent matter, and then the Colonial Secretary, who is
going abroad today, had to see me about another matter before he goes.
Therefore it is not surprising that the first rule in my department is
never do anything by day which can possibly be done at night; and it is
at night that the departmental work gets done."

The Bill provided for two Commissions to be set up, one for England
and one for Scotland, whose duty it would be to keep all the existing law
under review with the intention of developing and reforming it,

particularly its codification, of eliminating its anomalies, and of repealing its obsolete enactments and reducing them, as well as generally simplifying and modernizing the law.

Gerald admitted there was opposition to the reforms he proposed, but there always had been. Quoting many examples of this, he mentioned the long battle to get a Court of Criminal Appeal, when every sort of argument against it was used. "It was said that everybody would appeal as a matter of course; that you would have to have at least three courts working day and night throughout the year; that the costs would be astronomical, and that juries would convict lightheartedly, because they would say: 'If we are wrong, the Court of Criminal Appeal can always put us right.' Then, when new rules and a system of legal procedure were mooted in 1883, the Bar Committee (now the Bar Council) marched to the bar of another place to protest against rules that they said would never work and were quite impracticable; and they said that if they did work then all lawyers would be ruined. In fact, they worked extremely well and, so far as I know, the lawyers are not ruined yet."

There would be a certain number of Commissioners, he explained, responsible for a five-year programme, reporting to Parliament annually on what they had been doing and what they intended to do in the future, and, he concluded, he hoped that with the help of a Law Commission our law would better serve the needs of the people.

Although most of the peers taking part that afternoon were favourable, Lord Dilhorne and Lord Simonds, both previous Lord Chancellors, had many reservations which very nearly wrecked the Bill at the committee stage. Others who welcomed it at the time were the most eminent in the legal profession – Lords Denning, Reid, Wilberforce, Silkin and Tangley – thus giving it sufficient support to enable the Law Commission to come into being and perform invaluable service to this country. Leslie Scarman, a High Court judge of three years' standing, was its first Chairman, with four Commissioners, Neil Lawson, Norman Marsh, Andrew Martin and L. C. B. Gower, working with him.

In later years Gerald has often been asked if there was anything in particular for which he would like to be remembered during his lifetime. He has not hesitated to say the creation of the Law Commission. Whether this was also closest to his heart is arguable, for another which had a very special meaning to him was a cause which he supported and for which he laboured for over 40 years, the abolition of

Left: Off to court at a swinging pace.

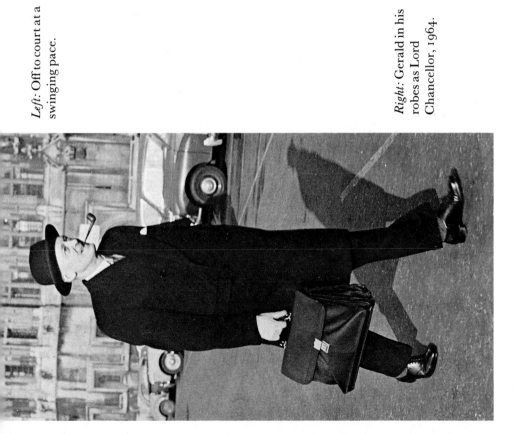

Right: Gerald in his robes as Lord Chancellor, 1964.

Above: Gerald taking the chair at a board meeting of the *New Statesman*.

Below: The Queen sharing a joke with Gerald in the Law Courts at the opening of the new Queen's Building in the Strand.

Above: The Chancellor conferring degrees on the Open University graduates, 1973.

Below: Gerald and fellow graduates, after receiving their degrees from the Open University, 1977.

Above: Gerald and Muriel Box at Mote End on their engagement, 1970.

Below: Gerald and the author, at Sydney Harbour, before leaving for Hong Kong, 1973.

the death penalty. A great number of Bills had to be dealt with and several years passed before he could devote himself to this objective.

Meanwhile, a debate on homosexual offences, initiated by the Earl of Arran as a result of the recommendations of the Wolfenden Report, required his attention.

The Wolfenden Report, which had been completed in 1957, was in favour of relaxing the law by allowing homosexual acts to take place between consenting adults in private, previously a criminal offence. This, it was argued, would eliminate some existing evils – fear of blackmail, fear of prosecution and harassment by the police, and fear of imprisonment if convicted of the offence.

On May 12th, 1965, the debate opened at three o'clock, and continued in lively fashion for over five hours. It was notable for the fact that only one woman, Lady Gaitskell, took part in it, as Gerald later pointed out. His views on the subject, like those of a great many other peers and several churchmen (the Archbishops of Canterbury and York and the Bishops of Worcester and Southwark), reveal an understanding and desire for reform of our antiquated law, which was causing much trouble and unhappiness to a section of the community who scarcely deserved the opprobrium they were receiving.

Dora Gaitskell's thoughtful comments on the Report during the debate are interesting: "The Wolfenden Committee recommendations were approved by twelve to one. If I had any grave doubts about my own attitude to this social problem, they were dispelled by the arguments in the minority reservation of Mr Adair. Why? Because I do not believe that homosexual behaviour between consenting adults is harmful to the community, or can have a serious effect on the whole moral fabric, as it is called, of social life. The whole moral fabric of social life looks somewhat tattered to me after I have read my morning newspapers, or even my Sunday papers. The misdemeanours between man and woman far outnumber those between man and man. . . . We persecute these men for what they are, and we do not persecute heterosexuals for many of the perversions in which they indulge – we treat these as private and confidential. We expect a degree of self-restraint from them that is absolutely unrealistic."

Gerald's contribution to the debate showed clearly where he stood, as the following extract indicates: "May I remind your Lordships that, after all, we are not talking about a word derived from the Latin 'homo' but a word derived from the Greek 'homos', meaning 'like' as opposed to 'heteros' meaning 'unlike'. The question which has not really been mentioned, except by the right reverend Prelate the Lord Bishop of Southwark, is the question: is it right – and I am not using the word 'right' in the theological sense but like the ordinary man in the street – that if two men, by themselves, choose to do things to one another – they can be sent to prison for life, yet if two women do what they like together it is not a criminal offence at all? This was mentioned, I remember, in a debate in another place. The fact that it was not an offence for women was mentioned by somebody who advocated the retention of the present law. He was at once asked: 'Would you make it a criminal offence for women?' but he declined to answer! . . . My Lords, I have never understood on what ground it is said to be less harmful. I appreciate that it is said that homosexual offences by men are inimical to family life. But, if that is so, I suggest that anyone with a divorce practice knows that the Wolfenden Committee were right on this point when they said:

> Cases are also frequently encountered in which a marriage has been broken up by homosexual behaviour on the part of the wife, and no doubt some women, too, derive satisfaction from homosexual outlets to prevent their marrying. We have had no reasons shown to us which would lead us to believe that homosexual behaviour between males inflicts greater damage on family life than adultery, fornication or Lesbian behaviour."

Lord Arran introduced the Homosexual Offences Bill barely two weeks later, and on May 24th its second reading was carried by 94 votes to 49.

Since the beginning of the year there had been ominous rumblings from Rhodesia, punctuated by visits from Mr Ian Smith to London and return visits to Salisbury by some of Harold Wilson's Ministers, including Gerald, who went out with Mr Arthur Bottomley, the Commonwealth Secretary, for talks on the Constitution, towards the end of February. Ian Smith had reluctantly agreed that they could meet representatives of all sections of the community, including imprisoned African leaders, in an endeavour to get first-hand information on the troubles fomenting there under White Rhodesian rule.

Harold Wilson, Lester Pearson (Canada's Prime Minister) and Sir Robert Menzies all found Ian Smith a somewhat devious character to deal with; he favoured secret interviews which he afterwards denied having taken place, and Gerald, after talks with him, could certainly confirm their opinion after trying to negotiate with the gentleman.

Before leaving Salisbury he was told by the Rhodesian rulers: "Of course we accept majority rule, because we accept the 1961 Constitution; and under the 1961 Constitution, as African educational and financial status improves there is, of course, bound to be African majority rule. Therefore we accept it." When Mr Smith was over in London, however, and was asked whether he would increase the amount of African education if the United Kingdom gave some help, he said: "No. We believe in education for its own sake, because the African who is to some extent educated is more use to us economically than one who is completely uneducated. But we do not believe in bringing African majority rule nearer, and we certainly should not agree to African education being expedited for that purpose. The Rhodesian Government would think it wrong to accelerate the educational advance of the Africans simply in order to improve their political status in the community." He made it very clear that the Government Party in Rhodesia did not believe in majority rule, and prophesied that it would never come in his lifetime (a statement often repeated). Mr Harper, their Minister for native affairs, went even further, giving Gerald his honest opinion that it would not happen for 200 years!

Throughout 1965 there were constant attempts by the Prime Minister to come to terms with Ian Smith and his Government over the question of majority rule and the Five Principles* which had been formulated by March 3rd on the conclusion of Gerald's and the Commonweath Secretary's visit to Rhodesia.

Time and time again these were vigorously discussed, amended and altered, and new suggestions were put forward by the Prime Minister to Ian Smith in an endeavour to prevent an illegal declaration of independence, commonly known as U.D.I. All to no avail, for on November 11th, 1965, the long-averted decision was taken and Rhodesia was in a state of rebellion against the Crown.

It happened on a Thursday. By the following Monday an enabling Bill was introduced in both Houses of Parliament to cope with the unusual situation. The discussion in the Lords started a few minutes

* These were: Unimpeded progress to majority rule; improved political status of the Africans; end of racial discrimination; and various guarantees concerning the constitution and the Rhodesian people as a whole.

after 2 p.m. and continued without a break until 12.30 a.m., when the Bill, having been passed in the Commons, came over to the Lords. There it was debated for another hour by the peers and subsequently passed, including all amendments, by 1.30 a.m.

Opening the proceedings, Gerald spoke for just over an hour, explaining all that had transpired between the Government and Rhodesia during the past year, ending in the tragic breakdown of talks with Mr Smith. In dealing with sanctions and other possible solutions he stressed the Government's opposition to using force.

> How far we should go is a matter of opinion. There are those who cry "Forward!" and those who cry "Back!". Some would like to do nothing, so long as it is not effective. That does not seem to be a very sensible point of view. Others would go further and use force. But it does not seem to the Government that, whatever the problems of Rhodesia are – and they are great – they could usefully be solved by force.

He dwelt on the basic philosophic difference between us and the Rhodesians:

> We of the Commonwealth and all Parties in this country have long subscribed to the view that we are trustees in the case of Colonies while we bring them to a stage of development when they can run their own country. This view is not shared by members of the Rhodesian Front – no doubt quite honestly. They say that all these countries would have been much better off if they had stayed under British rule. If by "much better off" they mean economically, I have no doubt myself that that is true, but what do we do when the African whose country it is says, "Well, thank you very much; on the whole I would rather be free and run my own country, even if I do not do it so well as a white minority"? How do we equate the scales: economic standard with being free?
>
> Some of your Lordships may have read an account the other day in a newspaper of a Salisbury barman with the average living standard in Rhodesia of about £1,250 a year – the African standard being about £200 a year – who said, "All these niggers are no good. They never will be any good." The thing that struck me was that he said it in front of his assistant, who was an African. People have feelings, and whether this desire for freedom and for running your own show

is rational or not, we in the Commonwealth have recognized its strength and have adopted the view which I have set out. It is true that these Rhodesians are the most loyal subjects of the Queen, and that 9,000 fought for us in the war. What they did not mention and what one could not guess from the advertisements in this country, on which they spent so much money, is that so did 15,000 black Rhodesians.

Concluding, Gerald said:

We in the Commonwealth believe that it is our duty in respect of all Colonies – and this is a Colony – to develop the inhabitants of the country so that they get to a position in which they can rule their own country. This is not the view of the Rhodesian front: they do not believe in majority rule. The situation which we have to face is that we have to consider what is necessarily involved in the whole relationship between white people and black people in Africa. . . .

At about 10 p.m., when the Lords had examined every aspect of the sorry affair, Lord Coleraine rose to pay Gerald a compliment on his lucid explanation of all the problems the Government had encountered. Since he was a member of the Opposition party, his comments carried more weight than if they had come from Labour.

I listened to his speech this afternoon with the greatest admiration for its objectivity and its absolute fairness. As he was speaking, I felt that if the noble and learned Lord had been in charge of these negotiations, not only for the last three or four weeks but over the last three or four years, the Rhodesian Government would have formed a different opinion from that which unfortunately they did form about the reliability and the integrity of British Ministers.

Many thousands of words have been written and spoken about the crisis and its aftermath. Now that legal independence has been won after fifteen years, it seems tragic the country had first to be torn apart in a prolonged bloody struggle which might have been avoided had a more reasonable attitude been adopted by its rulers. It prompts the question: "Is similar suffering to be endured when South Africa is faced with the inevitable results of her apartheid policies?"

Earlier in the year, during the summer recess, Gerald attended the Commonwealth Law Conference in Melbourne accompanied by Lesly and Carol. None of them had ever visited Australia before, and the occasion was a source of enjoyment and pleasure to Gerald since it enabled him to see his brother Cyril after many years of separation. It was a successful and fruitful trip, but when they returned Lesly complained of feeling ill.

Consultations with a specialist revealed that she was suffering from lung cancer. This was bad enough, but then came the shattering news that she had barely twelve months to live, since the cancer was at an advanced stage and quite inoperable. Faced with these grim facts, Gerald seriously considered giving up his work in the Lords in order to devote himself to caring for her, but Lesly strongly vetoed this. He also talked to Harold Wilson, intimating that he was thinking of resigning, but was advised that it might be better – depending, of course, on Lesly's condition – if he carried on for a while until he had given himself time to reconsider such a precipitate step. Thus persuaded, he continued to sit on the Woolsack and, since he lived above his own office, was able to be with Lesly whenever the need arose. He also had the help of Maria, a very capable Italian who had been their housekeeper for several years and who turned out to be a most sympathetic nurse.

Cabinets, debates, Bills (first, second and third readings), amendments and committees continued to form the pattern of Gerald's working days, and often the pattern of his working nights as well, generally until two or three in the morning. For after the daily session in the Chamber ended the Red Despatch Boxes would be opened up later and every telegram, letter and state document scrutinized in order to keep him *au fait* with events in the Commonwealth countries as well as in his own. Maria would often discover him fast asleep, still in his armchair, with his papers strewn about him, when she came in with his breakfast!

The year 1965 had seen the passing not only of those important measures for reform already touched on, but of several others, including Barbara Wootton's Death Penalty Bill and the proposal by Edith Summerskill of a Matrimonial Homes Bill (supported by Gerald), which would give a deserted wife the right to occupy, and not be turned out of, the family home.

In the following year the Theatres Bill, introduced by Lord Annan to deal with the pre-censorship of plays, was debated in February at great length. This was obviously a subject of considerable interest to Gerald, for his theatre-going had never waned, though latterly it had often been curtailed by late sittings in the House.

Since playwrights and producers had found the Lord Chamberlain's censorship of plays a source of irritation and deep frustration for roughly a century, various attempts at reforming the law had been made from time to time, but each had been unsuccessful. Lord Annan felt the situation should be remedied, and presented a strong case for a joint committee of both Houses to review the law and practice relating to it.

Participating in the debate of February 17th, 1966, were peers notable for their interest in the theatre, among them Lord Willis, Lord Goodman, two previous Lord Chamberlains, the Earl of Scarborough and Lord Cobbold, as well as Lord Harlech, an ex-censor of films, and Lord Birkett, a producer of them, for the cinema has problems with films similar to those of the theatre with plays but has dealt with them in a different way. Gerald's views on this touchy subject show that he strongly supported those who were in favour of the need for an inquiry, to the extent of abolition of pre-censorship. In this he had the backing of the Government.

He spoke early in the debate, plunging into the crux of the matter:

The question is: should theatres, like most other things in our country, be subject to the rule of law, of the courts, in the ordinary way; or is there to be pre-censorship? . . . What I have never understood is what is the difference, or should be the difference, between plays and books. We have laws which apply to books and under which people who publish obscene, seditious or profane books can be sent to prison, but I hope that we should all join in objecting to any pre-censorship of books. The difference has always seemed to me to be obscure. Sometimes, if the question is raised, someone will say, "If you read in a book that a woman had taken her clothes off and had a bath that would be quite all right; but it would be very different on the stage." Then everybody nods and says, "Yes, there you are, you see; there is a great difference between books and plays." But as soon as one comes to think of it, the whole thing is ridiculous, because any actress who did this would at once be "run in" by the police. . . . The absurd position we have got into to-day is . . . that you don't go to see a play unless you know the sort of play it is. Yet the very play which may be banned by the Lord Chamberlain may be brought into your home on television – and this, I understand, has actually happened. There have been plays banned by the Lord Chamberlain which, nevertheless, have been brought in, unasked, to the home. And when the set is turned on, young people say: "That is

interesting. I should like to see the rest of it." . . . A minor criticism
. . . is that it always seems all right to mention certain subjects
humorously, but you must not deal with them seriously. For a long
time, for example, it was perfectly all right to put a homosexual in a
musical show, so long as he pranced and wiggled about and moved
his hips, and everybody laughed at him. Whereas the playwright
who tried to deal with the subject seriously was not allowed to do
so. . . . How is it that the adults of all other countries can exist with a
theatre which is free and subject only to the same laws of obscenity,
sedition and blasphemy as apply to everything else, and that it is
only grown-up Englishmen who have to see their plays read by
somebody else beforehand who will tell them whether or not they are
to be allowed to see them? Whatever the right conclusion, my Lords,
there is clearly, I think, a case for an enquiry.

The debate continued with a considerable number of peers showing
their preference for abolition of the censor with the exception of Lord
Dilhorne, who had several reservations. After Lord Willis and the
Marquess of Hertford had expressed strong views for getting rid of it,
the former concluding that, "as an institution it is wrong. As an
institution it is false and it must go", and the latter saying, "I hope your
Lordships will agree with me that it [the theatre] has now grown up
and therefore no longer needs a nurse as a censor," Lord Kennet rose
and gave a well-documented and reasoned speech aimed at legal
reform which was long overdue. Incidentally, he referred to an action of
Gerald's relevant to the debate, saying:

> The situation between the Lord Chamberlain and the playwrights
> came to a head in two cases in 1958. One was the Theatre Workshop
> case, concerning a play put on by Joan Littlewood, which contained
> a large element of improvisation. A sort of text was submitted to the
> Lord Chamberlain and was approved, so far as it went, and the
> actors improvised, as they always have under Joan Littlewood,
> because that is her purpose in the theatre. They departed from the
> text, and in the course of their improvisations they said and did
> certain things which incurred the displeasure of the representative of
> the Lord Chamberlain who came to the theatre to see the play. A
> prosecution ensued before the East Ham magistrates. We have here
> a case in which something that appeared to the Lord Chamberlain of
> the day to be impermissible was sent for trial at law. Largely, I think,
> because my noble and learned friend the present Lord Chancellor

was far-sighted enough to give his services free – I do not think that this company could have paid for them – the company got off with a token fine, and Joan Littlewood and those associated with her have continued to be major ornaments in the British theatre.

The practical support which Gerald gave in the above case revealed that he was a man not merely of words but of action when help was needed. This was only one of a number of cases where he gave his services in a cause which he supported.

Lord Annan wound up the debate, and the motion recommending an inquiry into theatre censorship was agreed to, but it was not until two years later that the Bill, finally abolishing the particular function of the Lord Chamberlain in this country, was passed in both Houses on July 19th, 1968.

In the meantime Gerald had to cope with the serious problem of Lesly's health, which soon after the debate in February on the Theatres Bill deteriorated rapidly. During the first few days in March 1966 the end came, six months earlier than had been anticipated.

The loss of Lesly after a marriage lasting over 40 years affected him deeply, so much so that after Parliament was prorogued three days later he was confined to his bed, suffering from emotional and physical distress which continued for two weeks. Carol also felt the loss keenly. Many years later, when I came to know her, she recalled happy times spent with her mother as a child, particularly in the large garden at Oxshott which Lesly loved. She was at her best organizing exciting birthday parties. Carol remembers in particular a splendid children's fair, complete with a huge marquee, side-shows and childish games in which Gerald joined, allowing himself to be drenched with buckets of water every time a child successfully hit a target! Her sense of fun delighted Carol, but there were periods when, suffering from moods of black depression, she made life for those around her very hard to bear. When these passed there emerged a charming companion, generous to a fault and, in times of stress, most tender and compassionate. To the end she was devoted to Gerald and Carol who, as our conversation concluded, let fall: "Though the bad times were awful, the good times were marvellous."

The Easter recess came to an end and Gerald had recovered sufficiently to resume his place on the Woolsack, but it was many months before he took part in any social life. Shut away in the Victoria Tower, the light burned late as he dedicated himself to the copious work which came continuously to his desk.

ON FEBRUARY 25TH, 1966, Harold Wilson announced the date of the next general election: it was to be March 31st. After Parliament had been dissolved on the 10th, political campaigning by all parties began in earnest. When the results came through, the Labour party had made 40 gains and increased its majority to 97.

With this reassuring result, the Government went ahead for the next four years, and as far as Gerald was concerned the prospect of carrying out the law reforms and other measures he had in mind was encouraging. In May he was invited to Washington to deliver an address to the American Law Institute to celebrate its 43rd anniversary. By taking a long weekend, he was able to squeeze this in and be absent from the House of Lords for only two days. On the 20th he was in the U.S.A., and by Monday the 23rd he was back on the Woolsack, having given a long dissertation on English law compared with its American counterpart, not forgetting to mention the new Law Commission just beginning to operate in his country.

"That so much of such spare time as I have had," he told them, "should have been devoted to law reform is not a matter on which I have any regrets. My motive has not really been that of a lawyer interested in the law as such. My motive has been a hatred of injustice. I can't bear seeing anomalies in our law which cause injustice. I have wanted to see them put right."

The speech had its lighter side, for not only did he wittily describe the case of the bigamous marriage of the Duchess of Kingston, a unique affair which had taken place a hundred years earlier, but he also told the story of the Lord Chief Justice of Northern Ireland going to attend a law reform meeting in Dublin. He journeyed there by car, and on reaching a level crossing found one gate opened and the other shut, which sent him in search of the gate man.

"What's all this," he said, "one gate open and one shut?"

"That's all right," said the gateman, "sure we're half expecting a train."

Pressure of work at the House increased by such leaps and bounds in the late sixties that he was forced to remain in London, and, apart from a couple of trips in 1969 to Canada and New Zealand to speak to their law societies, no other official visit abroad was made except one to the Netherlands in 1967 to sign a treaty and address the Anglo-Nether-lands Society. While there he noticed a curious thing. Although it was Christmas week, when Father Christmas paid his seasonal visit to the stores, the main streets were practically empty. Shopkeepers explained the phenomenon, complaining that everyone was at home watching the *Forsyte Saga* on television and they might as well close their doors!

A project which Gerald had considered for some time required serious attention was an overhaul of the Assizes and Quarter Sessions in this country. Their administration had not changed radically for hundreds of years, in some cases since the reign of King John, and needed to be thoroughly modernized. In the 1870s the coming of the railways had forced a few reforms in the legal system and location of the courts, but otherwise it was vastly out of date as a whole and this caused delays in dealing with legal problems.

He came to the conclusion that a Royal Commission to study the situation and suggest reforms was the best way of tackling the matter. Thus in August 1966 he proposed to the House the setting up of a Commission headed by Lord Beeching.*

Many people criticized him for choosing a business man with no special knowledge of the law to carry out the work, but Gerald was confident that Beeching was the man to do it, since he had recently been responsible for a very thorough report on the railways and had a reputation for his down-to-earth ideas and efficiency. A previous Royal Commission had been composed of judges and lawyers, whereas Gerald was convinced that the real problem called for the talents of administrators of proven efficiency. The Courts had always been run by the judges, who turned out to be ineffectual administrators. A change was definitely necessary that would rectify this and make the smooth running of the courts speedier and more satisfactory, not only for the lawyers but for the laymen.

The legal luminaries in the House were in general accord that a great deal required examination and change, and thereafter the Commission was set up and began its work, which was not completed until 1970. Unfortunately Gerald at that time was unable to steer the Commis-sion's report through the House, as he was no longer Lord Chancellor,

* Others serving on the Commission were Sir George Coldstream, Sir Arthur Norman, Mr Leslie Cannon, Rt Hon. Lord Justice Phillimore, Sir Andrew Wheatley, Sir Denys Theodore Hicks, Mr Richard Bingham and Mr Hugh Purslove Barker.

but it was promptly taken over by Lord Hailsham soon after the Conservatives came to power. He approved its recommendations and they were embodied in the Courts Bill which was passed on November 17th, 1970. The consensus of opinion was that Lord Beeching and his team had produced a vastly improved plan for dealing with the muddle which had existed for centuries, and that it would enable the courts to be run on far more efficient and time saving lines. In fact, the work of the Commission was highly praised and its recommendations were not long in being implemented.

By the end of 1966 sanctions had been agreed against Rhodesia, and among the Acts supported by Gerald during that year were the Matrimonial Homes Bill, initiated by Lady Summerskill, and the Family Provisions Bill, which dealt with the economic position of a wife after the death of her husband. This also affected the financial position of the children, legitimate or illegitimate. Provision for them was greatly outdated, owing to the fall in the value of money, and the Bill was intended to rectify this.

The creation of the first Ombudsman in England had long been an objective of Gerald's, and in 1967 he was instrumental in bringing it to fruition, but not without some resistance from certain Government departments who were horrified at the idea of their files being made available to outsiders. The members of Justice were strongly in favour of the idea and published a report on it, which was supportive of Gerald's Bill. The conception of an Ombudsman was first tried as an experiment in Sweden in 1809; its adoption in this country took 150 years, and has since proved a valuable and progressive step. Gerald explained the main issues of the Parliamentary Commissioner (Ombudsman) Bill in February during its second reading:

The five basic points about the Bill are first the high status and wide measure of independence of the Parliamentary Commissioner. The second is that his function will be to investigate actions taken on behalf of the Crown. The sphere, therefore, is the Central Government on one side, and the citizen on the other. Thirdly, he is given unprecedented powers to provide for the examination of documents and obtaining evidence from Ministers, civil servants and private persons. Fourthly, the purpose of the investigation is to bring to light administration which has caused injustice to the citizen. Fifthly and lastly, complaints will be made to him through Members of the House of Commons; and it will be for the House to deal with

Ministers where they refuse to remedy an injustice in a way which the Parliamentary Commissioner recommends.

After a debate in the House of Lords lasting six hours the Bill passed both Houses on March 9th, 1967, when the Ombudsman became a permanent feature in our lives and henceforth of great assistance to British citizens.

In 1968 one of the most interesting issues to be debated in the House of Lords was its own reform. For some months Gerald had been sitting as chairman on an all-party committee, consisting of Lords Longford, Shackleton, Byers and Jellicoe, studying every aspect of the problem. This eventually resulted in a White Paper outlining a number of proposals to be considered by the Members of both Houses. These were discussed on November 19th, 1968.

Gerald, in opening the debate, voiced his opinion on the subject unequivocally, saying:

I think that anybody who has given long consideration to this problem will end by agreeing that there are four ways in which the problem may be approached. The first is: Let us abolish the House of Lords. I, of course, do not agree with that ... I am not an abolitionist for two reasons. First because one can observe that there are occasions, as with the recent Transport Act, when through a shortage of time the other place was not able to complete its own work; and, of course, a large majority of the Amendments made by your Lordships to Public Bills are accepted in the other place as being obvious improvements. How on earth it can be thought that one Chamber can do all its own work and all ours as well, I simply do not understand. ...

Secondly ... there is no other Western democracy of anything like our size that has not found from experience that it is absolutely essential to have another Chamber. There are, of course, smaller ones which have one Chamber: New Zealand, Israel, Zambia, I believe Liechtenstein, and no doubt some others. General experience has been that it is necessary . . . .

I haven't seen any two people who agree on a sensible alternative. . . . I believe that whatever Government is in power, it is absolutely unrealistic to think that the House of Commons will ever vote in favour of a Bill to establish an elected, and therefore rival, Chamber.

The third approach is: do not let us do anything. This again is being unrealistic. The reform of your Lordships' House has been hanging over our heads for years. . . . It is no good saying: "Let us do nothing" because this is not going to happen. The Government is pledged to introduce a Bill on this subject in this Session. . . .

Is it really possible to justify a Chamber which has a large, built in, permanent majority, for one particular Party? I do not believe i is. . . . Can it be justifiable that this Chamber should be in the position to annul any subordinate legislation in opposition to the will of the elected Chamber?

The proposals in the White Paper, summarized briefly, were that after every general election a sufficient number of life peers would be appointed by the Prime Minister, on the advice of a committee of peers, to ensure that the Government of the day would always have a majority over the Opposition but not over the Opposition plus the Cross-benchers. The existing hereditary peers could remain in the House of Lords but would only be able to vote on certain Bills. Their sons would not be allowed to attend at all, thereby eliminating the hereditary system. Only a certain number of peers would be allowed to vote, who undertook to attend regularly, and these would be paid attendance fees. They would be elected by their own parties in the Lords, with some existing hereditary peers not excluded from this group.

These were the bare bones of the scheme, the complexities of its operations being set out in much greater detail in the White Paper. When a vote was taken at the conclusion of the three-day debate, the Lords were in favour of the reforms by 251 to 56.

One would have thought this augured well for a Bill to implement the proposals, especially as its intentions had been outlined in the Queen's Speech at the beginning of the 1969 Session. The events which followed, however, took a strange and unexpected course. Harold Wilson introduced it three months later in the House of Commons on February 3rd, 1969, when the Second Reading was carried by 285 votes to 135.* Both Houses, therefore, were in complete favour of the

* Harold Wilson, speaking in the debate on the Queen's Speech, said: "First, the hereditary basis for membership [of the Lords] should be eliminated; secondly, no one party should possess a permanent majority; thirdly, in normal circumstances the Government of the day should be able to secure a reasonable, working majority; fourthly, the powers in the House of Lords to delay legislation should be restricted; and fifthly, its absolute power to withhold consent to subordinate legislation against the will of the Commons should be abolished."

uggested reforms, but during this second reading strong objections vere raised by two M.P.s from the opposite sides of the House xpressing diametrically contrary views. Michael Foot, the Socialist Member for Ebbw Vale, was against any reform whatever on the rounds that it might tend to increase the authority and influence of the Jpper Chamber, whose continuance, he held, was indefensible. Enoch Powell, then a leading Conservative, was ardently in favour of the tatus quo – i.e. the hereditary system – and against curtailing any of he Lords' powers and functions.

Gerald ascribed the failure in getting the Bill through the House of Commons to the fact that two important Ministers in the Labour Government who had strongly supported it had meanwhile been ppointed to different posts and were unable to steer its passage uccessfully: the Leader of the House, the late Richard Crossman, and Roy Jenkins, then Home Secretary, had been made Minister of State or Social Services and Chancellor of the Exchequer respectively. Neither Fred Peart nor James Callaghan, who replaced them, were nthusiastic about the Bill, taking the line prevalent among a minority n the Cabinet that if the House of Lords was left alone it would radually wither away through ridicule. During the Committee stage numerous amendments, arising mainly from the views of Mr Foot and Mr Powell, mounted steadily, and later, in the nine days' debate in the Commons, finally persuaded the Prime Minister to give it a "merciful elease" on April 17th.

The withdrawal of the Bill in the House of Lords caused dismay to hose who had striven hard to achieve a consensus between the political parties in order to reform the Chamber. Lord Alport, in announcing its vithdrawal on May 8th, praised their efforts and courage, saying: "I an think of no more remarkable achievement in the field of constitu- ional reform than theirs in assisting the Labour government towards a lecision to publish, first, a White Paper, and secondly, a Bill, the effect of which was both to strengthen your Lordships' House and to naintain a remarkable degree of continuity with regard to its composition." He went on to recall a statement by Edward Heath in *The Times* the previous month: "Of the Lords Reform Bill, Mr Heath aid the White Paper embodied the best proposals for reform yet levised and they would have produced a more effective House of Lords. He suggested that if Mr Wilson had not called off the inter-Party talks n a fit of pique, over the Lords' action in the Rhodesia Order last summer, the Opposition would have gone on fighting for the Bill."

This referred to the anger the Prime Minister had felt when th·
Lords voted against the Southern Rhodesia Act 1961, which impose·
a total trade ban on Rhodesia, ordered by the United Nations afte·
the executions carried out in Salisbury during the previous March. H·
was incensed by the built-in majority of Conservatives which killed th·
Bill, and the rumour that if a fresh order was made they would vot·
against it and so make Government policy unworkable.

Comments from all parts of the House almost unanimously de·
plored the loss of the Bill. Lord Byers, for the Liberals, referred to it a·
"an unmitigated tragedy". Gerald's final words concerning it expresse·
the views of many other speakers: "My Lords, I venture to predic·
that both the great Parties of the State will live to regret the demise o·
the Parliament Bill for differing but, nevertheless, compelling reasons·
I also think that it would not be wise for the Members of this House t·
do other than to recognize here and now that the failure to proceed fo·
the moment with our reform is an ill day, not only for your Lordships·
House but also for Parliament."

Lord Longford echoed his words: "If we really love this House, as·
am sure is true of everyone here, then it seems to me clear that w·
must try to improve the constitution in some way that gives us th·
standing in the public mind that will enable us to do our job. I hop·
and believe that this evil day will in fact be forgotten when proposals·
possibly different from these but not, I should think, much different·
are brought forward in the near future."

Fifteen years have passed and the "near future" seems as far off a·
ever. Over and over again Gerald, now in his eighties, returns i·
pessimistic mood from voting in the House, vowing he has wasted hi·
time. The large Conservative majority in the Chamber makes votin·
utterly pointless.

In 1969 important measures concerning marital issues were deal·
with, pre-eminently the Divorce Reform Bill, which Gerald strongl·
supported. This tackled the problems in earnest, and progressiv·
steps were taken to enable married couples seeking divorce to obtai·
their freedom more easily and with dignity.

Pressure of work in the House continued unabated. Law o·
Property, Human Rights, Matrimonial and Property Act, Animals·
Administration of Justice and Murder (Abolition of the Death Penalt·
Act 1965) followed in quick succession. The last-named excite·
Gerald's interest more than all the others put together, for th·
possibility of achieving the sweeping away of capital punishment fo·

good in this country, after so many years of campaigning, seemed at long last to be within his grasp.

It was during this particular summer that a correspondence between the Lord Chancellor and myself on legal matters relating to a book I had written on Marie Stopes, which had been continuing spasmodically since 1967, gradually developed into something of an entirely different character. I had recently divorced my husband, and was deeply interested in the new Divorce Reform Bill scheduled for June. Lady Edith Summerskill, a close friend of mine for several years, knew I was keen to follow its progress and invited me to the House to hear it debated. The robed and wigged figure seated on the Woolsack intrigued me, and the more I listened to its voice the more I was attracted.

I began to attend the debates in the House fairly frequently. Letters from me on the subject of the Bill followed, and resulted one day in early June in Gerald asking me to talk over its provisions and recommendations during luncheon in his flat in the Victoria Tower.* It was not until the autumn, however, when he invited me to the opening of Parliament and to the party which he gave afterwards, that our future together showed some signs of being inevitable.

Shortly before Christmas, on December 17th, the Death Penalty Bill was debated in both Houses of Parliament, and, since it promised to be of special significance and highly controversial, I went along with Edith Summerskill to hear the speeches.

The House of Commons had just passed the Bill by 343 votes to 185, with all three Party Leaders in favour of abolition, and next day it arrived in the Lords' Chamber. Harold Wilson describes the way it was received from his point of view as Prime Minister of the day.†

The proceedings in the Lords were attended with great drama. There was a packed attendance of peers, public and many M.P.s from the Commons. The debate was conducted at a very high level on both sides, but undoubtedly the greatest speech of the day, both for its content and manner and for the effect it had on doubters, was the concluding contribution of Gerald Gardiner, the Lord Chancellor. Some of the most discriminating parliamentarians and commentators of my acquaintance described it to me as the greatest

* A more detailed account of our meeting can be found in *Odd Woman Out*, my autobiography, published by Leslie Frewin in 1974.

† *The Labour Government 1964–1970: A Personal Record* (Weidenfeld & Nicolson, 1971).

parliamentary speech they had ever heard – and undoubtedly on
unprecedented in its power and effect in influencing the results o
the debate.

Norman Shrapnel, in the *Guardian*, was equally enthusiastic abou
its quality, calling it a "cliff-hanger":

Peers crammed themselves into every inch of space and stood ii
masses at the entrances: bishops were crowded off their rightfu
benches by ecclesiastical competition and had to perch elsewhere
the packed galleries craned forward in suspense: the steps wer
thronged with Privy Councillors – Mr Callaghan on one side of th
throne, Mr Sandys on the other, to name two. Who said the Lord
was dull? This was the true, unwhipped drama of debate. . . .
    Lord Eccles sounded as though his only concern was to save th
instant abolitionists from themselves. . . .
    Then came the Lord Chancellor with a speech gleaming with
kind of brilliance – casual in manner, devastating in content – tha
Lord Gardiner alone commands. . . .

Some of the salient points of Gerald's speech during the debate
which lasted two days, show clearly and vividly what he though
about the issue:

It has been a very long road from the days in the last century whe
we had capital punishment for some 220 different offences unti
now, when, apart from crimes of treason and treachery in the tw
world wars, there has been no execution for civil crime but murde
since 1861.
    In 1908 there was a big advance: we abolished capital punish
ment for children under sixteen. When my grandfather was twenty
one a boy of nine who had set fire to a house was hanged a
Chelmsford. In a previous year a little way back, a boy of seven an
his sister of eleven were hanged at Lyne. In 1922 we abolished capita
punishment for infanticide. In 1929 a Resolution in the House o
Commons calling for the abolition of capital punishment resulted i
the appointment of a Select Committee. In 1930 the Select Committe
reported:
    "Our prolonged examination of the situation in foreign countrie
has increasingly confirmed us in the assurance that capital punish

ment may now be abolished in this country without endangering life or property, or impairing the security of society."

Winding up his long and legally detailed speech, Gerald said:

My Lords, I have sought to deal with the matter by rational arguments. I have not involved myself in emotional arguments, those being the words used by people to describe other people's moral views with which they do not agree. But I should not like to conclude without making it plain that I do not think that the practice of putting men and women who are your prisoners to death, in cold blood, and telling them a fortnight beforehand that you are going to do so, is right. I believe it to be wrong . . . .

At a quarter to eleven it was decided to adjourn proceedings to the following day; 43 peers had already taken part, but there were another half-a-dozen still to come.

The next day these remaining speakers, including the Archbishop of Canterbury, the Lords Reid, Shackleton and Byers and Viscount Eccles, most of them expressing conflicting views, took only two hours in their deliberations. Gerald in his winding up speech dealt with some of the main objections to abolition:

When people say that there has not been time to think about the arguments, I must, of course, believe them; but I am surprised. Perhaps I am peculiar in having read all the debates on capital punishment in both Houses since 1810 and having sat in the Gallery for most of them during the 1920s and since. But the argument, certainly the retentionist argument, has always been exactly the same, starting in 1810 with the first Bill to abolish capital punishment for shoplifting, which was thrown out by the Lords; to 1811, when the same Bill was thrown out by the Lords; to 1813, when the same Bill was thrown out by the Lords; to 1816 when the same Bill was thrown out by the Lords; to 1818, when the same Bill was thrown out by the Lords; to 1820, when it was again thrown out.

I have always been fascinated to read what my noble and learned predecessors on the Woolsack have said. In 1820, when the House of Commons passed a Bill to abolish capital punishment for cutting down a tree, the noble and learned Lord Eldon got up from the Woolsack and said:

"It does undoubtedly seem a hardship that so heavy a punishment

as that of death should be affixed to the cutting down of a single tree
or the killing or wounding of a cow. But if the Bill passes in its presen
state a person might root up or cut down whole acres of plantation
or destroy the whole of the stock of cattle of a farmer without bein;
subject to capital punishment."

Well, my Lords, you see the argument never changes . . . I alway
think that the shortest statement of the retentionist position arose ii
1748, when William York was convicted of murder at Durham
Assizes. It was in that short period in our legal history when the tria
judge had the right himself to respite the death sentence. The the
trial judge, who was, in fact, the Chief Justice, was in very grea
doubt, so he asked all the other judges – few, of course, in those days
They had a meeting and sent him a short memorandum, which i
how we know what they said:

"He is a proper subject for the capital punishment and ought t
suffer it. Though the taking away of the life of a boy of ten years ol
may savour of cruelty yet, as the example of this boy's punishmen
may be a means of deterring other children from the like offences, an
as the sparing of this boy, merely on account of his age, will probabl
have a quite contrary tendency, in justice to the public the law ought t
take its course."

One ought to take public opinion into account, and indeed in th
other House they fail to do so at their peril. But I remember th
Attorney-General in 1948 saying: "We ought to distinguish betwee
informed opinion and uninformed opinion."

People do not realize that nearly every Christian Wester
democracy has abolished capital punishment. They know nothing o
the Select Committee or of the Royal Commission. They do not knov
that there is not a single country in the world where the abolition c
capital punishment has resulted in an increase of murder.

The argument on the state of crime is always put both ways. I
crime is increasing, the retentionists say that with all this increase ii
serious crime this is the fatal time to adopt abolition. If crime i
decreasing, they say that that shows how well the present deterrent i
operating and it would be pity to water it down. . . .

Gerald's final words before sitting down were almost in the nature o
a plea:

Of course, it is never the right time to abolish capital punishment.

ask your Lordships to take the view that the three Leaders of the Parties in the other place were right in thinking that the time has come now. . . . The Home Office will certainly go on with the figures and their analyses, and at any time it will be open to anybody, since no Act of Parliament is permanent in that sense, to try to bring back capital punishment. Therefore, I would suggest that the three Party Leaders were right in saying that now is the time, and I hope that your Lordships will say so.

And they did – by 220 votes to 174!

I had been present on this historic occasion, and felt intensely relieved when the result was known; the verdict of Shrapnel, "It has been a good week for Parliament", expressed my feelings precisely. Those of Gerald, after his 35 years of indomitable campaigning, can well be imagined.

SIXTEEN

THE NEXT SIX months were so intensely work-concentrated for Gerald that on one occasion he admitted to me that he was finding the pace almost too swift. Harold Wilson's energy seemed inexhaustible and his programme, even to his work-aholic Lord Chancellor, was becoming a strain.

The parliamentary session had come to an end on October 22nd, when the Queen's prorogation speech revealed the large amount of legislation that had been achieved. As Harold Wilson records in his book,* the number of measures passed in the previous six years was the highest in our legislative history, and they certainly looked as if they would be no less formidable in 1970.

On February 11th the Prince of Wales was introduced into the House of Lords. Before the ceremony I was present as a guest at a luncheon party given by Gerald in his flat, which produced the following comments in my diary:

During the meal Ireland and its problems were discussed, and I remarked that their troubles would never be solved until religion ceased to govern their lives. Gerald then came out with a story about Sir Leslie Scarman's visit to the country during the recent riots where he had been deputed to act as a kind of Ombudsman on the scene. He was greeted by a Minister who asked whether he was a Roman Catholic or a Protestant. "Neither," replied Scarman. "I'm an agnostic." "Ah, yes," observed the man, "but are you a Protestant agnostic or a Catholic agnostic?"

This put us all in a lighthearted mood, and when luncheon was over we went down to the Chamber to take our places. Never before had it seemed so crowded; it reminded me of the debate on the Abolition of the Death Penalty with its tense and excited atmosphere. Peers packed the seats and the aisles; even the gallery was overflowing. As the induction neared its end and the Prince, advancing to the Woolsack, shook

* Op. cit., p. 195.

Gerald by the hand, a loud cheer burst suddenly from all present – a startling sound in a place normally so subdued.

Later, during tea with Edith Summerskill in the Members' dining-room, Prince Charles came in accompanied by Lord Shackleton and Gerald. Chatting together they moved over to a table opposite, and were soon joined by Baroness Barbara Wootton and a couple of other peers. All proceeded to take tea, with the exception of His Royal Highness who, as Edith noted, drank only a glass of milk!

During March and April, despite much pressure of work on both our sides, Gerald and I managed to see each other with increasing frequency, having no doubt by then about our feelings towards one another. There were rumours of a general election in the air. Would it be in October or in the summer? The question was a tantalizing one for the press, but Harold Wilson was not telling. It was also tantalizing for us, since we were trying to settle a convenient date for our marriage. The beginning of September seemed the most suitable time, for it would be in the summer recess, and should there be an October election Gerald by then would be free to do some campaigning. Little did he know that even as early as mid-April the Prime Minister was contemplating an election in June. Harold had been keeping a watchful eye on the opinion polls, then registering a favourable attitude towards the Labour Government, and on May 12th, when the results of the voting in the district council and borough elections came through with the same message, he made his decision, unanimously endorsed at a meeting of the Inner Cabinet. Had he decided against a June election, he records in his book, he would "have been certifiable".

At his weekly audience with the Queen, he recommended the dissolution of Parliament, to which she agreed. In the evening there followed an announcement giving the date of the general election a month later, on June 18th.

Our plans had to be altered accordingly, and we decided the Gardiner wedding would take place just after the election. Having settled that, Gerald, prudently looking to the future, leased a flat in the Temple which was just then on offer, and we went along to inspect it on June 3rd. If Labour was defeated at the election, he explained to me, he would need immediate accommodation elsewhere. But if it wasn't, I queried? He said that in any event he was not continuing as Lord Chancellor; six years was enough on the Woolsack, and since he had recently celebrated his seventieth birthday the time was ripe for his retirement. This pleased me, for had he intended otherwise I knew I should see precious little of him, the House claiming the major part of his time.

Having made these arrangements for us both, Gerald set off on his electioneering tour for the next fortnight, his itinerary being Ilford, Cambridge, Gravesend, Wellingborough, Croydon, Chippenham, Bath, Gloucester, Saffron Walden and Southampton. Delivering a political harangue at each town, and then racketing on to the next with scarcely time to draw breath, seemed a gruelling programme for a man of seventy, but such a thought never appeared to enter his mind. I also did some canvassing in the coming weeks for the Labour party, in part to show solidarity, encountering some odd people in my peregrinations. One door I approached to knock at bore a metal plate above the letter-box bearing the inscription BEWARE OF THE CHILDREN! Another was opened by an old fellow who proceeded to tell me he had voted Labour for 40 years but was certainly not going to this time. "Why not?" I asked. He viewed me with disgust, exclaiming: "They taxed the pets' food, that's why! All those old-age pensioners with animals, having to pay tax on their food! Disgraceful!" The door slammed in my face.

I recounted these and similar incidents to Gerald when I joined him on the evening of June 18th in the Victoria Tower flat to hear the election results, but our laughter was shortlived. After the first six came through on the box he remarked gloomily: "The swing is bad – about 5 per cent. If it goes on, it means the Tories will be in by about 40 seats." I left soon after midnight, too weary to stay the course, having ferried people to the polls from early morning till they closed at nine o'clock.

Around 3 a.m. Gerald realized that his rough guess at the figures was proving only too true. Labour lost the election by 42 seats. Next morning, making my way over to the House, I found him looking more melancholy and depressed than I had ever seen him.

Fortunately there was little time in which to sit around and mope at the result, for his apartment had to be vacated by the weekend, which was spent packing his belongings and arranging for their removal to the Temple on the following Tuesday – a formidable operation after six years of working and living in the Victoria Tower. Within a few days he had regained his equanimity, and was writing in optimistic mood to me about our future:

Lord Chancellor's Residence.
House of Lords. S.W.1.
22nd June 1970

My darling,

We may seem an odd couple, but I think that this is a relationship which is rarely explicable on a rational basis.

I see no reason why we should not be extremely happy together. We are both very lucky in having enough money to live on. We are both intelligent and of a pacific nature. We shall both have separate part-time interests. I shan't get in your way. We are both mature. I don't mind what I eat as long as I don't have to eat a few particular things.

I just want to look after you without getting in your way. Come the end of August I shall be free of all commitments. It was, I think, better to start clear.

We have both worked very hard all our lives and in different ways been through difficult times. I think we are both entitled to a bit of fun sometimes. And to laugh a good deal.

Added to which we appear to be in love.

I can only say that I shall do my best and hope to make you a good husband.

All this sounds terribly pontifical which I didn't want it to be. All I meant to say was that I love you very much, that I am very relieved that I am no longer L.C. because of you, and that I am feeling very cheerful.

Blessings on your dear head,
G.

Paradoxically but characteristically, having admitted that our relationship could not be explained rationally, he proceeded to justify it for a number of rational reasons, as though to convince himself that he knew what he was doing, for which perspicuity people in love are scarcely renowned! We realized fully the risks we were taking, but fortunately were mad enough to gamble. Now, after twelve years, the gamble can be said to have come off far beyond any of our expectations.

Relinquishing the office of Lord Chancellor was a real wrench for Gerald, since there was so much more he wanted to accomplish. Any plans he had conceived for the reform of law in this country would possibly be shelved or would not be realized, he thought, for many years to come.*

* He was mistaken. Lord Hailsham, on taking office, put through practically all the legislation Gerald had set in motion in 1970.

When he left the Lord Chancellor's residence in a taxi loaded with luggage on June 23rd, practically the whole staff gathered in Royal Court to say goodbye, because they thought he was very "special" and were fond of him. As far as anyone can tell, this had never happened to anyone else in living memory, and probably not to anyone in the 900 years since the Lord Chancellor's office was created!

Sir George Coldstream, who worked closely with him from 1964 to 1970, in answer to my queries about Gerald when they were together during that period, wrote:

In my opinion, Gerald was the greatest architect of the reform of the law and its administration since the days of Lord Chancellors Cairns and Selbourne in the 1880's – far greater than, for instance, Lord Birkenhead.

One other thing: you mention G.'s personality. I always thought, will think, of him as absolutely the prisoner of his upbringing. His distinguished parentage, his upper class education, Harrow, the Coldstream Guards, Oxford, the Bar – he is, contrary to popular belief, fundamentally conservative in thought and manner! Nothing that he has said or done has altered my view of him. It is one of the reasons why he was such a magnificent champion of the Bar.

The idea that Gerald would be free of all commitments by the end of August was the only doubtful element in his otherwise accurate pronouncements. As long as I have known him, Gerald has never been free of commitments and probably never will be, although he managed to free himself of a small number on reaching eighty years of age. It is a joke in the family that he is incapable of refusing help to those who need his advice and assistance, resulting in his membership of numerous societies and groups and the presidency of an equal number of charitable and reforming organizations.

After the new Parliamentary Session opened on July 25th, 1970, we saw comparatively little of each other for several weeks, for Gerald began attending the House of Lords regularly, taking his seat on the Front Bench, until the summer recess, when he was free to have a long-standing holiday in Switzerland with his daughter Carol, who had just arrived from New York and agreed to act as witness at our wedding. On July 28th the announcement appeared in *The Times*, and a month later to the day we went along to the Guildhall in the City on a hot sunny afternoon and changed my name from Box to Gardiner. I discovered, during our honeymoon spent in exploring Istanbul, Venice and

Bellagio, that Gerald was an intrepid walker, as well as a meticulous planner-ahead. Our itinerary was so arranged by him that we should enjoy to the maximum all the places we visited. He spent hours poring over maps and guide books and was never lost for a way to reach his objective, however tortuous the route. This was a revelation to me, since my holiday travelling had always in previous years been by car, thus missing an enormous amount of fun in consequence.

When we returned to England Gerald came to live at Mote End, my home a few miles north of London in a very rural part of Mill Hill. He had visited the house before on several occasions, and taken a great fancy to the wide open spaces of the garden with its small lake, ancient trees and lovely views looking towards Arkley to the rear, besides relishing its quiet and peaceful atmosphere. It was a complete contrast to the House of Lords residence and the kind of flats he had occupied in London for the previous 30 years, which was no doubt part of its charm for him. He settled in easily and immediately began working in the garden, and soon his pallid cheeks were transformed by a healthy glow, noticeably absent from them while he sat for hours on end, day in and day out, on the Woolsack.

As well as resuming work in the Lords, Gerald acted from time to time as a judge with other Law Lords and also rejoined several of the societies from which he had had to resign on becoming Lord Chancellor. Attending the House most days of the week, to deal with the Party's legal problems arising out of the Bills coming up from the Commons, kept him as busy as ever trying to fit everything in. One of the societies he rejoined was unwittingly the cause of our first separation.

The International Commission of Jurists had arranged a Conference in Aspen, Colorado, to which a number of outside experts were invited to discuss "Justice and the Individual" and for their members to review the last three years' work and the future programme. Gerald had accepted the invitation and we had planned to go together, but fate decreed otherwise. At the last moment I suffered the mishap of a 'slipped disc' and had to abandon the idea, so he went alone. In Aspen his working hours, including Sunday, turned out to be from nine in the morning to about six in the evening, and as he had also agreed to speak on South Africa his time was fully occupied. Nevertheless I received a letter from him every day during his absence, keeping me fully informed of all that went on. From his account of his journey to Aspen I was thankful to have escaped its rigours. He wrote on September 8th from Chicago:

Darling,

I am not going to enjoy this at all but I *am* so glad that you didn't
come. You would have had that long wait from 10.45 till we finally
got off at 4.15 and then an 8-hour flight. Being a Jumbo Jet it had
taken ages to get through passports and customs. We had to wait
about half an hour before the right bus appeared. It was a $\frac{3}{4}$ hour
ride. . . . Changing at Denver for Aspen would have been another
very bad day for you.

I miss you dreadfully. With your back I should have cancelled, but
always hate letting people down. I am quite certain that you couldn't
have managed all this as you are, but it is very sad to be without you
in an enterprise which I am not good at anyway, although I know a
few of them quite well. Do take great care of yourself. You are my life.
I hope to find you ready for all kinds of things when I get back.

All my love, darling,

G.

It might be assumed, in view of Gerald's addiction to work, both here
and wherever his reforming societies led him, that we never relaxed
together and enjoyed ourselves or even had any of that "fun"
mentioned previously in a letter. Not so. Whenever Parliament was in
recess he took advantage of the break to arrange holidays abroad, and
over the succeeding years we usually spent a few winter weeks in
Madeira, Egypt, the South of France and Malta, while in the summer
recess we managed to explore bits of Denmark, Sweden, Finland and
Morocco. Sometimes I took writing work away with me, but on only
one occasion can I ever remember Gerald doing so. The moment he
returned to London Parliamentary work and the usual legal appeals
occupied most of his time, and the rest he gave to lecturing to various
societies all over the country, who imagined that since he had ceased to
be Lord Chancellor time lay heavy on his hands!

Over the succeeding years he agreed to be president of a number of
societies: The Howard League for Penal Reform, the Society of Labour
Lawyers, Help the Aged, the Birth Control Campaign and the Society
for the Defence of Literature and the Arts. As if these were not enough,
he added a few vice-presidencies to his list: The Town and Country
Planning Association, the Institute for the Study and Treatment of
Delinquency and Leeds University Law Society. Besides renewing his
links with the International Commission of Jurists he became Governor of the British Institute of Human Rights and a member of the

Council of Justice, and so the list goes on. It seemed as though he was incapable of saying "No" to any society which approached him and of whose objectives he approved.

In the autumn of 1971, as a result of terrorist attacks in Northern Ireland, considerable criticism of the questioning and treatment of prisoners there became a serious issue which had to be dealt with in Parliament. Gerald was asked to join Lord Parker of Waddington and Mr Boyd Carpenter to consider the procedures currently authorized for the interrogation of persons suspected of terrorism, and to report on them to the Government.

This committee, consisting of three Privy Councillors, was set up on November 9th and met regularly for the next three months. During this period it interviewed 33 witnesses and considered 25 representatives from members of the public, as well as ten from other organizations, including the Civil and Armed Services. During the three months' investigation of the problems Gerald became more and more uneasy as he found himself disagreeing with the views of his two colleagues. It was with relief that I heard he had finally sent in his minority report, which it seemed to me could not be faulted, from both the legal and the humanitarian point of view. He was extremely doubtful as to how it would be received, and almost certain the majority view would be upheld.

He pointed out in his statement that interrogation of prisoners in depth by hooding, the use of a noise machine, wall-standing and deprivation of diet and sleep had never been sanctioned in writing in any army directive, order, syllabus or training manual, and that therefore no Minister could lawfully have authorized their use. The procedures, in fact, were illegal. He also quoted the Third Geneva Convention, which provides that "no physical or mental torture, nor any other form of coercion, may be inflicted on prisoners of war to secure from them information of any kind whatever. Prisoners of war who refuse to answer may not be threatened, insulted, or exposed to any unpleasant or disadvantageous treatment of any kind." This was observed in World War II, when prisoners of war were dealt with in situations far more vital to our country's safety than those in Northern Ireland.

"In fairness," he said, "although the Minister for Home Affairs appeared to approve the procedures, he had no idea they were illegal and therefore the army and the constabulary had assumed in turn that

they were legal. . . . The blame for this sorry story, if blame there be
must lie with those who, many years ago, decided that in emergency
conditions in colonial-type situations we should abandon our legal
well-tried and highly successful wartime interrogation methods and
replace them by procedures which were secret, illegal, not morally
justifiable and alien to the traditions of what I believe still to be the
greatest democracy in the world.''

Edward Heath, the Prime Minister, accepted Gerald's minority
report in March 1972, and orders were immediately given to stop the
illegal methods of interrogation. Nevertheless, despite the outcome
some time later the Irish Government brought a case to the European
Court of Human Rights alleging torture by the British Government of
certain persons in Northern Ireland, although by then they knew the
interrogation procedures had been prohibited and altered. Britain was
found guilty of "inhumane and degrading treatment" but absolved of
torture. Other countries, however, were by this tardy judgment given
the impression that prisoners were still undergoing the sort of
treatment Gerald had persuaded the Government to stop. If the Irish
Government had wished to blacken Britain in the eyes of the world they
could not have chosen a better way of doing it, for nearly ten years later
accusations of torture by us in Ulster prisons continued to flourish and
be believed.

SEVENTEEN

JUDGING BY THE letters from a variety of people, Gerald's minority report had a very favourable reception. Much heartened, he resumed his normal routine in the Lords, which was only interrupted by two lectures that he gave in March at University College, London, and in Bristol. A third one in May, however, was requested from an entirely different quarter.

The Society for the Study of Greek Problems, consisting of a liberal group of people, founded by a former ambassador, Rodis Roufos, asked Gerald if he would care to address them on human rights. Their previous speakers had been M. Jean Ray, President of the European Community, and the well-known author, Günther Grass, and they wanted someone of similar calibre to follow on.

Although he went to Greece, Gerald never delivered his lecture on human rights. I accompanied him to Athens, where we were told on arrival that his mission was pointless – the Colonels would never allow it. They had in the meantime arrested several members of the society and deported them to isolated villages in northern Greece. Gerald asked for permission to visit them, but again we were warned that this would never be granted. After waiting several days, during which our hotel manager secretly warned us that our room telephone was being bugged by the police, the permit came through to enable him to see the banned officials, to the surprise of everyone. But there were certain provisos. None of the society's members was to accompany Gerald, and he was to travel alone except for his driver.

We set off one morning soon after dawn in a taxi driven by the ex-chauffeur of the ex-Deputy Governor of the Bank of Greece, Mr Pezmazoglu, one of those who had recently been deported to the north by the Colonels. The man refused to take a drachma for his services, which covered an eighteen-hour day and a drive of roughly 600 miles. Halfway there Gerald left me at the hotel in Volvos, while he went on his lonely drive over the mountains to the distant villages, where he eventually met the excommunicated members of the society and discussed their problems. At each crossing, as we travelled north, a military guard was posted to take note of our progress. I was told to

expect his return at around 4 p.m., but as five o'clock passed with no
sign of him, and then six, I was reduced to a state of acute anxiety
However, soon after six he turned up, blaming his delay on the dreadful
state of the rutted roads which had played havoc with the taxi's tyres.
We turned south towards Athens and arrived back exhausted at about
midnight.

We returned to England, and a year later, on February 19th, 1973,
Gerald described his experiences, in a debate concerning the Colonels'
dictatorship, in the House of Lords. As far back as 1969 there had been
a previous debate about the Greek situation in the House of Commons,
for not only was that country a NATO ally but it had fought on our side
in both World Wars, and the state of affairs existing there under the
military junta was causing profound concern. After Lord Beaumont of
Witley urged "the Government to use its influence towards the
restoration of political freedom in Greece", Gerald rose and addressed
the House:

For some years all over the world there has been what I think is a
tragic increase in the use of physical force and an increase by
totalitarian governments of the considered practice of torture of their
political opponents. Owing to the action of some brave writers we
know now what has been going on. . . . The degree of torture carried
out in Brazil is well known. In November 1969, the European
Commission on Human Rights, on massive evidence, found that
there was "an administrative practice of torture in Greece".

As we all know, in consequence Greece would have been expelled
from the Council of Europe if they had not, perhaps wisely, resigned
In today's *Times* at page 6 a statement dealing with Mr Alexandros
Panagoulis states: "According to reliable reports, Alexandros is kept
in a specially built unlit cement 'tomb' without running water and
has been repeatedly tortured."

My Lords, in June [1972] I was in Athens . . . to address a society
mainly of intellectuals who were ordinary democrats and, therefore
opposed to the Colonels' Government, while naturally taking care
not to say or do anything illegal. I had, of course, advised the Foreign
Secretary and our Ambassador in Athens of my visit. The night
before I was due to leave the Foreign Office rang up and told me that
the Colonels had that day obtained an order from the Greek court
declaring the society an illegal society as having gone beyond their
objects and the three officers of the society had been forcibly

deported to villages in the North of Greece for a year. They had not, of course, been charged with anything, or had any opportunity of saying anything at all.

My Lords, I imagine the Colonels thought I would not go, but I do not react very well to that sort of thing, so I went. . . . I motored altogether 600 miles in Greece to these rather inaccessible villages, over roads where your first puncture is not the trouble; it is when you get the second before you have mended the first that there is trouble. The officers were not allowed outside the last houses in the village. At the same time the Government obtained a similar order from the court dissolving the students' union because they wanted to elect their own officers instead of having officers appointed by the Colonels, and some of them also had been deported. All these people were given an allowance of 17 drachmas a day, which is not even enough to pay the rent of the accommodation they were forced to occupy. There is, of course, no social welfare in Greece. In those circumstances you can live only with the support of your family.

While in Greece I saw the last legal Prime Minister, more than one former Minister of Justice, and judges. After about a year the Colonels had dismissed about thirty judges who had given decisions that they did not like. I suppose that the first principal rule of law is closely bound up with the independence of the judiciary. They included Mr Sartzetarkis, the judge in the film Z. He appealed to the *Conseil d'Etat* and it ruled that his removal from the Bench was contrary to the Constitution and made an order that he should be restored to his position. The only result was that the Colonels dismissed the chairman of the *Conseil d'Etat*.

I went back in October to hear the appeal of the Society. This was obviously useless. . . . The society was limited to one oral witness only. The questions were all hostile ones. They were told: "Your objects include research. Who did research? You should have submitted the result to the Colonel in charge of education for him to decide whether it was right." On both occasions I met members of all political parties and those who had recently been tortured.

He went on to describe the lack of individual liberty and the rule of law in Greece, and ended: "Western democracy, I feel, must indeed be in a sad way if it is not possible to defend it without allies of that kind."

The collapse of the Colonels' régime came unexpectedly some months later, in July 1974, when we were happy to learn from the several

friends we had made in Athens that their relatives had been freed
and were taking their place in the new democracy which eventuall
emerged. The one who was not there to see this happen was the
secretary of the society, Rodis Roufos. The only reason he had no
been imprisoned by the Colonels was that they knew he was shortly to di
of cancer.

One morning in the early autumn of 1972 Gerald was visited a
Mote End by a gentleman who had driven over from Milton Keyne
in order to discuss a personal matter with him, which was presentl
revealed as we drank coffee together.

He was Dr Walter Perry,* and, with scarcely any preamble, h
divulged the point of his visit. Lord Crowther having recently died
the office of Chancellor of the Open University had fallen vacant and
urgently needed to be filled.

The Open University had come into existence two years earlier
Lord Crowther, who was the first Chancellor of the "University c
the Air", as it was called, had opened the Charter ceremony at th
premises of the Royal Society on July 23rd, 1970:

> We are the Open University. . . . We are open, first, as to *people*
> Not for us the carefully regulated escalation from one educationa
> level to the next by which the traditional universities establisl
> their criteria for admission. The first, and most urgent, task befor
> us is to cater for the many thousands of people, fully capable of ,
> higher education, who, for one reason or another, do not get it. . .
> Only in recent years have we come to realize how many sucl
> people there are, and how large the gaps in educational provisior
> through which they can fall. The existing system, for all its grea
> expansion, misses and leaves aside a great unused reservoir c
> human talent and potential. Men and women drop out througl
> failures in the system, through disadvantages of their environ
> ment, through mistakes of their own judgment, through sheer bac
> luck. These are our primary material. To them we offer a furthe
> opportunity.†

Dr Perry, who was the Vice-Chancellor, had come to ask Gerald
whether he would care to become Lord Crowther's successor.

* Later Lord Perry of Walton.

† *The Open University from Within* by John Ferguson, Dean and Director of Studies ir
Arts, The Open University (The University of London Press, 1975).

I looked across at him, wondering what Gerald's reaction would be to this most unexpected and flattering proposal. His expression told me nothing. Only the previous week we had been discussing the necessity of cutting down his various commitments, deciding that he should take on nothing extra in future. I held my breath. After a pause, Gerald murmured his very real appreciation of the offer, saying it had taken him completely by surprise and would need very careful consideration. There was an odd silence, then he suddenly turned to me and asked: "What do you feel about it?"

This put me on the spot, and he knew it. We had often expressed our admiration for the Open University and all it signified, thinking it one of the finest projects which the last Labour Government had supported and pushed through at the last moment against some real opposition, and for which it would perhaps be remembered when its other achievements were forgotten. I could not restrain myself from replying that I thought it was an exciting idea and one I felt would interest him enormously. Realizing I had gone back on what we had previously agreed, he smiled, since my reply had now let him off the hook.

"I do, too," he answered, "but I don't know whether I can measure up to such a prestigious job. I've never been a serious academic . . . but if you feel like taking a gamble, then perhaps . . . ?" He glanced tentatively at Dr Perry.

The Vice-Chancellor gave an eager response: "We most certainly do," or words to that effect. His satisfaction and relief were obvious, and so the matter was settled there and then. Some further discussion followed, and we both accepted an invitation to visit the new university as soon as possible to get some idea of the way this unique educational experiment was being conducted. As anyone knows who has read Lord Perry's informative book *Open University*,* the growth and success of its activities have been remarkable, the extent of its fame world-wide.

Several exploratory meetings followed between Dr Perry and Gerald. One, in the New Year, when he was introduced to the university's officers at Kettner's restaurant in London, resulted in his coming home to me and saying that there were so many things he was unfamiliar with concerning the day-to-day running of the university that he felt he would never fully understand all its intricacies unless he took an active part in its functions by becoming a student. I regarded this as just a fanciful notion on his part, not one to take seriously, and

* Open University Press, 1976.

dismissed it from my mind. However, in the following January, to my amazement, he announced out of the blue that he had received his course material on the Social Sciences, and would be settling down to read it forthwith.

The three years' study course for a degree was a fairly gruelling one, requiring regular attendance at Hendon for his tutorials, and during the holidays at summer school at regional universities (York and Bath) in the company of many young men and women. It was some time before any of them realized that the tall white-haired student of advanced years queuing for his lunch or dinner was the Chancellor of their own university. No one seemed to mind, some were even intrigued.

"What on earth is an old man like you doing here?" one of his fellow-students asked him during a summer course, and was astonished when he replied that he was her Chancellor. Talking to the students made him realize how difficult it was for many of them – especially middle-aged women who hadn't written an essay since they were fourteen – suddenly to have to grapple with this very different world. So at the monthly meetings with the Vice-Chancellor, the Chairman of the Council, the Secretary and the Treasurer he would always urge that most of the money spent on tutors and counsellors should be allocated to first-year students; thereafter most of them would have got used to it, but the first year can often be very hard. He was not himself dismayed by the essays, for he was used to writing opinions; but the economics course he found extremely tough. It was good, too, for the morale of the other students to know that when their papers failed to arrive on time the Chancellor was in the same boat!

Many of them eventually met him again when they attended the huge graduation ceremonies at Alexandra Palace or the half-dozen regional towns where he conferred degrees on 600–700 students at a time, shaking hands with each one individually. In 1977 at the Central Hall, Westminster, he himself graduated, and, as he strode to the platform in the wake of the trailing line of black-gowned graduands, long and resounding applause greeted him from the packed and excited audience. They were aware that he had broken new ground by being the only student to become a graduate at a university of which he was at the same time Chancellor.

Besides coping with his mass of reading material and taking examinations while preparing for his degree, Gerald went along to the House of Lords as usual, working on the new Bills, and he also attended meetings of the many reforming societies to which he belonged.

One of the most important, as far as he was concerned, which absorbed a great deal of his time from the moment he ceased to be the Lord Chancellor, was the Rehabilitation of Offenders' Bill, on which, as chairman of a committee set up by three societies – Justice, the Howard League for Penal Reform and the National Association for the Care and Resettlement of Offenders – he worked until 1973, when it passed its second reading in the House of Lords. This was the only Private Member's Bill Gerald had ever introduced in the House. It enabled people who had been convicted once or more often of a criminal offence, in civilian life or in the Services, in Great Britain or abroad, and had gone straight thereafter, to become rehabilitated persons. Under the new Act they would not be required to disclose past convictions, and it would be an offence for anyone to disclose such information, except in the course of official duties.

That, very roughly, was the nature of the Bill, whose legal complexities had been painstakingly worked on by the committee for more than two years. It was finally drafted by Mr Paul Sieghardt (a barrister member of Justice) with consummate skill, thus contributing largely to its successful passage through the House. *Living it Down*, the Report published by Gerald's committee, gives a full and clear explanation of the Act in all its detail. According to Tom Sargant (secretary of Justice), Gerald felt it to be so important that he personally paid for and addressed 350 copies, and sent one to every peer who might be interested. Since the Bill came into force in 1975 life has, in consequence, been made easier and far less harassing for at least a million people in this country.

On April 1st, a few weeks later, Gerald and I flew to Australia via New York, where we enjoyed a few days with his daughter Carol, saw some plays and generally exchanged home news. Then we continued our flight, reaching Melbourne on April 8th, to be welcomed by the Warden of Trinity College, who installed us in his attractive house in the university grounds, where we enjoyed his hospitality for a week. This was Gerald's second visit "down under", his last being in 1965 for the Commonwealth Law Conference. This time the meeting with Cyril, his brother, was not so happy, for the previous year he had lost his wife and suffered a mild stroke, rendering speech difficult. It was a particularly wretched blow to him, since like Gerald he possessed a beautiful speaking voice, and must have suffered deep frustration in consequence. However, he was able to attend the centenary celebration of the establishment of the university's Faculty of Law, to which Gerald had been invited as guest speaker, and was able to watch him receive an honorary degree of Doctor of Laws, and hear him deliver an unusually long and interesting address to the faculty in its magnificent assembly hall.

This was called the Southey Memorial Lecture, its theme being "The Likely Pattern of Future Legal Changes in the Commonwealth", and it was given on April 12th, 1973.

After dealing at length with the legal changes, Gerald turned to other things which he felt needed to be said:

For what changes, then, do we have to prepare? At what are the next generation aiming? They see a world in which greed and competition in all its forms and violence appear to predominate rather than love and co-operation. I should think that "Make love not war" is perhaps the best four-word slogan ever invented.

They see a world in which the developed countries are getting richer and the under-developed countries are getting relatively poorer. . . . They see a world in which – while a large proportion of its inhabitants are undernourished – too high a proportion of the world's wealth is devoted to armaments and the exploration of outer space. They see that the industrial revolution has led to a rate of extraction and consumption of raw materials which cannot continue, partly because of the pollution it causes and partly because the materials are not there. . . .

They know that at the time of Christ the population of the world was about 250 million, that it doubled in the next 1,050 years, and has since been doubling again at ever shorter periods and looks like doubling again in the following 45 years, and that this process – if not arrested – can only end in disaster. . . .

What then, are the demands of the next generation likely to be? I think, first, a demand for a simpler life, and a willingness to give up further extensions of material well-being so that others can have enough food; an increase in personal freedom and an increase in egalitarianism. . . .

There can be no freedom except freedom under the law. . . . Remember that freedom in a democracy is based on law, and that without respect for the law there can be no freedom and no democracy. . . .

Before returning home we paid a visit to Sydney, where a vast number of the legal profession assembled for an impressive luncheon. Afterwards a tour of the fascinating harbour was mandatory, as well as the new opera house which was soon to be opened by the Queen. A few days later we reluctantly bade our friends and relatives farewell and took plane to Hong Kong, a scheduled stop on our way home to enable us to meet Robert Gardiner, Cyril's son. While we were there Gerald met the Chief Justice, who afterwards wrote to Robert to say how much he had enjoyed his talk with "your distinguished uncle. Quite apart from his brilliant intellect, he is a man of remarkable humanity for whom I have the deepest admiration."

Almost immediately we learned by cable that Cyril had collapsed and died suddenly the day after we flew from Melbourne, leaving Gerald the only surviving son of Sir Robert Septimus.

"It was as if," Robert said, "Father willed himself to keep alive until he would see you again. Your visit made him very happy."

When we arrived home Gerald had a great deal to catch up on, particularly his Open University work. He also had to prepare himself for an event some weeks ahead: his first degree-conferring ceremony on June 23rd. In a way it was in the nature of a double event, since he was being given the degree of Honorary Doctorate of Law by his own university, his second that year.

It transpired that I was the only person close to him to be present at the Open University ceremony, which, to a laywoman like myself, was stimulating, colourful and heartwarming. I noticed how small was the proportion of females sprinkled among the long line of graduands receiving their degrees, but as year succeeded year I was happy to note that their number increased considerably at each ceremony I attended, until the last one, in 1977, showed something approaching an equal proportion of young men and women.

Apart from a short session in Geneva in October to attend a conference of the International Commission of Jurists and our yearly weekend at Chichester to see the plays and enjoy ourselves in that charming old town, the programme for the rest of the year for Gerald was work, work, work.

EIGHTEEN

THE YEAR 1974 had seen the fall of the Prime Minister, Mr Edward Heath, followed by Labour taking over the reins with Mr Merlyn Rees appointed as Secretary of State for Northern Ireland, where the troubles and difficulties had mounted to such an alarming degree that another inquiry in depth was deemed necessary.

Merlyn Rees formed a committee and approached Gerald to become its chairman, which he accepted. It was to "consider, in the context of civil liberties and human rights, measures to deal with terrorism in Northern Ireland". Since the acceptance of Gerald's minority report the situation, ever volatile in Northern Ireland, had radically changed, for the province was now under direct rule from Westminster.

The first meeting of the committee which was eventually to produce the "Gardiner Report" was on June 19th, the last on November 22nd, and during those six months the seven members met approximately every alternate week in London and Belfast to do their work. Three newspapers in Ulster gave notice of the inquiry and asked organizations and individuals to offer their views with written submissions about the pressing problems, while the urgency of the task was emphasized. After visiting the Crumlin Road, Maze and Armagh prisons, hearing 97 witnesses, studying 157 memoranda and listening to complaints about the security forces, the courts and the police, the committee presented a unanimous report, subject to one reservation by Lord MacDermott which did not materially affect the result.

The main bones of contention which the committee had to deal with, in reference to civil liberties and human rights, were detention without trial, arrest on suspicion, and trial without jury; but the most significant, and one which has caused serious repercussions even to the present day, was the argument of certain prisoners convicted of murder, bombing attacks and similar terrorist crimes against the population, who insisted that they had political status and therefore merited special privileges which were denied all other prisoners sentenced for equally serious crimes. These had been granted to them by the previous Home Secretary, and now had to be looked at afresh.

When conditions prevailing in the Ulster prisons came under scrutiny in relation to the European Convention for the Protection of Human Rights 1950, it was found that in time of war or other public emergency the United Kingdom (which had ratified the Convention in 1951) had been within its rights to take the measures it did to deal with terrorism in Northern Ireland, and that it was not in breach of international agreement in so doing. However, the Committee recommended that the emergency powers should be limited both in duration and in scope, particularly detention without trial and trial without jury. As a result, detention without trial was stopped. The committee was also in favour of discontinuing trial without jury the moment witnesses ceased to be intimidated or threatened for attempting to give evidence at trials, which was the only thing preventing the courts from trying cases with a jury and which was considered ultimately desirable. In the event trial without jury has remained in force.

The situation with regard to "special treatment" for political prisoners was much more difficult and disturbing. On investigating the three prisons, and after interviewing many of the male inmates, the committee found that Protestants and Catholics had been segregated into two alien groups, and that the latter (who mainly supported the I.R.A.) were not required to work or perform any prison duties but spent nearly all their time marching and planning activities in army style directed by their own chosen leaders, who refused to accept other prisoners assigned to their section if they regarded them as undesirable. The idea of devoting their energies to training and carrying out military manoeuvres was to make sure they would be ready, should an amnesty ever come to be granted, to prosecute their political aims when they were released. This was paramount in their minds. In effect they ran the prison compound much as they liked, suffering little interference from the staff, and were allowed more visits from relatives than other prisoners who were not in the "political" category.

The committee came to the conclusion that the introduction of the "Special" category status had been a serious mistake. Paramilitary organizations were encouraging the convicted prisoners in the misleading notion that they would not have to serve their full sentence in the event of an amnesty. The report* states firmly that: "it should be made absolutely clear that 'special category' prisoners can expect no amnesty and will have to serve their sentences. We can see no justification for

* Published in 1975.

granting privileges to a large number of criminals convicted of very serious crimes, in many cases murder, merely because they claim political motivation. It supports their own view, which society must reject, that their political motivation in some way justifies their crimes. Finally, it is unfair to ordinary criminals, often guilty of far less serious crimes, who are subject to normal prison discipline."

To help remedy the situation the committee suggested as an urgent necessity the building of a new-style prison, equipped with workshops, etc., and the elimination of the compound system; instead, they proposed that the prisoners should be housed in cellular accommodation which would be easier to supervise by the staff. They stressed that: "The present situation in Northern Ireland's prisons is so serious that the provision of adequate prison accommodation demands that priority be given to it by the Government in terms of money, materials and skilled labour such as has been accorded to no public project since the Second World War."

This was plain speaking indeed, and the recommendations were acted upon. The Government made an immediate start on the building of a new prison which, when it was completed a couple of years later, the Minister, now Mr Humphrey Atkins, claimed to be one of the most modern in Europe.

The view subsequently expressed in the Gardiner Report that the special status of political prisoners should not be recognized or given preferential treatment, was upheld by the European Commission on Human Rights. Nevertheless, it has been regarded by the I.R.A. as a valid reason for the hunger strikes and the "dirty protests" prevailing in the Maze prison, which persisted for a considerable time, and was even put forward several years later as the motive for the attempted assassination of Gerald in 1981.

The report was a lengthy one of 78 pages and represented months of intensive, careful study and final composition. I was surprised to learn (as I am sure others may be) that all the work done on governmental committees is unpaid, being given freely by those asked to sit on them. Only travelling expenses and cost of their lunches are allowed, though their work may occupy them for many months, as this one appears to have done; or it may even go on for years, as a considerable number do, with the general public singularly unaware of the labour which is given "for free", emanating from some of the finest brains in the land.

The removal of the "Special Status" category in the Maze prison infuriated the I.R.A. and those paramilitary prisoners who had been deprived of their privileges. Thereafter they waged a "dirty campaign", refusing prison clothes, wrapping themselves in blankets and ceasing to clean their cells, persistently smearing the walls with excrement; and, when this failed to have any effect on the Government, one by one they went on hunger strike. The propaganda value of the hunger strikers' deaths which followed was devastating, and the I.R.A. exploited it far and wide, particularly in the U.S.A.

Thus, nearly six years after Gerald and his committee made their report, nothing but trouble had ensued. "Political Status" was the issue for which it was remembered and held responsible, but stopping detention without trial, and the earlier minority report of Gerald's which resulted in the discontinuance of undesirable and inhumane methods of interrogation, appeared to have been totally forgotten.

Some years later, in 1981, he was asked to chair a meeting at Queen's University in Belfast by the Joint Sponsored Conference on the Administration of Justice in Northern Ireland, to which were invited individuals and organizations representing a wide spectrum of political opinions: the Peace People, the National Council of Civil Liberties, a professor of Law from Belfast University College and other members of the legal profession, church groups, prison representatives, police and the Northern Ireland Office – though not all these attended. Topics discussed included the Diplock Courts systems, arrest, interrogation, and complaints procedure.

When I understood Gerald was about to accept the invitation I was filled with apprehension, and asked him to make sure of adequate police protection in case of trouble, as I was fully aware that the Provisional I.R.A. had long memories and were not exactly friendly towards him. He said the organizing committee had assured him he would be given ample protection from the moment he arrived at the airport to the moment he left. This was faithfully carried out by the provision of a special branch car and driver.

On the Friday evening I saw him off, crossed fingers and hoped for the best. The following night I met him at the station at about 9.30, and during our drive home he told me that the conference had gone very well, the organizer saying that but for his presence only half the audience would have turned up. In all, about a hundred people attended the meeting.

During the morning break he had been approached by a supporter of the hunger strikers in the Maze prison and asked if he would be willing to speak to them later about the prisoners' problems. Gerald answered:

"Of course. I'm happy to talk to anyone", and arranged to be at the main door of the university at two o'clock, when he could spare half an hour before the afternoon meeting. After lunch he went to keep the appointment at the scheduled time and waited nearly half an hour, but as no one appeared he returned to the hall. At five o'clock he left the university to catch his plane back home, pleased that nothing had gone amiss. Naturally I was relieved to hear all this, and that my instinctive fears had all been groundless.

On Sunday afternoon our telephone rang, and on answering it I heard the voice of a friend in Sussex asking: "Is Gerald all right?" Mystified, I assured her he was fine and working away peacefully in the garden. She explained that the radio at four o'clock had given the news that the I.R.A. had attempted to blow him up by putting a three-pound bomb under his special car the previous afternoon. Fortunately he had left for the airport by five and the bomb, which had been timed to explode at 5.30, apparently failed to do so, having been insecurely taped to the underside of his car. It had dropped on to the road and was discovered later and defused by the army disposal squad without mishap.

For some time afterwards Gerald was deeply affected by the incident, though he said little or nothing about it. I was told that a member of the Belfast Brigade of the I.R.A., who claimed responsibility for the murderous attack on him, had rung up a Belfast newspaper in the morning and told the editor that Gerald had refused to meet a deputation from the hunger strikers and was going to suffer the consequences. When apparently it was learned that he had already agreed to speak to them the paper received a cancellation of the previous statement, but the attempted assassination went ahead.

Gerald's views on Northern Ireland, after his experiences there during the past few years, were despondently negative. When the power-sharing conference at Sunningdale had broken down in 1973, killed by the all-out strike of the Ulster workers which paralysed the province and terrified people by its explosive violence, hope for a solution gradually faded away, and for him the outcome spelled total failure. He felt strongly that Protestant and Catholics should press for the education of their children at the same schools and end segregation. He believed that the separation between young people who never learned each other's views because they were of different faiths was lamentable, and that there was no hope until such a situation could be rectified. Only today comes the rumour that a few groups are attempting to achieve this, but the church is not in the least sympathetic to the notion, and it will be a long, slow process, if it ever gets off the ground at all.

Meanwhile the tragedy of Northern Ireland continues, and despite all attempts by peaceful people to heal its wounds the hatred between North and South persists and exacerbates its problems; it will never cease until the two sides weary of the killing, the bombing and the terrorism which make their lives a misery and their economy bankrupt.

The events connected with Ulster in 1974 and 1981 having been linked together for convenient reading, it is now possible to revert to others, in the years between, which were of some significance in Gerald's life.

On January 1st, 1975, he opened *The Times* as usual, to find that he was to be made a Companion of Honour by the Queen. This happy beginning to an otherwise ordinary, hardworking year was followed by another heartwarming one in 1976, when he heard he had passed his final Open University examinations. As I have already described the ceremony when his degree was conferred on him by the Vice-Chancellor in London, to enlarge upon it would be superfluous, except to add that we were both heartily thankful that the years spent slogging away at the courses were over at last and that we could thenceforth relax and enjoy a little more leisure together. This turned out to be over-optimistic, for, on going through the diary for 1977, I see that in addition to his Parliamentary labours in the Lords we went to Vienna in April to attend a conference of the International Commission of Jurists. It lasted roughly ten days and Gerald worked as hard as ever, but the visit allowed me the chance to explore that lovely city, which unfortunately was denied to him.

On returning to London at the end of the month he was promptly off again on a series of weekly trips to Nottingham, Newcastle, Southampton, Birmingham, and finally back to Alexandra Palace, conferring degrees on the year's graduands.

Carrying out the duties of Chancellor for the past six years had been a fascinating and informative experience for Gerald, far more than he had ever expected it to be. Nevertheless, it had been arduous, and kept him fully stretched the whole time. For a while he sat back and reflected. He was now seventy-eight, and gradually coming to the conclusion that the moment was ripe for a man of his age to step aside for another, someone younger and more vigorous, perhaps, who would continue the good work. Having made up his mind, Gerald therefore offered his resignation, and on January 1st, 1979, was pleased to hand over the reins to Lord Asa Briggs.

Sir Walter Perry, who had worked as closely as anyone with Gerald during his years at the Open University, later expressed an academic view of him:

> In Lord Gardiner we found a Chancellor who brought wholly new qualities to the task and new honour to the University. Not only does he bring to the top of the pyramid his wisdom and humanity; he is to be found at its very base, as an undergraduate student who has completed and passed two full credit courses, and who knows what it is like to be on the receiving end of our complex system.

Gerald's farewell speeches at the two dinners given in his honour by the students and the members of the Open University staff were among the best and liveliest he ever delivered.

These speeches were not by any means his last, for coming up shortly was one he made on opening a 2,000-strong meeting at the Central Hall, Westminster, at what he considered to be an unusually important event and one he was glad to chair and support in every way possible, the Campaign for the World Disarmament Convention launched by Lords Philip Noel-Baker and Fenner Brockway on April 12th, 1980. The meeting, a forerunner of others all over Europe and the U.S.A., stressed the dangers of the arms race, and the campaign culminated in subsequent years in enormous demonstrations by the peoples of France, Italy, Holland and Germany, which became so vociferous that Governments of NATO countries could no longer turn a blind eye or a deaf ear to their protests against nuclear warfare. The NATO Governments began to express fears of the movement and of the possibility of having to curb their own desires for more and more deadly weapons of destruction by indulging in smear campaigns insinuating that the World Disarmament Campaign was backed and controlled by Communists.

Ten days after the convention Gerald participated in a debate initiated in the House of Lords by Lord Philip Noel-Baker, together with other eminent speakers including Lords Zuckermann, Carver, Gladwyn and Ritchie of Dundee. It was outspoken and stimulating, but the over-all tone was pessimistic to a degree, with warnings of impending doom from many speakers. Lord Mountbatten's speech in Strasbourg in May 1979 was repeatedly cited, and Gerald could not refrain from expressing his views on the way it had been treated in this country:

> Having had the pleasure of knowing Lord Mountbatten, it seemed to me extraordinary that, with one exception, his speech was never reported or referred to in any national newspaper. Does anyone doubt for a moment that if Lord Mountbatten had made a speech saying that we were getting behindhand in relation to the Russians, and that we must have more and more nuclear arms, that would not have been published? I said "with one exception". *The Times* is the exception because *The Times* was not being published at the time the speech was made. Therefore, I wrote to Mr Rees-Mogg and suggested *The Times* might like to publish the speech. He said it would want some special occasion and said he could not. Ultimately, it was published in *The Times* but only as a paid advertisement. It seems extraordinary that people must pay *The Times* to put in a speech of a man of this character. I gladly agreed to the campaign sending a copy of his speech to all Members of Parliament with a brief note from me. I have had a good many replies, some rather odd. One was from a noble duke writing from his ducal castle who said that as soon as he saw the speech, he thought it a clear sign of senile dementia.
>
> What has disturbed me is the number of letters suggesting the whole case against nuclear war was very much exaggerated, and that if only we had enough civil defence, if only we had enough fall-out shelters, we should get through it all right. . . .
>
> It does no service to anyone to pretend that there is any defence against a nuclear attack. . . . I am persuaded that if we go on with nuclear armament, it is only a question of time, and probably only a very few years, before there is a nuclear war whether by design or accident. I think it not at all unlikely that it will start by accident. It was President Eisenhower who made it plain that we are not going to get Governments of the world to agree lightly unless the people of the world insist on it. That is the object of the campaign.

For a man who is by nature an optimist, Gerald's view of the world and its prospects is singularly bleak, his only hope being that a saner attitude in international relations will eventually prevail.

In April 1981 we travelled to Newcastle where the university had asked him to deliver their first Convocation lecture. He called it "A

Ramble around Age". Since he was to achieve his eighty-first birthday the following month, he felt there was some justification for his conclusions concerning it. One of his qualifications, he remarked, was his "lifelong interest in the subject. I cannot remember a time when I did not think that old people had too much to say in our affairs and young people not enough say." He concluded his talk thus: "In a world faced with an atomic war, which I think we shall probably have – whether by accident or design – within the next five to ten years, unless within that period we can achieve nuclear disarmament and spend the money instead on the starving areas of the world, and with all the great difficulties caused by the increasing rate of change, surely it is possible that the minds of those in their late teens and early twenties may be better equipped to see us through our problems than minds that are old and tired? After all, they could hardly make more of a mess of the world than we have."

A ᴠᴀsᴛ ɴᴜᴍʙᴇʀ of people have known Gerald Gardiner, and opinions of him vary wildly, but all would no doubt agree that a streak of personal reserve in his character prevented them from assessing it in any real depth.

Since the end of this book is imminent, the question, "Which is the real Gerald?" remains to be answered. Personal letters and documents he rarely kept, except those of especial interest, and if some of the details as to time and place are found to be inaccurate, then this may be attributed to the overburdened memory of an eighty-year-old. Their substance is true as he remembers it.

The puzzling nature of Gerald's personality can best be illustrated by the quite dissimilar views of two men who followed him in the office of Lord Chancellor. First, Lord Hailsham: "He reminds me enormously of a seventeenth-century divine. He's got a high sense of purpose and morality, and very austere morals, I would have said. He's not without humour, but he's not a warm, approachable man."

Second, Lord Elwyn-Jones: "He's a man of great humanity, of great modesty, immense intellectual ability and great personal friendliness."

Yet a third, a barrister colleague, Louis Blom-Cooper, remembers appearing in cases with him: "He was always terribly nervous. One felt he was a dramatic actor with all the nerves actors have and yet tremendously controlled. A rather isolated, remote figure with a slightly cold appearance, but it wasn't coolness at all. Underneath this exterior was a real fire burning inside him, particularly on matters he felt passionate about." Mr Justice Howard possibly encountered this fire on the occasion when he referred to him as "that dangerous Socialist fanatic"!

Finally, Lord Hailsham concluded: "Everybody who knows him intimately would, I think, recognize that he has got a warm heart inside rather a glacial exterior, and which is the real Gerald you must make up your own mind."

No matter how many facts are collected about a life, the interpretation of them may vary greatly in the search for truth. Many different assessments will still be made of my subject, which is inevitable, for I myself have no hesitation in admitting that there are depths in Gerald which have set me a problem and which I have found difficult to plumb, since his personality presents a complex mixture of wisdom and youthful ingenuousness, acute logicality of mind and unexpected sentimentality, besides steadfastness of purpose and strange streaks of obstinacy which are hard to reconcile. Small wonder his fellow undergraduates at Oxford called him "the unflappable Gerald", for in times of stress he could be likened to a rock-bound lighthouse impregnable in a stormy sea.

This became more evident several decades later in the House of Lords, where he remained on the Woolsack for hours at a stretch when any other Lord Chancellor in living memory would have been happy to relinquish his duty to a deputy. C. H. Rolph, who has known him for 30 years, relates that once, when he was waiting to see him, an official in the Lord Chancellor's Department said to him: "I've been in this House forty-five years and I've *never* known a man do that job so conscientiously. It's amazing. I don't know how he keeps awake!"

A considerable number of individuals, mostly lawyers or judges, regard themselves as having been his special protégés and speak of it *sotto voce*. Most of them are right, Rolph says, for as far as he can see Gerald picked no losers and they owe their advance to his interest and encouragement. "They are far too numerous for there to be anything 'special' about them. There was no trace of nepotism in this respect. Gerald Gardiner knew just who were the best people for the job and saw to it they got appointed."

Speaking of Gerald's personality, he remarked that "he always seemed to need the 'set occasion' to call up his quietly assured persuasiveness – the court of law, the debating chamber, the board-room, the public meeting. Away from these, he seemed shy and propitiatory. At a cocktail party he would have no 'small talk', and in the growing eminence of his later years this often seemed to leave him defenceless among the prattlers, so that one felt (needlessly, no doubt) protective about him. People briefly acquainted with him sometimes said he was stand-offish and cold, but they were totally mistaken.

"In Court, his speeches and judgments were devoid of rhetoric. They were factual, and he always made the facts more telling by recounting the more outrageous or 'sensational' of them with careful under-emphasis. If, as he once hoped to do, he had become an actor he would have been a Ralph Richardson rather than a John Gielgud, and he could only have played Donald Wolfit for comedy. In Court, it was the actor in him that controlled the timing in his speeches and the urbane, incisive thrust of his questions. No Court of Appeal, I would guess," says Rolph, "has ever had to say to him 'Mr Gardiner, may we remind you that you are not addressing a jury?' Nor has any jury had to endure, at his hands, the embarrassment which such a rebuke might reflect.

"On any committee he chaired, he was always in his seat well before the appointed hour, and on the stroke of that hour proceedings began. He was ever ready to address meetings, whatever the kind of accommodation (I've shared platforms with him at some extremely grotty little local halls and committee rooms), to participate in debates, to give evidence to Parliamentary and other inquiries concerning matters of law reform he considered important – capital punishment, sexual offences, prison reform, censorship, police powers, the administration of justice."

One of the few critics who openly acknowledged differences between them was Richard Crossman, his Cabinet colleague from 1964 to 1970, who wrote in his *Diary*: "Very soon the usual tension between the Lord Chancellor and me was in the air. We differ on most things. He is a tight-lipped Quaker liberal and I am a rather slap-dash unliberal conservative socialist." His views of Gerald had a chameleon quality, changing radically according to the support or non-support which Gerald was giving him in his current political manoeuvres. In 1965 Crossman wrote: "Of course the fact is that though he is Lord Chancellor, he is a real political innocent, uncertain and unsure of himself and nearly as out of place in our world as Vivien Bowden. But he is so good, and so noble, and so much in Harold's good books that I will do what I possibly can to help him."

Which of these views is one to accept? Gerald himself, when confronted with them, smiles: "But I've never claimed to be a politician. I am a lawyer. I am not even pre-eminently a lawyer, but one who is obsessed by any injustice caused through bad law which needs to be remedied." He explains that the "usual tension" between himself and Crossman was due to the latter's intense dislike of lawyers, which was the result of an antagonism that always existed between Richard and his father, Mr Justice Crossman, a judge in the Chancery Division. Clement Attlee often played tennis with Justice Crossman and learned of their disagreements, and when he became Prime Minister was so greatly influenced by his friend that he never gave Richard office in his Governments. Crossman was forced to wait thirteen years before being appointed to office by Harold Wilson when Labour won in 1964.

Gerald's loves and hates present a curious mixture. Of the latter, injustice, cruelty and interference with the liberty of the individual are paramount. As to his loves, he has an affection for most of the arts, but his deep and lasting devotion to the theatre is undoubtedly the principal; yet having to renounce an acting career for the study of law never proved a matter of regret to him in later life. Taking the stage in a law court eventually became an infinitely more attractive proposition, while putting on the advocate's "silk" gown and the ceremonial robes of the Lord Chancellor for state occasions was always enjoyable. After all, an essential part of play-acting is dressing up, and this was in his bones. Although by nature anti-Establishment, he usually dresses conventionally. This, he admits, is deliberate, in order to reassure people, when he is propounding ultra-left-wing ideas, that he is not necessarily "way out" or in the least trendy! At home he relaxes in the simplest clothes, slacks and a sweater for gardening and household chores. While his tastes are generally speaking modest, he confesses to sophistication in one particular: "I always have my hair cut at the Savoy – it's the one luxury I allow myself!"

He has various pastimes: watching first-class tennis is one. His pleasure in it is perennial, and he never misses going to Wimbledon each summer, but participating actively in the sport has no appeal for him, although the video game of tennis delights him by its ingenuity and the opportunity it gives him to relax and completely forget work. When he was Lord Chancellor, tickets for Wimbledon tennis week were – and even to this day still are – given to the staff of the Lord Chancellor's office. They remember with delight, according to Pat Malley (his Assistant Private Secretary from 1964 to 1970), his warmth and generosity of spirit, especially one evening when he chartered a launch to take over a hundred of them (including husbands and wives) on an evening trip down the Thames. Pat Malley said: "Buses were hired to take the guests to Tower Hill; drinks were provided on arrival at the launch which he had hired from the Port of London Authority; and a most lavish supper was served for all the guests. The fact that the July night proved to be a disaster so far as the weather was concerned, with torrential rain and the awning over the bar collapsing before the party had sailed under Tower Bridge, made the event even more jolly. He moved around the guests with a shy informality in an effort to meet members of his office with whom he did not come into daily contact."

Yet when he officiated at the opening of Parliament parties, which took place in the large drawing room of his "Residence" overlooking the Thames, he entertained in a most conventional manner to suit the leading politicians and dignitaries of Church and State. Things must be *comme il faut*! "The office staff," said Pat Malley, "regarded him with affection and deep respect, and he was always referred to as a 'perfect gentleman'."

Wilson Wiley, his contemporary at Oxford and a staunch friend over the years, expresses considerable admiration for him privately and professionally. He remembers, when he first became a solicitor, sending Gerald his firm's account, which Gerald returned with a letter saying it was much too small and enclosing a cheque for double the amount. "Who else would do this?" he asks. He also recalls a judge remarking on Gerald's "marvellous courtesy", saying that if he ever met an acquaintance in the street and stopped to talk, he would never be the first to break up the encounter. Wiley added: "Perhaps because he has always felt so strongly about the reforming work he was engaged on he never had any small talk, and for this reason some people – particularly those who are shy themselves – never feel cosy with him. He is not an extrovert by any means, nor an introvert, but always ready and interested to listen but reticent to air his views."

Gerald admits freely to his diffidence of approach to people. "I'm not a hail-fellow-well-met chap like Lord S——" (naming with a mischievous smile a well-known Judge). "They said of him that nobody ever patted so many people on the back and called them by the wrong Christian name!" Nevertheless, Wiley agrees that some found him very frightening as an advocate, the direct gaze of his "cold blue eyes" striking terror into them. Desmond Wilcox, after interviewing him on BBC television, also confessed to a sense of fear when facing him. Gerald, on hearing the reactions, was quite surprised, exclaiming: "Why, I wouldn't hurt a fly! I wonder why they feel that way about me?" Before I knew him well myself I felt the reason was clear. Had I ever been a witness under cross-examination by him, I should no doubt have had similar fears. The intensity of his gaze makes one feel that he is probing for the truth to the very marrow of one's bones. Should the recipient feel even faintly guilty, the onslaught would be devastating.

Wilson Wiley summed up his feelings about Gerald: "To me he has always seemed an extraordinarily saintly sort of person, and the amount of good he has done for individuals is incalculable."

Since his partial retirement (he still attends the House of Lords a few days a week) his main interest is gardening, devoting several hours a day to keeping Mote End in trim. The rest he spends in reading *The Times*, *New Statesman* and magazines of a strictly legal nature. On holiday, however, he indulges his catholic taste to the full, getting through novels, biographies and a variety of current publications at great speed. While he is fond of light, popular music, operas and symphonies on the whole leave him cold; and although in the early twenties he joined the Film Society and attended its Sunday night shows, he much prefers the theatre to the cinema. It is only on rare occasions, when I can assure him there is an exceptionally good film on locally, that I can persuade him to go along and see it.

Had I attempted to cover all the court cases and social reforms in which Gerald has been publicly active for nearly 60 crowded years, this book would have been too long for even the most patient reader. Pruning was important, and therefore I aimed at the salient facts in his life, omitting others, such as his contact with Charlie Chaplin and the help given over the reissue of his old films; the advice on problems of censorship which he was called upon to offer the publisher of the famous novel *Lolita*; his involvement in the Vassall Tribunal and in the early stages of the thalidomide case (which he had to abandon on becoming Lord Chancellor). I have also had to omit his persistent strivings to obtain legal aid for those unable to afford it, or the support he has given the Birth Control Campaign, Writers and Scholars International and other demanding causes.

This account of his life and work (virtually synonymous), and the quotations from some of his more important speeches, may go some way towards an understanding of Gerald's philosophy and aims.

He would agree, I am sure, that in his personal relations he is a very private man, often extremely shy and sensitive in making friendly contact with people; but when the initial hurdle has been overcome the reserve vanishes, and he is frank and outgoing, and no one could be more affectionate. His kindness reveals itself not only to those with whom he comes in daily contact outside the home, but extends within it to a marked degree. Nothing is too irksome, nothing too difficult for him to cope with in an attempt to smooth out and soften rough edges. He is a man of habit (an inveterate pipe-smoker) and a firm time-keeper, favouring a fairly strict routine both in public and private life, yet paradoxically flexible when it suits him to be, flying off to foreign parts at the drop of a hat if he can see his way to alleviating pain or injustice by so doing.

In his eightieth year he was made an honorary member of the

Garrick Club, which he had joined in the twenties, following in the footsteps of his father, who became a member in 1895. This delighted him, especially as on the same day Laurence Olivier and John Gielgud were accorded a similar privilege.

It seemed a fitting place to hold a party to celebrate his eightieth birthday, and so it was arranged. His daughter Carol made the journey from New York to London to be with him on May 30th, while his two nephews, Robert and David Gardiner, flew in from abroad to swell the number of colleagues and friends gathered together in a flower-filled room. Lord Elwyn-Jones, who succeeded him in office in the last Labour Government, gave a felicitous and witty speech, bubbling with his usual amusing anecdotes, thus setting the tone for a happy occasion, while Robert Gardiner read my birthday wishes to Gerald which I hoped would also express the feelings of those present.

GREETINGS TO AN OCTOGENARIAN

The burden of the years seems light to him,
Though others feel it more than weighty.
Rejoicing in his strength of wind and limb
He finds, to his surprise, he's eighty!
What if his hair be white, the spirit's young
And ready in defence of human rights.
While virtues of the old are seldom sung
His should be echoed from the heights.
We'll not forget injustices he fought,
This man of patient spirit and of peace –
The garlands that we bring him now, unsought,
Are those of love and trust. Long may his lease
Of life continue happy and content,
Is our united wish and our intent.

On first being approached about his biography Gerald was reluctant to have it written, but eventually, after considerable persuasion, agreed that perhaps it was more sensible to have it done while he was still alive than when he was not around any more to vouch for its accuracy. Having at last completed a work which has been a sheer labour of love throughout, I offer it as a tribute to a rare spirit, and one I am proud to have known.

APPENDIX

During the Parliamentary period April 18th, 1966 – November 27th, 1967, Gerald addressed the House as Lord Chancellor on the following subjects:

Aberfan disaster, Attorney General's Statement
Acoustics of Lords' Debating Chamber
Advertisements (Hire Purchase) Bill
Age of majority, Latey Committee's Report
Air Corporations Bill
Appeals from Quarter Sessions
Arbitration (International Investment Disputes) Bill
Barristers and professional negligence
Brighton Marina Bill
Bus Fuel Grants Bill
Capital Allowances Bill
Centenary of Canadian Senate
Companies Bill
Consolidation Bills, Motion
Consolidation Bills Joint Committee
Countryside (Scotland) Bill
Criminal Appeal Bill
Criminal Justice Bill
Criminal Law Bill
"D" Notice System: Radcliffe Committee's Report
Development of Inventions Bill

Divorce and marriage reconciliation grants
Divorce Laws
Edinburgh Corporation Order Confirmation Bill
European Economic Community
Family Provision Bill
Forestry Bill
Fugitive Offenders Bill
General Rate Bill
Home Affairs
Industrial Injuries and Diseases (Old Cases) Bill
Irish peers
Judicial Business:
    Appeal Committees appointment Motion
    Appellate Committees, appointment Motion
Judicial Offices (Salaries) Order 1966
Judicial precedent, Statement
Justices of the Peace and Stipendiary Magistrates
Land Commission Bill
Land Registration Bill
Leave of Absence, Statement
Lord Chancellor's visit to Washington

SHORT BIBLIOGRAPHY

Adamson, Iain: *A Man of Quality*, Frederick Muller Ltd, 1964
Cannon, Olga and Anderson, J. R. L.: *The Road from Wigan Pier*, Victor Gollancz Ltd, 1973
Cooke, Colin: *R. Stafford Cripps*, Hodder & Stoughton Ltd, 1957
Crossman, Richard: *The Diaries of a Cabinet Minister 1961-1966*, Hamish Hamilton Ltd and Jonathan Cape Ltd, 1975
Davies, A. Tegla: *Friends' Ambulance Unit*, G. Allen & Unwin Ltd, 1947
Eden, Anthony: *Full Circle*, Vol. 1, Memoirs, Cassell & Co. Ltd, 1960
Faulks, Sir Neville: *No Mitigating Circumstances*, William Kimber & Co. Ltd, 1977
—— *A Law unto Myself*, William Kimber & Co. Ltd, 1978
Ferguson, John: *The Open University from Within*, The University of London Press, 1975
Gardiner, G. A. and Curtis-Raleigh, Nigel, editors: *The Judicial Attitude to Penal Reform*, Stevens & Sons Ltd, 1949
Gardiner, G. A.: *Capital Punishment as a Deterrent*, Victor Gollancz Ltd, 1956
Gardiner, G. A. and Martin, Andrew, editors: *Law Reform Now*, Victor Gollancz Ltd, 1963
Hill, M., and Williams, L. N.: *Auschwitz in England*, MacGibbon & Kee, 1965
Hollis, Christopher: *The Homicide Act*, Victor Gollancz Ltd, 1964
Jackson, Robert: *Operation Musketeer – Suez 1965*, Ian Allen Ltd, 1980
Nutting, Anthony: *No End of a Lesson*, C. Tinling & Co. Ltd, 1967
Perry, Walter: *Open University*, The Open University Press, 1976
Rolph, C. H.: *The Trial of Lady Chatterley*, Penguin Books Ltd, 1961
—— *All Those in Favour? The E.T.U. Trial*, André Deutsch Ltd, 1962
Rose, Gordon: *The Struggle for Penal Reform*, Stevens & Sons Ltd, 1961
Thomas, Hugh: *The Suez Affair*, Weidenfeld & Nicolson Ltd, 1967
Tuttle, Elizabeth O.: *The Crusade against Capital Punishment in Great Britain*, Library of Criminology No. 4, Stevens & Sons Ltd, 1961
Wilson, Harold: *The Labour Government 1964-1970, A Personal Record*, Weidenfeld & Nicolson Ltd and Michael Joseph Ltd, 1971
International Commission of Jurists: *Bulletin No. 8*, 1961
Report of Committee: *Living it Down*, Stevens & Sons Ltd, 1972

INDEX